The Love That Matters

Your Grace —

Thank you for your
faith in me and your
support. God bless
and keep you always!

The Love That Matters

Meeting Jesus in the Midst
of Terror and Death

Charles H. Featherstone

Foreword by
Audrey West

CASCADE *Books* · Eugene, Oregon

THE LOVE THAT MATTERS
Meeting Jesus in the Midst of Terror and Death

Cascade Books
An Imprint of Wipf and Stock Publishers
199 W. 8th Ave., Suite 3
Eugene, OR 97401

www.wipfandstock.com

ISBN 13: 978-1-62564-910-2

Cataloging-in-Publication data:

Featherstone, Charles H.

   The love that matters : meeting Jesus in the midst of terror and death / Charles H. Featherstone ; foreword by Audrey West.

   xvi + 236 p. ; 23 cm. —Includes bibliographical references.

   ISBN 13: 978-1-62564-910-2

   1. Featherstone, Charles H. 2. Christian biography. I. West, Audrey. II. Title.

BX4827.F43 A3 2015

Manufactured in the U.S.A.   12/19/2014

To Michael Sultan and Angela Joy Nelson,
who asked for this book
long before it was a possibility

Contents

Foreword

I FIRST MET CHARLES Featherstone in a classroom at the Lutheran School of Theology at Chicago. He sat close to the exit, as far from me as possible, as if he was preparing for a catastrophe that demanded immediate escape. The course was Introduction to Biblical Greek, required for students beginning their first semester in the master of divinity degree program and preparing for ministry as pastors in the Evangelical Lutheran Church in America. As his classmates buzzed into the room with energy fueled by lunch and the first day of school, Charles sat quietly at his desk. Watching. Waiting. Wary.

As a member of the seminary's tenured faculty, I was well acquainted with the fear of learning a foreign language that plagued many of my students, who worried that their dreams of pastoral ministry would be thwarted by the intricacies of Greek syntax, not to mention an unfamiliar alphabet. It was soon obvious, however, that Charles had a gift for languages, as he would occasionally reference Arabic or Russian while unraveling the knots of Greek grammar. He consistently scored at the top of the class. I wondered, then, why his wariness was not assuaged by my cheery exhortations to the class that "babies in Athens learn Greek, so can you!" Evidently there was something more than academic performance at stake for him, something more threatening than failure.

Only later, when he shared some of his story with me, did I learn the depths of his fear, and how much higher were the stakes. And why an escape route was so crucial.

The Love That Matters recounts the odyssey of a man who "ached . . . for the affirmation that I mattered to just one human being." It is a memoir of fear and friendship, of seeking and being found, of life turned upside down and made new again. It is a testimony to faithfulness—God's faithfulness—encountered in and through some of the darkest, most terrifying experiences of life.

Most of all, this is story of love.

Deeply scarred during a childhood characterized by brutality and humiliation, as well as a disastrous stint in the army, Charles Featherstone lands in college in San Francisco in the late 1980s. There he encounters beauty and poetry in the Qur'an and converts to Islam. Over the next decade and a half he is welcomed into multiethnic Muslim communities wherever he goes, among them a studious and peaceful group in Utah and a collection of wanna-be jihadists in Ohio.

His quest for "home," that is, an experience of safety and rest, drives him to "tough places, marginal places, difficult places, even frightening places." Through his studies and work as a journalist he crisscrosses the country and the globe: from Southern California and Logan, Utah, to Washington, DC and New York City; from Dubai, in the United Arab Emirates, to Saudi Arabia; from an office directly across from the Twin Towers of the World Trade Center to a basement complex at CIA headquarters. And, eventually, he finds his way to a small Lutheran church in Virginia and the seminary in Chicago.

The book is not a travelogue, however. Charles Featherstone's memoir offers rich theological reflection on his encounter with "a God who simply would not leave me alone no matter where I was or what I was going through." The particularities of this story belong to Charles and to those whose lives interconnect with his, especially his wife, Jennifer, but they also exhibit deep resonance with a cloud of biblical witnesses.

Like the Israelites who were led out of bondage at the exodus, Charles discovers that God is with him even (especially) in the wilderness of deprivation and despair. Powerful, unbidden experiences at prayer evoke the voice that came to Elijah in the middle of the night as well as the exhortation repeated throughout Scripture: "Do not be afraid." There is also Jacob, who demanded a blessing after wrestling all night with a mysterious angel, and who received in return a permanent limp, a sign of both his own perseverance and of the God who would not let him go.

Throughout the journey, brutality and terror are unwelcome companions in places that are supposed to be safest, while friendship and hospitality are found among the least likely people, "where the grace of God, a God who simply will not give up on God's people, meets the real mess and ugliness of human life." Charles Featherstone invites his readers to stand beside him at the foot of the cross and to see—really see—what our fear and anger are capable of doing to one another. Then he testifies to a love that is greater than all of that, "a love which defeats death and suffering by going through it with us."

"I didn't choose this life," he writes. "It chose me."

The semester after he aced New Testament Greek, Charles enrolled in my course "Jesus and the Gospels." This time he abandoned the safety of the back of the room for a seat in the second row. A few weeks into the semester the class discussed the Gospel of Mark's portrayal of Jesus's disciples: how fear clouds their understanding, even as "insiders" to Jesus. Mark's narrative suggests that the disciples will understand Jesus only after the cross; until then they cannot grasp that God's power is manifested most fully in and through this suffering Messiah. Despite their confusion, however, Jesus persists in showing them what it looks like to be caught up in the nearness of God.

Charles waited after class that day to ask me a question. Amazement tinged his voice. "The disciples didn't *have* to understand, did they?"

"What do you mean?" I asked. "The disciples," he said. "They didn't get it; they didn't understand. But that was okay, wasn't it." This time there was no question, just a growing confession of faith that the God who had brought him to this place had loved him even before he knew or understood what that meant. "We don't have to understand," he whispered. "God doesn't require that."

I resigned my professorship at the seminary about a year later, turning my attention and energy toward the care of my terminally ill father. Before I left, Charles and Jennifer invited me for coffee and related some of the remarkable events that had led them to Chicago and that form the heart of this book. I remain thankful that they did. Conversations such as these offer new insights, both settling and unsettling, leaving us wanting to know how this particular, compelling story will continue to unfold. This book is an invitation into that conversation. I invite you to come along for the ride—to capture a glimpse of the thing that matters most of all.

AUDREY WEST

Acknowledgments

The Love That Matters is an act of love, an attempt at faithful witness. A reconciling witness. I won't go so far as to say I harbor no resentments—I am human and have lived with some hurts for a long, long time—but I have come to realize that too much good has come from even some of the most awful things that have happened.

Even with all the cruelty, there has been a lot of kindness. A great deal of grace. And that has mattered more. Much more.

There are names (or full names) I have not used, either because I do not want to hurt the people and places involved or because I don't want to start pointless arguments. A few names have been changed, either to protect people or simply because I have good reason to suspect they wouldn't want to be associated with me at this point in their lives.

I'd like to start by thanking Rod Dreher at *The American Conservative*. Without Rod, you would not be holding this book in your hands. This began as an e-mail response to something Rod had written on his blog. Rod asked if he could publish my response, and the reaction I got from that e-mail was overwhelmingly positive—something I didn't quite expect.

Among the people responding was Charlie Collier, a senior editor at Wipf and Stock Publishers, who wondered, would I be willing to make that essay into a book?

I'd also like to thank Lew Rockwell and everyone at The Ludwig von Mises Institute in Auburn, Alabama. Some years ago, I wrote an e-mail to Lew after reading a piece on his website I had an issue with, and Lew encouraged me to write for him. So I did, and found lewrockwell.com a place of kindred souls when it came to expressing my opposition to war, all forms of state violence, and my intellectual and moral issues with the state itself. I know that for many people my views on these things aren't "reasonable."

But I have come by them honestly. And sometimes, the world needs to hear unreasonable things.

And a special thanks to Marie Copeland for teaching me how to write.

There are my parents, Charley and Carol. More than anything, I want to say I love both my father and mother very much. Because to anyone reading this, I suspect it's going to seem that I don't. I am glad they are both in my life. Truly. Especially my father, who wasn't much of a father for the longest time. I would also like to thank Jennifer's parents, Ruclare and Patricia, especially for their help and support during seminary.

Now there are a whole mess of people I want to thank, everyone who appears in this book (named and unnamed), and some who don't but who have been important to me. I apologize that I do not remember everyone.

I would like to thank all those people who over the years have been my friends, colleagues, classmates, and collaborators, but especially Gary Pedvin, Marck Weiss (who during an awful year was the only friend I had), Kai Brothers, Pat and Don Jankiewicz, Kyle Brodie, Franklin Bruno, Ron Johnson, Dan Clucas, Karen Keane, Frank Webb, Ed Crane, Jeff Smith, John Barger, Talal Hattar, Trish Khleif, and most especially Dr. Sean Foley, who lets me come up the mountain with him every now and then.

And I would also like to thank everyone I've ever worked for and with, including Robin Arthur, Joel Dreyer, Pete Woelper, Mike Wennergren, Mark Tarallo, Ros Krasny, Stephen Burns, John Siciliano, Deborah Kinirons, Scott Reeves, David Givens, Erin Zaro, Dr. Ahmed Shukani, Dr. Sabria Jawhar, Moinuddin Ali Khan, Shibbu Itty, Michael Sultan, Allison Radomski, everyone at *Khaleej Times*, *The Herald Journal*, *The Saudi Gazette*, The Saudi Press Agency, and Energy Intelligence.

Everyone at Peace Lutheran in Alexandria, Virginia, but especially Christine Howlett, Cathy Kroohs, Paul and Sue Sticha, Jim and Cathy Nice, Elliot and Vicki Haugen.

For everyone at Bethel Evangelical Lutheran Church in Chicago, Grace Lutheran Church in Westchester, Illinois, and Amazing Grace Church in Watseka, Illinois, especially Bruce and Jocelyn Bennett, Sam Widemon, and Pat Jackson.

For all the professors I've ever had who challenged me, believed in me, and supported me: Tom Johnson, Aguibou Yansane, Peter Mellini, G. Wayne Bradley, Robert Baum, Jon Anderson, Tarek Yousef el-Magariaf, Mark Swanson, Peter Vethanayagamony, Linda Thomas, Ray Pickett, and Audrey West.

And to all the pastors who have somehow influenced me: Barry Neese, Mark Olsen, David Miller, Cheryl Pero, Maxine Washington, Albert Starr Jr., Craig Mueller, Michelle Sevig, Tom Gaulke, Roger Crum, Bishop Paul Landahl, Robert Lesher Jr., Cynthia Hileman, and Metro Chicago Bishop Wayne Miller.

To everyone I worked with and studied with at the Lutheran School of Theology at Chicago, especially Angela Joy Nelson, Mark Fisher, Allison Williams, Tiffany Demke, Bridget Thien, Dr. Bridget Illian, David and Angel Holland, Aaron Decker, Pastor Eva Guldanova, Francisco Herrera, Pastor Paul Moonu, Pastor Mamadou Diouf, Patricia Bartley, Jim and Pam Maxey (and their horde of wonderful children), Peter and Dana Perry (and their daughters, Ruth and Esther), and Emilie Pulver.

Thanks to a few people who don't really belong anywhere else, mostly for just being there: Kathe Bills, Abbie Baron, Kate Murray, Breanna Rouse, Matt, and Amber.

And especially Erinn and Melissa.

I have no words to thank Kurt Hendel and Rosanne Swanson, who despite it all did not let go of me. Even when letting go would have made a great deal more sense.

Nor do I have words to thank Abdullah al-Hamdan. *Jazakumallahu kheiran, ya akhi.*

And a big thanks to the crew at the West Aurora Starbucks, where most of this book was written: Jazmine, Leah, Jenna, Will, Cassandra, Donald, Beth, Allie, Taylor, Ashley G., Ashley B., Jose, Tayrn, Beckah, Alyssa, Suzie, Destiny, Jim, and Jen.

Now, Jennifer and I are big fans of author and child advocate Andrew Vachss, especially his series of Burke novels. We like the "family of choice" his main characters create and the commitment to adopt, and to take responsibility for, the people you meet along the way who need your care. And wish to care as well. And so I would like, more than anything, to thank my "family."

To my "baby brudder" David Barnes, who has always been there, especially when things were particularly awful. Who always told me, "Never give up." And whose cheerfulness is something of an inspiration.

To Patrick Visel, who helped keep me grounded, and who showed me a kind of faith and faithfulness I'd never seen before.

To Vince Gay, who tried to fire me the first time we met in 1988. Honestly, I can think of no better basis for the deepest and most important friendship I have.

To Joy Proper, who probably didn't need another "sibling," but the same sky fell down upon us both, so she got one anyway.

To Michaela Besedova, who walked into my life in the summer of 2012 and said to me, "You will be my daddy and I will be your daughter." Having done this, she is teaching me a whole new kind of love that I didn't think I would ever get to experience.

And finally, I want to thank my wife, Jennifer. She loved me into being, and without her, I hate to think what would have become of me.

1

Who Are You?

MY VERY EARLIEST MEMORY is of praying mantises.

It was 1972, I think, and we were living in a little house on the missile range at White Sands, New Mexico. I was four, helping my mother in the front flowerbed, or maybe just playing while she worked. I don't remember.

But I remember the mantises. There was a brown one, and a green one. Ever the naturalist, my mother was very concerned that I respect these little creatures, appreciate them, not hurt them, and especially that I not be afraid of them.

I wasn't. In fact, I let them crawl on my hands and arms. And I remember how big they were, covering my hands, from the tip of my longest finger to my wrist. They were huge, magical creatures.

Many years later, when I was sixteen and we lived in Upland, California, I was wandering in our backyard, in between our beehives, and watching all the various bugs that made their homes in our flower gardens.

We had a bunch of praying mantises, all different colors—green, brown, yellow, even a white one. I picked up a brown mantis, held in it my hand. It wasn't happy to be there, but I gently kept it from escaping.

My mother was out back. Weeding, I think. But we didn't work hard on that flower garden. It was wild.

"Mom, is this as big as praying mantises get?" I asked.

"Yep, it sure is."

"Hmm." I thought for a bit. "I remember them being so much bigger."

I told her about White Sands. She smiled, and laughed.

"Chuck, of course they would seem much larger. You were very small. Now, you're almost grown up."

The mantises hadn't gotten smaller. I'd gotten bigger. But because I hadn't seen one, or held one, in a long time, there was no way for me to know that.

Perhaps this would have just made sense to most people. But it was the kind of thing that I wouldn't have considered until I held a praying mantis in my hand. That's how I learn: by touching, feeling, experiencing. And then I behold the wonder—of discovery, of the world, of change.

This book is a work of memory, and as such, it is flawed and imperfect. I have had to consider—as I have gotten older—what seemed bigger to the mind of the younger me that really wasn't so big. Memory isn't a simple recording of facts. Memory is also filtered, again and again, through years and layers of meaning and experience, as new experiences help give new meaning to old ones.

To acknowledge the nature of memory is not to say I have made this story up. Everything I relate here really happened. Everyone I write about, I really met.

But what has changed over time is meaning. I understand things differently at forty-six than I did at twenty-six. Or at sixteen. This story is an attempt, from a very particular place, to make sense of the purpose and ends of my life. It is not by any means complete, and there are other ways to relate all this. I accept that. It is the story of my struggle—to find a place in the world into which I had been born, a world that was all too cruel and unwelcoming at times. A world in which too many people didn't seem to know what to do with me.

It is also the story of my encounter with God, a God who simply would not leave me alone no matter where I was or what I was going through. And it the story of a love that transformed me. Slowly, and without my wanting it to.

This book is also an attempt to answer a question.

In January 2010, while I was studying for a master's of divinity at the Lutheran School of Theology at Chicago, I was looking for an intensive January class to take.

My classmate Joy Proper was over one afternoon, and she, my wife Jennifer, and I were drinking cocktails. Joy and I had become close friends following a shared misfortune, and she came over frequently for drinks and dinner.

"You are going to take the two-week emotional intelligence course with me!" she said.

Cheeky girl, telling me what I was going to do. But Joy didn't want to be in the class alone. She also pointed out, given the difficulties I was having in seminary, that the class would show I was serious about becoming more emotionally aware of both myself and those around me.

It was two weeks of general silliness, somewhere between annoying and unpleasant. I have doubts about such classes and what they can accomplish—they've always felt a little like Maoist self-criticism, and group encounters have always frightened me a little.

In that class was another classmate of ours, Adrianne Meier, who is now a Lutheran pastor in Ohio. Adrianne is a short, sweet, and sometimes very intense person—I always liked her. And for some reason, early in the second week of the course, we were asking questions of each other.

Adrianne looked at me.

"I have one question for you," she said, tensing up. "Who?! Are?! You?! Because every time you say something interesting, you say it's a long story, and then you *never tell the story!*"

She was right, and I could feel a whole world of frustration in the way she asked the question, as if she'd had it coiled up inside her for months, just waiting to burst out.

And in that moment, given all that had happened, it felt like the entire Evangelical Lutheran Church in America was asking that question. As well it might.

This book is my answer. A couple of years too late, maybe. But this is the long story.

The very long story.

2

Brother Umar

SOMEONE WAS POUNDING ON my dorm room door.

I opened it. There stood an unshaven young man, smiling a big, stupid smile. In his arms was a bag bulging with wine and beer bottles. He looked at me.

"My girlfriend just dumped me, and I'm going to get drunk. If you're a really good friend, you'll help me drink this and save me from myself."

There was no saying no, of course, and the young man standing in my doorway knew that. We also both knew how this would end, that I would indeed save him from himself by drinking far more than he did. The first time I'd gotten so drunk I had to crawl to my dorm room, threw up more or less in one of the garbage cans (one of my hapless roommates cleaned up the mess), and then passed out, fully clothed, in the shower with the water running.

I never got that drunk again, despite the fact this happened a couple of times. But John Hartwell had this strange power over me.

It was sometime in the spring of 1988, my first semester at San Francisco State University. Johnny was perhaps the sweetest and most troubled man I've ever met. (I called him Johnny until he graduated from medical school and became a surgeon, when I started calling him "Sawbones.") We met in Russian class. They'd given me several semesters' worth of credit for all the Czech I'd studied at the Defense Language Institute in Monterey, but I figured it would be pointless to let all that Slavic grammar go to waste.

It was a struggle at first, learning to properly pronounce Russian, what with all that Czech in my head. One of my instructors, a very short and saucy Russian woman named Katya, critiqued me one day as I was reading something.

"You speak Russian like a Ukrainian," she said. It was not a compliment.

At any rate, Johnny and I bonded quickly over shared experiences. Like me, he had been in the Army at DLI and had not finished. I don't recall exactly why his military career had come to an early end, but I think it had something to do with the lingering amoebic dysentery he'd gotten while a high school exchange student in Morocco.

He later told me that he'd been sexually abused by a scoutmaster when he was eleven or twelve, and he'd decided the best way to handle the pain of that was through drug abuse and promiscuous sex. In high school, his drug of choice had been LSD, and he'd become quite an acid head. He also had an affair with a female teacher twice his age. After high school, he came back from North Africa with a more-than-casual interest in Islam. He had become a believer, of sorts, but the Islam he practiced was very unique to him, one that didn't stop romance, drinking bouts to commiserate the end of romance, or sex in the meantime.

"The Qur'an says 'Go into your wives.' I'm just doing what my *Allah subhana wata'ala* has told me to do," he explained.

Johnny was sweet and broken. He was also crazy. When he felt manic, his favorite phrase was "zombie bird-head," and his eyes could sometimes get Charles Manson-wild, his smile big, and he'd start riffing nonsense. "I am at 90 degrees to the universe!" Which was either a statement of obvious fact or a deep observation about the tangent he suddenly found himself on in that moment. Sometimes it was insightful nonsense, often it was delightful and entertaining, but mostly it was nonsense. I wish I could remember more of it.

John Hartwell and me in the backyard of his parents' house, summer of 1992. Jennifer and I visited on our way to Ohio State. And yes, he's wearing underpants on his head.

When people got mean, or something disagreeable happened, he would always smile. "Fuck 'em if they can't take a joke," he'd say.

Occasionally, we'd sit in class—he only took one semester of Russian at SF State, and it was the only class we took together—and he'd whisper obscene comments to me about the very pretty red-haired girl with the sexy knees. But his tastes tended toward "dark and dewy" girls with big brown eyes. I helped him drink his way through the end of a relationship with a Vietnamese girl, and later with an Indian girl he once called "my little Hindu fertility goddess."

He wouldn't stay at SF State for very long. Johnny was a brilliant, abused, aimless child of the suburbs, and he wasn't really sure what he wanted—or was called—to do. He transferred to the California Maritime Academy in Vallejo, just up the bay from San Francisco, to study naval engineering, and I visited him once or twice while he was there. I noticed the little motel with the hourly rates just outside the entrance and thought, "This is Johnny's kind of place."

Once, the phone rang a little after one in the morning. It was Johnny. He was on guard, and most of what came out of the phone was incomprehensible nonsense. Even for John Hartwell.

"Do you know what time it is? Are you high?" I asked groggily.

"Oh maaaaan, you have no idea! I am 90 degrees to 90 degrees! I am the zombie bird-head!"

He did not finish his degree program at the maritime academy.

But Johnny wasn't just a bundle of pain and confusion and badly controlled urges. He could be thoughtful and incisive. He loved my songs, and was especially proud that I wrote him a song when the "Hindu fertility goddess" dumped him. He was very, very bright, and while politics and current events were of little interest to him, he could hold his own when those things came up. Once, not long after we met, we were talking about something related to the Middle East. I forget exactly what, but I remember I disparaged a particular source of information as not trustworthy.

"Why, because it's Palestinian?" he asked me. The statement struck me. It was a question I'd never been asked before, and one I would give some thought to.

This was a particularly sore point for Johnny. Not only because he was nominally Muslim, but also because he had a Palestinian uncle. It wasn't just a matter of right and wrong for him, it was a matter of family.

Once, we took a weekend road trip to visit his uncle and aunt in San Jose. When the traffic on U.S. 101 got heavy, I got anxious and started swearing. Stop-and-go freeway traffic has always made me feel stupid and angry, though I have gotten better about it over the years. Johnny tried his best to calm me down—"You need to learn some Zen," he said. He didn't know any koans, but I'm certain that if he had, he'd have taught them to me.

I'm not sure how John Hartwell managed to become an orthopedic surgeon, but he did. And apparently a very skilled and talented one. He never really escaped his personal demons and, despite being married, had affairs with nurses and got caught pilfering the pharmacy at the hospital where he worked. He was sent to rehab not once, but twice. And as all this was happening, he was diagnosed with a form of multiple sclerosis that eventually left him unable to work as a surgeon and gave him seizures that would hospitalize him for weeks. We regularly corresponded by e-mail at the time, and that's when he told me much of his life story. His marriage had ended, and he was planning on moving to Morocco to marry a Moroccan girl, someone related to the host family he stayed with when he'd studied there twenty years earlier.

"I hope you come visit me. And when the night is warm, we'll all sleep out on the roof underneath the stars, we'll each go into our wives and practice making them pregnant," he wrote. Some things didn't change.

And then in early 2004, the e-mails just stopped.

Not long after, I got a message from the imam at the *masjid*—literally, place of *sujud*, or prostration, where Muslims gather and pray to God—where he worshiped. John Hartwell had died in his sleep, from heart failure probably related to the seizures.

I miss him. His was a sweet, gentle, wounded, and deeply troubled soul. He was a kindred spirit.

One evening at SF State, Johnny handed me a small piece of paper. It was a list of books from an outfit called Tahrike Tarsile Qur'an, an Islamic book publisher located in Queens.

"You need to get a copy of the Qur'an and start reading it," he said. "Who knows what God will say to you when you do?"

I had come all the way north to San Francisco for a change. I was twenty years old, and I was running. From the miserable suburb of Upland, California, where I'd spent the last ten years. From the callousness, cruelty, and abuse that abounded there. From a military service that had ended embarrassingly badly. From a self I'd hoped I could leave behind—a person no one seemed to want and no one wanted to love.

But I was running *to* something as well. I was running toward hope, that in this new place—this great big city where I could get lost—I could become a new person. Find a place, and even some people, I could belong to. How I longed for that.

And I was running to God. There was an ache, in my soul, that wanted to know God.

And yet I was almost completely adrift. I had no real way of understanding the world, no story bigger than mine to help me make sense of things, and make sense of my life. I had not been raised with a religious faith—my parents are both nonbelievers, more or less. And this was good, since God was not involved, not named, and not used as a justification for any of the abuse I'd suffered at home or at school. It meant that I could go find God on my own. But that same freedom also meant I had neither guide nor map. I had no idea where I was going. Or how to get there. I believed in God. I had no doubts there. But I had no idea what that meant, either. While in high school I had dabbled in the majority Christianity of the Southern California suburbs—it was impossible to escape premillennial dispensationalism in early 1980s Southern California, as it was the default understanding of "Christian"—but it could not help me deal with any of the situations I found myself in: my loneliness and suffering, the mess that was army life in Panama. And when I saw the extent to which that Christianity justified American power and American order—things I had been on the wrong side of, or had seen the dark underside of, since I was very young— then it was clear to me that Christianity had nothing of value to say.

It had nothing to say to or about the suffering of the world. Not when it happily excused, or actively endorsed, or even caused much of that suffering. Oblivious or complicit, it hardly mattered.

So, I looked over that small catalogue Johnny had given me. Tahrike Tarsile had several translations of the Qur'an, and I had no idea which one to choose. In the end, I think I sent them five dollars for a simple, hardbound English-Arabic version. The book arrived more quickly than I had expected, and I was excited. I had no idea what might be inside this simple, austere book, with its plain green cover and simple gold title. What would I find?

I found *surat al-fateha*, "The Opening," the first *surah*, or chapter. This is not the translation I read then, in 1988, but the translation made by Dr. Muhammad Muhsin Khan and Dr. Muhammad Taqi-ud-Din Al-Hilali for Dar-us-Salam Publishers in Saudi Arabia. I've been reading this translation since the mid-1990s, and I like it because the English is a fairly sparse and literal rendering of the Arabic that, I think, conveys the power and poetry of the language in a way many translations do not. When quoting this translation, I have removed all of Khan and Al-Hilali's parenthetical additions to the text.

> In the Name of God, the Most Gracious, the Most Merciful.
> All praise and thanks to God, the Lord of all creation.
> The Most Gracious, the Most Merciful.
> The Owner of the Day of Recompense.
> You we worship, and You we ask for help.
> Guide us to the Straight Path.
> The path of those whom You have bestowed Your Grace, not of those who have earned Your Anger, nor of those who have gone astray.

The Qur'an felt strange, but amazingly beautiful and very compelling. I found it oddly poetic, like the language inside was bursting, barely able to contain exactly what it was trying to say. I wanted to read more, to drink these words in, to fill my body with them.

It felt like God was speaking directly to me.

(The Qur'an was not all John Hartwell gifted to me. He turned me on to Joseph Heller and New Orleans soul band The Meters, and kept shoving Kurt Vonnegut novels at me as well.)

I began to go with Johnny to pray with the Muslim students at SF State. They welcomed me, that group of Palestinians, African Americans and others, in an honest and sincere way no one ever really had before. They didn't push when I told them I was interested, though most were happily convinced that once I started reading the Qur'an, that would be enough to persuade me to become Muslim. They showed me the basics of prayer—the physical movements of *salat*, or what I have taken to calling "Muslim liturgical prayer"—and some of the words I needed to know as I prayed. I didn't memorize very much, as it was a lot to know. But I did pray with them.

Someone told me to read *surat al-'alaq*, "The Clots," if I hadn't already. It was the first thing revealed to the Prophet Muhammad, and they are powerful words. Below I have rendered the first word, *iqra'*, as "recite," because that is my understanding of what it means, though Muhsin and Al-Hilali render it as "read." It can be understood either way.

> Recite! In the Name of your Lord Who has created.
> He has created man from a clot of blood.
> Recite! And your Lord is the Most Generous.
> Who has taught by the pen.
> He has taught man that which he knew not.
> Nay! Verily, man does transgress.
> Because he considers himself self-sufficient.

> Surely, unto your Lord is the return.
> Have you seen him who prevents
> A slave when he prays?
> Tell me if he is guided
> Or enjoins piety!
> Tell me if he denies and turns away?
> Knows he not that God sees?
> Nay! If he ceases not, We will catch him by the forelock,
> A lying, sinful forelock!
> Then let him call upon his council.
> We will call out the guards of Hell!
> Nay! Do not obey him. Fall prostrate and draw near to God!

In these words I felt the power of God—the power to create us from the humblest bits of nothing—a God who calls us into being and teaches us. Everything we are depends on the words, on the mercy and actions, of God. The words were wondrous, and they began filling me.

I was hungry to meet God, and here I was, meeting God.

But also in these words there was resistance. God watches those who rule, those who make laws, those who molest and abuse and prevent, and God will hold them accountable. Our call, when faced with the power of the world, when faced with those who call a lie the truth, is to obey God.

I'd never seen anything like it before. The Christianity I had been a part of for a time in high school was focused almost entirely on the world to come. After a brief enthusiasm, I lost interest in the world to come (whether Heaven or Rapture or Millennium); I wanted something to speak to the here and now. And Islam spoke to the here and now.

As I continued to read, over the next few weeks, I found in the words of the Qur'an a God very interested in how human beings lived and treated each other. In fact, how we treated each other was the basis for how God would judge us, and not merely because we believed the right things. The Christianity I had experienced really didn't ask anyone to *do* anything. All that was needed was to believe and hope for the end of the world. It cared almost nothing about mercy, compassion, or empathy.

But in this Islam, God cared not just about our souls but our bodies, our lives, and our lives with each other. Islam also didn't have to apologize or justify any power or order I'd experienced or even knew much about. It spoke to suffering by saying, "Your obligation is to be kind and do good to those around you." God also empowered us to struggle against power, but mostly that involved rejecting the moral legitimacy of that power and its order, and standing proudly apart. And that was a place I'd been since I was at least six years old.

We aren't just formed by words. We are also formed by the people around us. And the Muslims who welcomed me, taught me to pray, guided me on what to read, and answered my first questions—African Americans and Palestinians—were themselves people who lived lives on the wrong side of power. And who knew what that meant.

Islam was also about dignity. I could see it in the way the very religious Palestinian and African American Muslims acted and lived. It was a combination of rigorous self-discipline, treating others with kindness and respect, a confident assertion of the self and a steadfast refusal to accept as legitimate the overwhelming judgment of the world—that your life amounted to little, that you were a problem and not a person, and that what little you had could be taken from you at whim.

The world could always do those things—and not think twice about it. But you wouldn't surrender to the world, or make it any easier, or grovel. You weren't what the world said you were.

I had a few fairly close acquaintances among the Palestinians, and we spent some time together. I got to know their stories, and learned a little what it meant to grow up in Gaza or Ramallah under Israeli military occupation. What it meant to be a Palestinian student living and studying in the United States.

I got my name, my Muslim name, not long after meeting Ijaz. He's a hard person to describe. He was a Pakistani who had been born in the United States and raised in Saudi Arabia (I believe his parents were both educated professionals), and was living with his uncle and aunt in San Francisco while he studied at SF State. He'd lived something of a sheltered life, took being Muslim seriously, was terrified of his uncle, and had a very bent sense of humor.

For example, one day I came into the journalism department to find a handwritten note from Ijaz in my mailbox: "Let's go gay and move to the Castro and open a hair salon."

Ijaz chain-smoked and laughed profusely, a very quiet laugh that sounded like he was wheezing. He was a keen observer, and also somewhat paranoid, telling me several times about incidents in Saudi Arabia that had convinced him he was being followed by the police.

Once, he glimpsed the crudely drawn Ku Klux Klan and neo-Nazi propaganda on the garage wall of the motorcycle gang next door.

"What is this Aryan bullshit?" he said. "I'm far more Aryan than they will ever be." Ijaz decided that Charles was not a proper name for a Muslim. He'd taken a couple of days and given the matter a little thought, and then came over one afternoon to tell my name was now Umar.

"After Umar ibn Al-Khattab, one of the closest companions of the prophet. He was a big man, like you. He was also emotional, and tended to act on impulse, without thinking. He was one of the best Muslims."

He put his arm on my shoulder.

"You shall be Umar."

Did Abraham have any idea where he was going when God called him to leave his home and his people?

I don't know. God tells Abraham to "go from your country and your kindred and your father's house to the land that I will show you." God makes some promises to Abraham—to make him into a "great nation," to bless Abraham and through him "all the families of the earth." But Abraham has no idea where he's going, and he won't really know until he gets there. Until God tells him, "This is the place."

As for the promises, they are given to him, but they aren't really for him. The land of promise isn't his—it belongs to descendants he will never know—and he never really settles but wanders from place to place, finding sanctuary as he can and occasionally bailing out his nephew Lot when Lot finds himself captured by hostile kings or trapped in a sinful and inhospitable city.

But he never has a home. He wanders, with his family and all his worldly possessions, his entire life. He even has to bargain with a Hittite for a cave in which to bury his wife Sarah when she dies.

"I am a sojourner and a foreigner among you," he tells the Hittites at the beginning of Genesis 23. Abraham has no ground to call his own.

Having roots, being settled, belonging to a people and a place—it seems so natural, so normal, so essential. It is how most people live, or desire to live, or think they ought to live. "A wandering Aramean was my father," begins the prayer Moses taught Israel in Deuteronomy 26, a prayer of offering and a prayer of thanksgiving Israel is to give following the first harvest in the land of promise. Our fathers wandered, and we remember, Israel says. But we are home now. We belong here. This is our place.

Yet, so many of the central figures of the Bible, beginning with Abraham, are wanderers. Strangers among their own people. Even outsiders. Because God called them to wander, to leave home and family, to live very strange lives (consider what John the Baptist wears and eats, and how he lives), to trust and proclaim the promise of God in word and deed. The settled people have a priest who accepts their sacrifices, presides over their worship, and celebrates and comforts them, but it takes a prophet—someone ripped away from place and people—to truly proclaim God's words of judgment, repentance, and forgiveness. To be deprived of past, of people, of place, is to be able to see more clearly the promise of God for the future, a future that is much bigger than the hope for ample rain, good harvest, many children, or victory over enemies in the current struggle.

I won't go so far as to say I am a prophet, or even prophetic. Others have used that word to describe me, even comparing me to Jeremiah. But like Abraham, God called me to wander. To be a stranger. And not just in space and time, going from place to place, but as a "foreigner" among a "foreign" people as well. People who would teach me another language and show me hospitality, mercy, and compassion.

And how to be hospitality, mercy, and compassion.

I'm not sure, even as I know that Jesus has called me to follow him, to tend and feed *his* sheep, that my wandering is over. It is the wanderer's calling, the stranger's vocation, to remind God's people that, as settled and secure as we may feel, as rooted to place as we may be, we really are strangers in this world. We are exiles, refugees who have been brought "out of Egypt with a mighty hand and outstretched arm, with great deeds of of terror, with signs and wonders" (Deut 26:8). We are aimless in the wilderness, given only our day's bread for the journey. Like our crucified and risen Lord Jesus Christ, we have no place to lay our heads. Not really.

3

Pollywog in the Sun

I HATE THE QUESTION, "Where are you from?"

I get asked it a lot and I never really know to answer. When I worked as a reporter in Washington, DC, and New York, just about everyone was from somewhere else. And "where are you from" didn't tell you anything important about someone anyway. So, the question you got asked was, "What do you do?" or "Who do you work for?" And that was an easy question to answer. I'm studying at Georgetown. I'm a reporter on Capitol Hill, I cover natural gas markets or the United Nations. I work for BridgeNews. I'm the defense correspondent for the Saudi Press Agency. I work for *Oil Daily*. I did something. I could even say sometimes I did something fairly prestigious. Even important.

But "Where are you from?" It assumes that everyone is from somewhere, has roots, family, connection to a people, a place, and that connection says something about who you are. That you have a home, a place where you belong and a people you belong to. That knowing will tell people something.

And some don't belong to a place. Or a people.

My life began—or rather, I took my first breath—late on the afternoon of Tuesday, August 22, 1967, a little after five p.m. "Just in time for supper," my mother would often say. I entered the world on a U.S. military base, Ft. Lewis in Washington state, where my father, Charles Leslie Featherstone, was an Army lieutenant supervising the rifle range, helping train recruits bound for Vietnam. He would soon join many of those recruits in the jungles and fields of Southeast Asia. I remember nothing of Ft. Lewis. We didn't stay there long enough. At that time, no one in the U.S. military stayed anywhere for very long; I think we moved every sixteen to twenty-four months.

That would be the first ten years of my life: moving from base to base, assignment to assignment, going wherever orders sent us. My childhood home isn't so much a place as it is an institution—the United States Army.

Home was also, for me, the packing and the moving, learning to live light, exploring someplace new, meeting new people, and the expectation that, in a year or two, I'd do it all over again.

Unlike me, both my parents do come from somewhere: eastern Washington state. My mother was born Carol Marsh, the first child of a reasonably well-off farming family from the Cheney area. There were times as a child when, upon my being introduced to distant relatives, they would almost always say, "Oh, you're Carol's boy!" That's who I was. At the time, it felt strange to be called that, as if I was not my own person. But now, as I recall those visits to people whose names I don't remember and whose relation to me I was never clear about to begin with, it has a comforting feel to it.

My mother's family sprawled across the countryside, a little like the scrubland pasture and the volcanic rocks and the rolling hills of eastern Washington, and she struggled mightily to escape what felt to her like the constant and oppressive presence of her family and a community always watching her, always seeing what she did and talking about it.

My mother's great-grandfather, Josiah Graves, had the good fortune in the 1860s of being one of the very first white men to settle in that part of the country. He was able to pass on much of what he homesteaded to his daughter Josie—my great-grandmother, whom I was fortunate enough to have known when I was young. Josie married Clarence Marsh, and he farmed and ranched the homestead until he died of cancer in 1933, when his oldest son (and my grandfather) Howard was fifteen. Despite being the oldest son with a family farm in the midst of the Great Depression, Grampie (that's what we called Howard) was able not only to finish high school but also studied for two years at university in hopes of becoming a veterinarian. Until his mother Josie yanked him home and told him in no uncertain terms he was going to run the farm.

Grampie had a younger brother, Melvin (whom we all called Mike), and the two of them ran the ranch. I use "ranch" and "farm" interchangeably to describe The Marsh Brothers operation because not only did they grow wheat and barley, but they also ran several hundred head of Hereford cattle.

Howard and Melvin married two of the three Schmidt sisters, Christine and Mary. The Schmidts came to the United States from Germany in the early 1920s. Howard and Melvin were apparently gifted musicians, able to form most of a band (between them, they played the guitar, the violin, the accordion, and the piano, though probably not all at once). Useful in the

1930s, when dance halls needed live musicians. It was at a dance, I believe, that Howard and Christine met. They married in 1941.

They were wonderful grandparents, Howard and Christine—my Grampie and Grammie. We would visit the ranch every other year up until I was a teenager, and the ranch was one of the very few consistent things in a life that was constantly changing. Life had a very different rhythm there, work wasn't off on a base somewhere, but just about right in front of you. It was in fields full of alfalfa and grain, it was the cattle that wandered nearly everywhere except in the well-kept, fenced-in yard around Grammie and Grampie's little white farmhouse. It was in the machine shop, where Grampie would tinker. He had an actual anvil and used it to shape and mold metal, which this obsessive watcher of Bugs Bunny cartoons thought was just the coolest thing ever. It was in gathering eggs in the henhouse with Grammie, something I did when I was very small. It was in the veritable ark of animals that lived on that farm—feral cats, coyotes, snakes, badgers, porcupines, deer, a colony of bats, a pond full of turtles. It was in the large family suppers we would have during harvest time in mid-August, where family stories were told. Over and over again.

Grampie, me, and Grammie on the front porch of our house at Ft. Bliss, El Paso, probably in 1969.

I wouldn't have finished university without Grampie's generosity. My grandfather gave me an amazing lesson on grace in his willingness to give, in his unwillingness to inflict whatever resentments he may have had on those around him. He would not let them get in the way of caring for the people he loved, and he was adamant—whatever opportunities he lacked, he would encourage and support his children and grandchildren to pursue.

Grammie and Grampie were also insistent: farming was not for me. They tried to make sure it held no attraction, that I would never be interested in any way in this work, this way of living. I was allowed to work at harvest the summers between my sophomore and junior, and then junior and senior, years of high school. It was a taste of farmwork—greasing the combine, driving a grain truck to the elevator. But it wasn't real work. Not like the hired hands. Over and over again, Grammie told me I had a greater calling, another calling, a better calling. That I was too good to be a farmer.

I have no idea if farming would have ever been attractive to me or not. It wasn't something I ever considered as a possibility, so I suppose Grammie got what she said she wanted. Not long ago, as I looked back on my life and considered what my options could have been had I actually seen myself as having real options when I graduated from high school, it occurred to me that I could have asked to work for a summer on the farm. Or a year. I don't know if my grandparents would have accepted. I would like to think they would have. But honestly, I do not know.

The ranch was another world for me. Not home, but not strange either. It was a refuge of sorts, a place I could go to and know that I could sit in the middle of a field, or a pasture, and be still and silent, hear nothing but the whisper of the wind in the warm August air.

Or on a moonless night in November, look up and see so many stars, the rough backbone of the sky, and know darkness so deep that the only difference between the sky and the ground is that the sky is full of stars.

My father was in Vietnam for my first birthday. And the war would fester in his life for years. We moved to Ft. Bliss near El Paso, Texas, and I think I might have a memory or two of the place, but they are fleeting—something to do with cinderblock bookshelves.

Dad, me, and Mom in the living room, Ft. Bliss. Those Polynesian masks would
hang in our living room throughout the 1970s, and by the age of seven, I had
named them after television newsmen: Walter Cronkite, Eric Sevareid,
and Howard K. Smith. Because that's who they looked like to me.

From El Paso we moved to the little military community at White
Sands. We stayed there for two years, but one of those years my father took
an assignment on Kwajalein Atoll as part of his work with Safeguard, an
early antiballistic missile system. It's in White Sands I have some of my earliest memories.

One afternoon—in Alamagordo, I think—my mother left me alone in
our giant blue Plymouth station wagon while she went into a J. C. Penney.
I decided to practice driving the car, got behind the wheel, and shifted the
transmission into neutral. The station wagon then coasted out of its parking
space and blocked traffic. I remember faces, kind of, people yelling at me.
Horns honking. I think I may have honked back.

Military communities can be tight-knit, and that was a help, because I
had this habit of taking off my shoes and wandering around, sometimes off
into the desert. At White Sands, someone was always looking out for me.

I vaguely remember preschool in White Sands. Marsha, who lived
down the street and was five years older than I was, decided she was going to

be either my big sister or my second mother. She would walk me to school, demand I hold her hand as we crossed the street, and I would spend time at her house after school. I remember, vaguely, a wonderful model train setup her older brother had, a great and detailed wooden city filled with all sorts of things to amaze a four-year-old. It seemed to fill a whole room.

**Marsha and me one bright October morning in 1971,
most likely on our way to school.**

I was always running away from Marsha, and she was always complaining to my mother. "Butch ran off again!" she would cry.

Ah, "Butch." That unfortunate name.

The geography of southern New Mexico and southwest Texas is burned into my soul, and it feels comforting, familiar, with its clear, wide skies, its flat scrublands and its jagged mountains. If there's a place that feels like home to me, it is this kind of desert. I love the desert. It is why the Indian Ocean coast of the United Arab Emirates felt so good, so familiar. It was New Mexico with a beach.

Living in New Mexico, we were very close to my father's parents, who had retired to Roswell after a lifetime working for the U.S. government.

My grandfather, Charles Thayer Featherstone, was a giant of a man, with an imposing personality as well. He was the middle child, born in 1907. And the family was well-off enough that Grandpa could go to university, which he did, getting a degree and becoming a teacher. His older sister Marion not only got a university degree, she got a master's at Stanford, and would go on to teach home economics at the University of Idaho in Moscow, retiring the year I was born.

Grandpa—that's what we called him—didn't get married until he was in his early thirties. That might not be strange today, but it was back then. Avis Primmo was young—much younger than Charles—the daughter of a French Canadian father and a good Swedish Lutheran mother. My father, Charles Leslie, was the first of three sons—Harvey and Davis are my father's younger brothers.

We would visit Grandpa and Grandma in New Mexico every year we didn't go to Cheney.

Sometime in the mid-1930s, Grandpa went to work as a teacher (or administrator of education programs) for the Civilian Conservation Corps. Like many men of his era, he served in the army during World War II, but he was never sent overseas, the war coming to an end just as he was being prepared for the invasion of Japan. He was then charged with the task of helping demobilize the millions of men coming home from the war, which he did for a year or two until leaving the army and going to work for the Bureau of Indian Affairs.

As I write this, it has occurred to me just what it is I know about my mother's family and my father's family. And how different that knowledge is. I know a lot about the Marshes, but I actually knew very little about Grampie. I learned some in conversations we had late in his life, but most of what I know specifically about Howard Marsh I learned only after he died. However, I know a lot about Grandpa Featherstone—though until my father and I started working on our relationship a few years ago, I knew very little about the Featherstone family.

I think a lot of this has to do with how very different the two families were. The Marshes were not just a family, but a clan. Family gatherings were big events, especially at harvest time (the only time I tended to be there). Family stories were told when we gathered, but they tended to be about people who were no longer there, or people who were not there now, or the way things used to be done. Stories weren't quite told by everyone, but they were everyone's stories.

Grandpa and Grandma arrived in Roswell with only their youngest son in tow. Grandpa, I think, fancied himself something of a biblical patri-arch (minus all the wives and concubines), and so family gatherings were focused on Grandpa in a way Marsh family gatherings weren't or couldn't be focused on a single individual. Grandpa did the storytelling. So, many of the stories were about Grandpa's time in the CCC, in the army, flying around Alaska for the BIA, the earthquake of 1964. There were family stories, many dealing with how many windows his three baseball-playing sons managed to break. And Grandpa was a really good storyteller. But his stories were adventures, and were always told that way. And he did most of the telling.

After the Featherstones settled in Roswell, Grandma went to work for the Social Security Administration and earned her bachelor's degree. They also became very involved in the little Lutheran Church there in Roswell, and you can't look at the collages of church activities there on the walls of St. Mark's without seeing Grandma's face at least once in each of them.

Grandpa and Grandma were always very critical of the fact that my parents raised me without any religion. I was insulated from this conflict— my parents insulated me from a lot of things, and I'm not sure whether that was good or bad.

My mother's family has little use for religion, though my mother has dabbled in various kinds of spiritualism. She was confirmed in a Lutheran church but doesn't have an awful lot of respect for the church or for clergy, having seen too much hypocrisy, intolerance, and cruelty in her youth.

My father was, of course, raised Lutheran. Grandma's faith was deep, stamped on her by her Swedish immigrant mother. Grandpa was raised Methodist, but he became Lutheran in order to marry. "A man should become whatever religion his wife is," Grandpa once told me. The Featherstones raised their three kids as Lutherans, and I didn't know until recently how seriously my father took his faith as a teenager. He led Bible studies, read in worship, even received a scholarship to Midlands College in Nebraska and considered becoming a pastor. Baseball took him to Washington State University, where he was involved in the campus Lutheran ministry. But he told me he was beginning to have some nagging questions about faith—how to reconcile the God of the New Testament, a God of Love, with the God of the Old, who seemed to be nothing but a God of Wrath? Did Jesus really have to die in order for human beings to be forgiven?

But he told me that he truly lost his faith in 1968, somewhere northwest of Saigon, on a day his unit had captured a North Vietnamese soldier. There were no specifics about what happened that day—even when he opened up about Vietnam later in life, he still kept many of the details to himself—except to say, "A loving and merciful God would not let us do what we are doing."

From White Sands we moved to Colorado Springs, where my father was apparently attached to the general staff at Ft. Carson. We lived in a big house off post with a big yard, and I started kindergarten that year at a nearby school.

I sort of remember my kindergarten teacher, Ms. Radford. I don't remember what she looked like, but I remember the kindness of her voice. There was a story she read every day, about letters of the alphabet that were trapped on a desert island. Down the street lived my best friend, Rosanne. We went to school together, we played together all the time, and she was the youngest child in a huge family of what I think were "Jesus people." They sang songs and did all sorts of family stuff together. And they had a trampoline in the backyard. I remember wanting to be part of their family. So much so, I actually snuck into a family picture taken in the backyard.

One evening, scrambling with Rosanne's siblings to get into the house, I tripped over a rosebush and banged my forehead on a great big rock. It bled rather profusely, though there wasn't much damage.

I have still have that scar on my forehead.

My best childhood memory of my father comes from this period in Colorado Springs. For a time, my mother went to modeling school in Denver, and that meant I got stuck in daycare at Ft. Carson. It was horrible, and I hated it.

One morning, I was dropped off early, in a giant room full of other children, a television blaring. There was an older woman watching over us who reminded me a little of my Great-grandmother Schmidt, and I remember telling her, "I don't want to watch television. Can I do something else?"

"You will watch television because everyone else is watching television! Now go sit down!" she yelled.

And then in the middle of the afternoon, then my father would come to rescue me. There he was, in his green dress uniform, ribbons on his chest, brass glittering in the afternoon sun, and he would pick me up. A time or two, or three, he got me a bubble gum cigar. It was a magical moment, and I still cannot see army dress uniforms without feeling a little of what I felt those afternoons, that comfort of being rescued.

Otherwise, my father was kind of a dour and distant figure. I was both in awe of him and frightened of him. I wanted very much to please him, and would come to realize I couldn't.

After Colorado Springs, my father started a master's program at the Naval Postgraduate School in Monterey, California. We lived in a little military housing complex called La Mesa Village, and it had its own school.

I loved being a kid in Monterey. La Mesa Village was a huge, open complex of small row houses and multifamily apartment buildings. There were playgrounds everywhere (and it was always fun when the playgrounds got new beach sand, digging through the piles to find the occasional gray sand crab). The community itself was surrounded by forest, and there was lots of space to play and hike and explore in. I was a budding naturalist and explorer, and if you'd asked me at the time, my career goal was to become a paleontologist and wander the Gobi Desert in search of dinosaur bones.

My best friend was Kendall, and we did just about everything together. I climbed every tree I could—the twisted California oaks were great for that. I collected tadpoles and raised them to frogs, watching carefully how many didn't make it. I had a lizard, a salamander, and I took care of Kendall's rat for a weekend. He also gave me a tarantula, which I eventually set free. When his parents moved out of La Mesa Village to a house in Pacific Grove, I spent the night once and had a wonderful evening watching a hoard of raccoons assault a pile of cookies on his back porch.

In all this, my mother was amazingly supportive and very nurturing. She made me an explorer's kit, including a treasure map she "aged" with the help of a little fire and a used tea bag. She made up stories, and I would draw pictures to go with those stories. (One was eventually published in *Highlights for Children*, without my pictures.) She helped me care for my menagerie (and even replaced all the pollywogs after she accidentally left the bowlful of them in the direct sun, and they all died when the water got too hot) and took me to special classes offered at a nature institute in Monterey.

I even found a fossil, one afternoon, as Kendall and I were hammering limestone rocks on a cliff overlooking the road to La Mesa Elementary. A shell, it looked like a scallop, and the rock opened right up to it as I split it open. I wish I still had that rock.

But some of the worst things my father ever did to me happened in Monterey as well.

I was seven, maybe, and had done something worthy of being grounded. I don't recall what. Which meant I was restricted to our house and our tiny front yard. Grounding was my parents' favorite punishment, and I was grounded often enough to know how the rules worked. But there were lots of kids to play with. So there I was, grounded, in my front yard, doing something, and I think someone I knew wandered by and enticed me away. I knew the risks.

My father found me in a nearby playground, his big white belt in his hand. "You'd better get back home!" he yelled. And I got up. And started walking. And he whipped me with the belt. And I started running. And he ran too, right behind me, the lash of that belt falling on my back as I ran all the way home.

I've known people who've suffered much worse. But this event is seared into my mind, beaten into my soul. I know it happened to me, but I remember it oddly in the third person, as if it happened to someone else, another child all together, as if I'm sitting on the hillside in front of our house watching it happen. Silently watching this grown man flog a seven-year-old, my voice unable to speak. I'm trying right now to remember the pain, a pain so intense I had to sleep on my stomach that night, my back black and blue from the beating.

My mother made my father apologize. He'd beaten me before, and he would again, though never as badly. He used his belt a lot. I knew that I wasn't safe.

It was about this time that fear began to overwhelm me. I was so terrified, especially of boys, that I could not use the bathrooms at school. So— and I'm ashamed even now to say this—I started peeing my pants regularly. I didn't want to. But I was so afraid. I was also deeply ashamed.

Of course, kids teased me about this. And every adult seemed to think the best way to handle this situation was to humiliate me. As if just a little more mistreatment was going to solve the problem. One night—it was a Sunday evening—my father decided that because I was no longer a big boy, I was going to have to wear diapers. I cried. And cried. And cried. And he just rubbed it in a little deeper. I lay there in bed, humiliated, and he sat there, telling me this was going to happen, as if somehow telling me this was a compassionate or merciful solution.

It didn't happen. I'm not sure why.

There in Monterey, I wanted a bicycle. I didn't have one, and when the neighborhood kids there on Halsey Lane went around on their bikes, I sometimes managed to keep up in my wagon, my right leg bent underneath me, and my left leg dangling out, propelling me along. If they didn't go fast or far, I could keep up. And I don't remember whether or not I was teased about this—a little, I suspect—but I certainly felt left out and humiliated. I remember asking my parents for a bicycle. "No," I remember them saying, "you don't know how to ride a bicycle."

"But I can't learn if I don't have one!" I responded.

I also remember somehow thinking that if I learned how to ride a bike, there'd be no reason for them to say no. So one afternoon, after school (I don't recall if this was first or second grade), I asked a friend if I could borrow his bike and teach myself how to ride. And far away from Halsey Lane, I got on his bike, fell down, got up, back on the bike, pedaled a bit, and fell down. Again and again. This seems epic to me now—that it took days and days of effort. But it probably only took a couple of afternoons. The event is so woven into my personal mythology that I really have no idea anymore.

Eventually, I figured it out. I could stay up. And pedal. And go. I could ride a bike. It was exhilarating. I'd done it! And . . . there was no one watching, no one to say "Good work!" or "Congratulations!" or anything else. There was no one. I'd managed it all by myself. I had no one to share this feeling of accomplishment with. That lesson stuck with me for a long, long time—that I was completely on my own to learn how to do the important things in life. No one would be there to help, to show me how, to share the successes—or the failures.

In the end, it didn't matter. There was no deal with my parents. That was all in my imagination. I'd taken the initiative, taught myself something very hard, and all for naught. I got a bicycle, but only later, in Virginia.

My father's violence, unfortunately, taught me how to be violent. There was a girl, about my age, seven or so, her name was Christian. We were friends—not very close, but for a while, we spent a lot of time together. She had allergies and drank soy milk and had a map of Disneyland on her bedroom wall. She was a pretty little girl, with long blond hair and a sweet face.

But Christian had another friend in the neighborhood, Kim, and Kim did not like me at all. And as Christian spent more time with Kim, she spent less time with me. I got jealous, and very angry. I began to envision what I would do to her, how I would make her stop. (Were these the same kinds of visions my father had, or did he just simply act on impulse, without thinking?) I would take her to a nearby pine tree, pretending to show her something, and then hit her, all the while demanding she stop seeing Kim. And that's exactly what I did. I don't how many times I hit her. More than once. She ran crying home. Our friendship was clearly over at that point. I tried to apologize, but her mother—in an oddly kind way—said that I'd already done enough, and that I just needed to go away. Which I did. Her family moved soon after.

This is a hard and shameful memory to have. I hurt someone, and I hurt her badly. And I think *haunted* might be a good way to describe how I feel about the horrible thing I did to her. I was only seven, and I lived with my father's sporadic but awful violence, though that's only an explanation and not a justification. If it's any consolation to anyone, I never did anything like that again.

What shocks me most right now is that I didn't get into trouble. I fully expected the beating that would come at home. But it never came.

Fear was beginning to dominate my life. I was never sure just how much I could trust my parents. I was frightened of my father and felt unprotected by my mother. Truth is, my parents should never have been married to each other. Watching their marriage was like watching a film in a foreign language without the benefit of subtitles, trying to discern something of plot and the inner lives of characters from their actions while at the same time trying to decipher the language. It was foreign, strange. Things were mysterious, frightening, incomprehensible. There was love, but it had to commingle with violence and self-centeredness and indifference and cruelty. It was hard, sometimes, to tell what was what.

And this fear became a toxic vapor that seeped into everything. I remember in Virginia reading in a children's answer book about capital punishment, not quite getting the concept, and wondering—would my parents do *that* to me? What sorts of things might I have to do for them to see fit to kill me? Could I even know?

Still, in Virginia, school worked for me. It was something of a refuge. I had friends, was challenged by my studies, found teachers who seemed to care. And home was tense, but not as bad as it could be. As it had been.

Then, in 1977, we moved to Southern California. And it all went to hell.

4

"I Am Lovable and Capable"

MORE THAN ANYTHING, I remember her voice.

It was a gentle voice, and she spoke kindly to me as she told me we'd be spending some time together, in this empty classroom, talking to each other. She would also show me some pictures, some special pictures that she had brought with her, and ask me to tell her what I thought was happening. She wanted me to make up stories. And as I made up my stories, describing what was going on in the pictures, the events that had happened, the things the people in the pictures were feeling, she responded with "hmmm" and "interesting" and "what else do you think is happening here?"

And she wrote down what I said. On a big white pad.

I want to say she had big brown eyes, and long brown hair, but I don't think so. I don't remember how she looked, not really. And I don't remember her name. But her voice, that I remember.

The pictures she showed me were drawings or sketches done in an old style, maybe from the 1930s or 1940s. Like people in old movies, or in old family photos. I remember one picture she showed me, there was a woman in it, in the center of the picture, and the face of a man in the corner. It was a frightening face. The man hurt her, I think I said. We talked a bit about the man, about how I had described him. "Are you sure?" she asked. "What else do you see?" And then, I think, we went on to another drawing. And another story.

How long this went on, I don't remember. As with the story of teaching myself how to ride a bicycle, I have trouble with measuring the time of things so distant in my memory. It was at least an hour a day for several days, I think. But how long? I don't recall. It may have been for only the one day, but I think it went on longer than that.

The young woman was a psychologist, and my fourth-grade teacher told me one day I was supposed to go to this classroom to help her with a "special project." I suspect the real reason I'd been sent to see the young psychologist was because I'd yelled several times in class, even once leaping up out of my chair and threatening another student. Perhaps the people at Citrus Elementary School wanted to find out what was wrong with me.

I say "suspect" because I was never told. Here I was, an object, a thing in need of management, being talked about. Over the years, many people, especially in positions of authority and responsibility, have likely spent many hours talking about me, trying to figure out what to do with me. Many meetings, much paper, lots of reports, serious conversations and difficult decisions. Talking about me only as a problem needing to be dealt with.

Occasionally, these authorities would talk to me. They almost never talked with me.

The psychologist came close. She may have asked why I yelled in class. I don't know if I told her, or whether, by this point in my young life, I'd become so mistrustful of adults and authority figures that there was no way I could be honest. I don't remember. All I really remember is how sooth- ing and comforting her voice was. That she spoke kindly to me. She may have been sent to evaluate me, to be professional, but her kindness stood out. There was very little kindness in my life at the time, very little com- passion, sympathy or understanding. I missed the time we spent together when she was done.

If I'd been up to telling the truth, being honest about why I had screamed and threatened and leapt up in my fourth-grade classroom at Citrus Elementary, I would have said it was because that was the only safe place for me to talk back, push back, fight back against what had become incessant abuse and torment from other students. They couldn't bully me in class and get away with it.

It is hard for me to think straight about Citrus Elementary School in Upland, California. I have very few good memories of the place—learning to play the clarinet in sixth grade with the district music teacher, a kind man with a deep voice and a craggy face, is one that sticks with me. It was a place where I was incarcerated, abused, tormented. It was a place where I was not welcome, where I was not safe, and it was a place I could not escape.

Sometime during first grade in Monterey, I think, I had my IQ tested. I don't remember the test, and like most things involving me and official processes at school, it was done and I don't remember being told either what was being done or the result. There were people I've met along the way who were apparently told what their results were, but I never was. (Some years ago, my mother told me that my father, upon looking at the test results, said, "He's so smart he scares me." But she didn't tell me what the test results actually were. I still have no idea what my IQ is.) As a result, I got labeled "gifted," and schools had to deal with me accordingly.

At R. O. Nelson in Newport News, Virginia, that meant that all us "gifted" fourth-graders were bussed to another school on Wednesday, where we had special classes, doing intensive work. We published a small newspaper, and I remember a project that involved being split up into teams to create civilizations—including a language and artifacts to bury—and then digging up the opposing team's artifacts and trying to decipher their "civilization" from what we dug up. The work was substantial and a lot of fun. I enjoyed school in Virginia.

It would be a long time before I would enjoy school again.

As a smart, sensitive, bookish kid at R. O. Nelson, I'd been able to fall in with a few other smart, bookish kids. They were there. I had friends. Despite what home could be like, things worked.

But not at Citrus. There were, so far as I recall, no other smart, bookish kids in the fourth grade. At least none I made friends with for very long. (And let's not start with how little sensitivity was valued . . .) The main interest at Citrus was sports—soccer and baseball. I'd played basketball for two seasons in Virginia, but that was just long enough to realize I was no good at basketball (could never master the layup; in fact, I could never even figure out how to do a layup). I was utterly uninterested in sports—that was my father's thing. Here I was in a sport-obsessed community in which nothing else really had any value. Soccer and Little League were all that really seemed to matter.

I tried to be interested, and I even played baseball for two seasons. But I was too afraid of the ball to take a swing and I wasn't a particularly good fielder. My father could have taught me some things, I suppose, if he'd been interested. If I'd been interested. But work took up a lot of his time. And time with my dad was always fraught with the possibility it would end in his demeaning or insulting me, or simply hitting me. I'm glad most of the time he was uninterested. That was simply easier to deal with.

I couldn't even fake an interest in sports. So there was little or no common ground between me and most of the kids I went to school with. No place to meet. We almost didn't speak the same language, and I found them rough and crude.

What they really were was cruel.

The tormenting began from the very first day. Strangely enough, prior to arriving at Citrus Elementary School, I do not ever remember anyone teasing me about my name. I suspect someone somewhere did. But I don't remember it. My mother had also saddled me with the nickname of Butch. All of the Charleses had nicknames—Grandpa's was Chick, my dad's is Charley. And apparently, I struck my mother as a Butch. So that's who I was, and everywhere we went, that's how she introduced me.

And God, how I hated that name.

I think the first thing another fourth-grader did was make fun of my name. In that rough-and-tumble culture, I was likely being tested. Could I take it and then dish it back? Could I play a rough contact sport, get down and dirty in the scrum with everyone else? Was I one of them? My reaction—I cried—proved I couldn't. That I wasn't. I'd never heard anything like this before, never been treated like this, talked to like this. What had I done to deserve it? I was just the new kid.

From that moment on, I was everyone's favorite target for abuse. And it did not stop. Not for the two and a half years I was at Citrus Elementary. In class and at recess. There was the name-calling, the being made fun of, the humiliation. Not being allowed to play with anyone. I think I was beaten up a time or two, but it didn't happen often, if it happened at all. All it took was the threat of being beaten to terrorize me. I knew what a beating was—my father was good at it—and I was terrified of being hit. He may not have been hitting me in Southern California, but that threat was always there. I knew what he was capable of. I lived in fear of the man. So, I was easy to bully.

I'm not going to name my tormentors here. Oh, I remember them, first and last names, after all these years. They are impossible to forget, that horde of Davids and Mikes, accompanied by a Kevin, a Tom or two, a Stacy, a Leslie and a Debbie (yes, the girls tormented me too), with their hateful sneers, their cruel judgments and nasty words. And they were all smaller than me, every one of them. (Well, not true. Debbie and Leslie were taller.) My being bigger didn't make a difference to them. They weren't afraid of me. No one at Citrus Elementary was afraid of me. Not even the girls. It wouldn't have made any sense to them to be afraid of me.

It didn't take them long to discover that I peed my pants. And that just made them giddy. My fear of boys, and of using the bathroom, was only heightened by the whole experience of being bullied at Citrus; I tried as often as I could to use the restroom during class, but that didn't always work. It was one more thing they could always make fun of me for. And they did.

I don't remember the name of my fourth-grade teacher. She tried to be kind, I think, but was mostly ineffectual. She also had health issues and was gone for a while. One of her replacements was an older woman, old enough to use "cross" as a synonym for angry, and her approach to my being bullied was to tell me it was my fault for failing to be nice enough to the kids around me. "You need to be a better friend," she said. She wouldn't tell anyone to stop teasing or tormenting me. "I'm not going to fight your battles," she told me one day, angrily. And she meant it.

Grammie and me up my favorite climbing tree, the fruitless mulberry in our front yard in Upland, California, summer of 1977. I *told* you she was an awesome grandmother.

Occasionally, though, some teacher would force everyone to allow me to play at recess, usually softball or soccer. But everything I did wrong, every mistake or failure, every missed pitch or dropped ball, became one more reason why I shouldn't be ever be allowed to play in the first place. So, usually, they'd force me out of the game sometime before recess was over. I don't remember what else I did during recess, at least not in fourth and fifth grade. I think I read a lot, sitting underneath a tree somewhere in Citrus Elementary's vast green space. School was boring, and I took to reading to keep my mind busy. There were some people who would tolerate having me play foursquare, I think, and some game that involved using one of those red foursquare balls in a handball court (not Buttball, because that wasn't allowed, and I wouldn't play that until junior high school).

I did tell my parents once, not long after it started. It was at dinner, we were sitting around the table, and I remember my father's response: "People are going to tease you. You just need to learn to deal with it." Not helpful. My mother's advice was even worse; she told me I needed to understand that the people who teased me probably had hard lives at home. Why that was supposed to explain their teasing me I wasn't sure. But I quickly determined that my parents could not be trusted. I may have mentioned the problems a time or two, but I never really talked to them about this again.

In fact, no adult could be trusted. No one in a position of power and authority could be trusted. Because they didn't want to know. Or because if they knew, they didn't care. And they certainly weren't going do anything to help. I was alone. I was on my own. This much was clear.

It got much worse in fifth grade, in large part because my fifth-grade teacher, Ms. Johnson, joined in the abuse. When I think of a monster, she is who and what I think of. She was a hateful, angry woman who couldn't seem to say anything without yelling. She played favorites with her students, and all her favorites were my tormentors. She belittled and insulted students she didn't like, even going so far as to hit them. She never hit me, but I remember her hitting a girl one afternoon—a socially awkward and unpopular girl whose name I don't remember—because that girl couldn't or wouldn't stop chewing on her hair. Ms. Johnson had frequently berated the girl, and then one afternoon, as we were doing some class project, she walked up to the girl—who was sitting quietly at her desk, chewing on her hair—and whacked her in the side of the head with her hand.

"I told you to stop that! When will you start listening to me?!"

I'm not sure it fazed any of us. We'd long since gotten used to the brutality.

The two fifth-grade classes at Citrus were "team taught." There was a moveable wall between the two classrooms, and it would come down every now and again. I don't remember the other teacher's name, only that I recall her looking like a very angry Toni Tennille. Discipline, if what we had at this point can be called that, was enforced by an in-class process of public trials. Once a teacher accused a student of violating the rules, he or she would be tried in front of the whole class, with some students publicly testifying and others forming a "jury" and voting on a punishment. These didn't happen often, but they were horrific to watch when they did.

I somehow managed not to get tried—the prospect terrified me—but that didn't mean I was safe from Ms. Johnson. She was always saying something cruel, calling me stupid, telling me I was incapable or incompetent. One afternoon, she stood there, in front of the whole class, and told them *all* how stupid I was, and how she was going to fail me and make me take the fifth grade with her all over again.

She laughed while I sat there and cried.

At some point during the school year, Ms. Johnson decided to implement a new bit of curriculum designed, I suppose, to improve self-esteem and how we treated each other. She had us write "I Am Lovable and Capable" on a piece of paper, and every time someone said something that hurt us, we were supposed to tear off a little bit. At the end of the day, or the week, or whenever the end of this was, we would show what remained of our paper to everyone, with the hope that others would see just how hurtful their words and deeds were.

I confess that at this point, a little bit of me held out a wonderfully and stupidly naïve hope: "Finally, they will see, and know, and things will change." I dutifully complied with the assignment, but by the end of the afternoon the exercise seemed pointless—so much had been taken out of my paper. I tore up what was left and tossed it in a wastebasket.

"I have no paper left," I told Ms. Johnson.

"That's because no one likes you!" she responded. As if I'd finally learned something.

One day at recess, a sixth-grader decided for some reason to make me his special project. He would find me, and if I was near the school building, he would threaten to beat me up and then force me to stick my nose in a corner. He was loud and big and I took his threat seriously. If I moved, he would threaten me again. If I wasn't near the building, he would come and find me (I couldn't outrun anyone). I don't remember how long this went on. Not very long, I think, because it offended the sensibilities of another sixth-grader, Brian Allen, who intervened, and threatened the boy who was bullying me. I don't know whether Allen did this out of a sense of honor and decency, or whether he disliked the other boy that much, or what. He didn't do it out of any real concern for me, because he wasn't interested in me otherwise. But it was the closest anyone ever came, in all of this, to standing up for me.

Because no one else ever did. Not ever.

The fifth grade that year put on a presentation. We sang the songs from *Free to Be . . . You and Me*, one of those 1970s feel-good things that was supposed to show how we are all okay with people being who they are. I don't remember the actual presentation itself, but I do remember singing those songs—I still hate those songs—and I remember one particularly bad rehearsal. It had been a long day, and I had not been able to leave class to use the bathroom. So right there, as we rehearsed, I peed my pants. I can remember it happening quite clearly now. The room was dark, we were standing on risers—I was in the upper right corner as you look at the audience—and Ms. Johnson figured out what was going on, grabbed me and sent me to the restroom. It was too late by then, of course. I think there might have been a change of pants available. But it was not like my teachers to save me from any humiliation.

I do remember the two teachers sitting me in their office, and then deciding—as so many had before—that the very best way to get me to stop doing this was to humiliate me. And do it angrily. Do I want to keep doing this? they asked. When it gets hot, do I want to smell bad? Do I have any idea how hard my life is going to be if I don't stop this?

Yes, I knew exactly how hard it was. Right now. Because everyone insisted upon making it hard.

I think I cried. I cried a lot. They had no sympathy for me, but then people rarely did. My crying just seemed to prove all the more to everyone around me that I was worth abusing. That I deserved to be treated like this. That I *needed* to be treated like this.

The kindest thing Ms. Johnson ever said to me? She gave me a certificate at the end of the school year, after promising several times to fail me (and then clearly not doing so), that read, "Most Likely to Grow Up and Use Big Words." And I suspect for her, that was still an insult.

That year, the year I was in fifth grade, the year I was ten, was the loneliest and most miserable year of my life. School was a morass of almost constant violence and abuse, a place where I was not safe and certainly not valued. I had one friend, Marck Weiss, who kept me connected to humanity. At school, he had it as bad as I did, but much worse at home. In fact, my family was something of a refuge for him. But I remember Marck fondly. He was all I had.

There were a lot of mornings when I would wake up wondering, "Why? Why do I bother going through all this? What if this is all there ever is? What's the point of going on?" Because at the age of ten, I was afraid, truly afraid, that this life of loneliness and fear, and having to deal with abuse on all sides—from kids and adults alike, at home and at school—was all there was ever going to be. So what was the point of going on? If this was all life was going to hand me, there was no point. No point at all.

And one day, somewhere inside of me, I heard a response. I don't know if the voice was mine, or if it came from outside of me. It was too long ago.

"No, this is not all you will feel," I was told. "Because if the pain, the loneliness, is all there is, it would not hurt. It would just be. Because it hurts, it means there is something else, something that will not hurt. And so, you will get up, and go to school, and you will live through it, because out there, somewhere, is a time and a place where there won't be hurting and loneliness. And you will live to get there."

I will live to get there.

And this is what gave me the strength to live through some incredibly awful days. I couldn't trust the world, what it said about me, its judgments and labels—whether those labels said "stupid" or "gifted"—but I could trust what I felt. It was the only reliable truth I had. And however this realization, this understanding, this hope, came to me, it was every bit as real as the awfulness. It was the only thing that would keep me alive and going.

It was not easy. I found a little bit more joy and belonging in sixth grade, mainly because I had a few friends, but not much more. The place I was living for was a long way away.

It did not take too long before I began to start hearing my tormentors in my head, their words as my own thoughts, and considering, as I acted, what they might say. Even if they weren't there. And I started to act, sometimes, as if they were watching, as if the first thing someone might do would be to make fun of me, or insult me, or threaten me.

There was a girl in sixth grade, her name was Nancy. She just showed up one day. Nancy was a tall and somewhat ungainly black girl, but she was friendly. And I remember one afternoon walking home with her, partway, and we talked, and catching no end of grief from the mob of Davids and Mikes. I wasn't sure how to act. On the one hand, here was someone being kind to me, trying to be something like a friend. On the other hand, I would have done anything to have avoided the attention, the name-calling and the insults. I hated the attention, and tried to avoid it whenever possible. Mostly it wasn't possible, but I was so frightened. I don't think I treated her well, as kind as she was, but I also don't think Nancy stayed at Citrus Elementary very long. Whether she was visiting, or her parents did something smart and sent her to another school, I don't know. But she lucked out, not being there very long.

I heard their cruel and savage words and their mocking laughter in my head for many years afterwards, and there are several young women from Upland High School I probably owe apologies to because I couldn't or wouldn't reciprocate their attentions or interest because of this.

Even as my father got older, and by this point he was in his late thirties, he continued to play sports, though he'd given up everything but softball. He played in a league sponsored by General Dynamics, and every week for a couple of summers, we'd go down to the Pomona Division's recreation center and watch my dad play.

By "we," I mean my mother. She'd watch. I wasn't that interested. So I'd wander around, sometimes finding someone else I could play with. (For a time, there was a girl, a year or two younger than I; we became fast friends, and I'd help her look after her little brother, who was maybe three or four.) The recreation center had a playground and was right next to a very busy Union Pacific train track. I loved watching trains—they were loud, intricate, and going somewhere. Somewhere that wasn't where I was. Somewhere else, somewhere far away.

One evening, about dusk, I was playing alone in the playground. I did that a lot, play alone. I am an only child, moved a lot, and I had what some adults would refer to in a very patronizing way as "a very active imagination."

Besides, being by myself at this point in my life was really the only time I was safe, the only time I felt really secure and at ease. I was sitting on a swing, maybe, or a merry-go-round, lost in my own world, when a man came over to me. He was shabbily dressed, very unkempt, had a face full of stubble. He spoke with a very pronounced accent—one I've never been able to place—and he smelled funny, a sickly sweet smell I would later come to know as the telltale sign of a life spent drinking too much fortified wine.

He said hello. He may have asked me my name, I don't remember. I don't think he ever told me his. He sat down on a bench and asked me to sit next to him. Which I did. I think we talked, though I don't recall if we talked for very long. He did most of the talking.

At some point, the man asked me if I would pull up my shirt. And I did. And then he rubbed my stomach. I remember his smell, his rough hand, and him telling me in that strange accent of his, "You're very pretty. You have a very pretty tummy. A very pretty tummy."

This happened a couple of times. That's all he did, and never tried to do anything more than that. And then one day, he was gone.

I never told anyone about this. (In fact, I wouldn't tell *anyone* about this until I was well into my forties.) Whom would I have told? My mother? My father? A teacher at school? I'll tell you what would have happened. They would have yelled at me, found some way to have made this my fault; they would have punished me for it. No, there was no one to tell, no one to trust.

But there's another reason I never told anyone about this. I know now what that man was doing, and the far worse things he could have done to me had he wanted. But at the age of ten or eleven, living in house where I feared my father's violence, welcomed his indifference, and knew neither of my parents was going to make much of an effort to protect me from anything or anyone—and going to a school where I faced daily abuse and humiliation—what that man did to me didn't seem like ill treatment. I knew what abuse was like. I lived with it every day. What he did . . . felt good. His voice was strange, but at the same time, he said nice things to me. He said them kindly. His hand was rough, but it was gentle. He didn't hit me. He didn't threaten me. He didn't make fun of my name. He never called me stupid. He said I was . . . beautiful.

What an awful place to put a child, where the words and acts of a pedophile are the only kindness he or she experiences. What an awful place.

It would be too much to say that I began to resist, or even fight back, in sixth grade. That wouldn't come until the next year. But I began to push back a bit at the society around me. I had experienced much of the previous two years as a profound rejection—I was simply not wanted by the world in which I lived, by the people who lived in and ran that world. So, I would not want the world, either. If I was not allowed to belong, and no points were given for attempts to do so, then I would simply stop trying, accept that I was an outsider, an alien, an interloper, uninvited and unwelcome and unwanted. I would assume whatever that meant and hold hard to it.

So, sometime in the sixth grade I simply stopped saying the Pledge of Allegiance. I couldn't, at the age of eleven, tell you why. I think I could have said they were meaningless words no one seemed to believe. Certainly not the "liberty and justice for all" part. (Now I have a full-fledged theology that tells me the pledge is idolatry, but not even I had such fancy words back then.) It was something we were forced to do, something that everyone did without thinking. Well, I would think about it. And when I thought about it, I decided it was wrong. I would rise and stand with the rest of the class, but I would not place my hand on my heart and I would not repeat those idiotic words. And I haven't said them since.

Strangely enough, no one made an issue of it. I've read all the times over the last two decades kids have gotten into trouble by refusing to say the pledge, and I think, "How did I get away with this?" Not even during the year or so I spent in the Boy Scouts—and I was a terrible Scout, though I had fun with a group of boys who actually didn't hate me—did anyone ever make a stink over my refusal to say the pledge.

As I tried to make sense of the frequently brutal and overwhelmingly unpleasant world I lived in, I began to focus my anger at the very human institutions and structures in which I found myself. There was no God in my life to blame, but there was school. There were teachers. There were parents. There was authority. There was something I was becoming aware of called the state. The world was organized on purpose for this brutality. None of this was coherent at first—it was a feeling that had yet to find many words— but I knew I was in this incredibly brutal place because people put and kept me there. This whole edifice of school had been built intentionally, arrayed and organized and funded, so that people like me could be bullied, abused, and tormented.

Because no, I did not see all of this as a mistake, something gone horribly awry, some aberration in need of reform, but an intended order and purpose of the institution and the organization from the very beginning. Citrus Elementary could not have worked without all the violence, without the bullying. It was a cheap way to reward obedience by giving that mob of

Davids and Mikes nearly unrestrained power to abuse those weaker than they. It gave those kids, who could have potentially been huge troublemakers themselves had they organized in that direction, a place in the hierarchy. It maintained "peace" and "order" at a price no one with any influence, importance, or value had to pay.

I wanted to trust the people in authority. But I had learned I couldn't. I was a child, and a rather sensitive one at that. I very much wanted to trust and to belong. But there was no one to trust, and there was nothing to belong to. The authority figures in my life—my parents and my teachers—had proven indifferent to my well-being, and were all too often intensely cruel toward me. They sometimes spoke nice words, words of caring and concern—"I Am Lovable and Capable!"—but they never meant it. Ever. Their words were only used to beguile and disarm, as a setup for the next humiliation.

Between school and home, I began to understand power in a very simple and brutal way: as the ability to inflict pain and suffering with impunity. The key word here is *impunity*—if there were consequences, if there were a check, someone or something that could or would step in to prevent or even punish, then there would be no power. There may be cruelty and violence, but real, raw, brutal power needs to be able to say, "You are at my mercy. No help is coming, because there is no one who can or will help you." It needs law. It needs righteousness. I have come, over time, to appreciate and even understand there are other kinds of power (I have to in the vocation to which I have been called), but even now, this really is fundamentally what I believe.

And I grew increasingly angry. Angry at the world. Sometimes, beginning in that spring of sixth grade, I would sit in class, or in my room after school, and imagine how I could make the world pay. How I could make it suffer as much as I had, make everyone around me feel the hurt they had so long inflicted upon me, even if for a brief moment, and even if that moment meant my destruction. It would be enough. Once I learned about nuclear war, I began to dream of it, to imagine how wonderful it would be. To see the world set on fire. To watch the panic in those around me, and know that they, too, would die. Just as I would. Their suffering just as pathetic as mine, their power utterly meaningless at the end of the world. It would be enough. I envisioned it over and over again, in daydreams. It was beautiful to imagine.

The destruction of the world. That would be revenge enough for me.

Once, during my first pastoral internship, I had to prepare a lesson for the junior high school confirmation kids on Abraham's sacrifice of Isaac.

In seminary, I'd done a little work on the passage that makes up nearly all of Genesis 22. But I don't think I'd ever really read it. So I sat down with the scripture and began to read. And that afternoon, alone in the office I shared with the pastor, it just hit me. That bit of scripture tore me up, brought me to tears, to a deep and sorrowful place where I just had to sit for a while. And let the story work with me. Work *in* me.

When we tell this tale, we make it all about Abraham and his faith. His willingness to follow the command of God without question, even if it means killing his son. Destroying the very child of promise that so much of the drama of the preceding chapters has been all about. Abraham is tested, and we think of that in terms of passing or failing. Does Abraham pass? Why yes, he does. His willingness to do what God asks, without question or objection (where was the Abraham who was willing to bargain with God over the fate of Sodom?), means he passes. At the last moment, God spares Abraham the need to follow through by suddenly providing a sheep. Abraham proved he was serious. God is satisfied. And all is well with the world.

But we miss what "test" really means here. The implication of the Hebrew is not to pass or fail, but rather to examine something, to learn or discover something new. God wants to know something about Abraham, something God didn't know prior to all this.

And when we make this all about Abraham, we miss the other important person in this story—Isaac. He's not just an object, not just a thing. He's a person, the child of laughter. He sees and hears and feels.

That day, I connected this story with my childhood. *I was Isaac.* I was bound and hauled out to the wilderness and tossed roughly on to a woodpile. And it felt like no one said stop, like no one stayed the hand.

Did I really matter so little to God? And yet, I was not dead. Only the living can ask this question, after they've stared at the sky and beheld the hand and the dagger pointing down at their throats, ready to slice veins and bleed them out.

We live as both Abraham and Isaac in a world where we know exactly what God is capable of. God has asked us to do the unspeakable—annihilate the child of promise, exterminate the people whose land we've been given. And God now knows we'll do this, too. At least, we'll make a good attempt.

But what Isaac knows, that's the greatest horror of all. Not only do we know what God is capable of asking, but we know what those closest to us—those who are supposed to love and care for us most, who are supposed to protect us, nurture us, and teach us—we know exactly what they are willing and able to do. And to do without question. Or objection.

We live with this horror. We live in it.

What makes this livable for me is the knowledge that Jesus comes and shares it—*all of it*—with us. We hold the dagger, and Christ is the sacrificial victim, likewise bound there with us, gazing up at a cold, gray sky. As God, he could stay the knife, knock it out of our hands, toss us into the air and make the very ground itself open and swallow us whole. Or free us from the ropes. And yet, the incarnate child of promise does nothing.

God has learned exactly what we are capable of. And instead of fighting it, or preventing it, or staying it, God gives in. God surrenders. To us. To our violence. To the worst we can do. Or imagine doing.

5

Gulag

It was lunchtime at Upland Junior High School, and I was looking for a place to sit.

I asked if I could join a group of boys at one of the covered picnic tables—the nice thing about Southern California is that usually the worst weather you have to prepare for is rain, and so the lunch area was outside—and they seemed okay with that.

But one boy, James, another seventh-grader just about my size, was not. He wore a heavy, ill-fitting coat and had a mop of straight brown hair. And he said something insulting to me. I don't remember what.

I barely knew James. He wasn't one of my Citrus Elementary tormentors, and I'd only met him that fall. Our paths rarely crossed; we didn't have many classes together, never spoke to each other, and barely even had anything to do with one another.

Yet here he was, saying I wasn't welcome. Saying something worse than that.

And something in me . . . snapped. I had taken this for more than two years. There would be no more. I acted without thinking, on pure impulse, dropping my lunch and lunging at James. He rose, and punches were thrown. Pretty quickly we locked, like two very tired boxers, swinging at each other occasionally. I'm not sure our hearts were in this, struggling as we were, but we had joined battle and we were going to grapple and punch until someone made us stop. Kids gathered, formed a tight circle around us, cheering, egging us on, throwing things at us. There were few things more exciting than a fight at lunch. Eventually, a couple of teachers or lunch monitors pulled us apart and, after a brief interrogation, sent us to the vice principal's office.

The vice principal of Upland Junior High School that year was a big man with a wide nose and giant ears; he looked a bit like a caricature of a union boss or a Chicago ward heeler. I saw the inside of his office a fair amount my seventh-grade year. I don't remember the specific conversation, but the verdict was quick: a three-day suspension. Which was fine with me. I still had no love for school.

That was my first fight at Upland Junior High School. I had never fought before, and I think my mother feared I was becoming one of her worst nightmares. During my years at Citrus Elementary, she would occasionally talk about the bullies she had known at the country schools she'd attended in Amber and Cheney—big farm boys, brutal and cruel. I think she was afraid that if I started fighting, I would become one of them. Whatever the reason, I had, for a long time, felt morally and emotionally disarmed by both my parents and my teachers. I understood that I was not allowed to fight back.

But at some point in the seventh grade, I stopped caring. I stopped being quite so afraid. Partly, it had to do with being in a new school, a new circumstance with new possibilities and some new friends. But it also had a lot to do with the fact that for some reason, most of my worst tormentors didn't follow me to Upland Junior High School. A few did, but not many. They were not legion. I was no longer tormented on a daily basis.

I know that middle school/junior high is a much-maligned experience in America. I sympathize. I remember hormones and cliques and cute girls and gym clothes. I suspect there were few twelve-year-olds more socially awkward than me. (A girl who sat and talked with me on a bus told me, when I was in eighth grade, "You don't know how to flirt, do you?" I was humiliated, and I had no idea how to respond. But she was right. I didn't, and wouldn't really learn until I was in my thirties.) But I can actually say that junior high school was far better than what came before it. Compared to elementary school, it was pleasant.

That fight with James was the first of several. I'd like to feel all heroic and say "many," but that would be a lie. There didn't need to be many. Just enough to learn to claw back a little dignity and self-respect.

One lunch period, I was playing Dungeons and Dragons with a group of friends on the loading dock end of the lunch facility. I was never very good at D&D and didn't really like the game all that much, but I played a lot in junior high. Because friends were friends; I took them where I found them.

One of the Mikes who had followed me to UJHS walked by and saw us—specifically, he saw me. This Mike was one of my cruelest tormentors. He was a little guy, with bulging blue eyes and straight blonde hair. And he never passed up a chance to insult me or threaten me, in or out of class.

Seeing us playing that game, Mike said something. It was an insult, of course, because he couldn't exhale without saying something cruel or nasty. But he made a mistake that day—he was alone. And I was not. And he was within reach. So, just as I acted on impulse with James, without thinking I grabbed Mike by the neck and threw him up against the wall. I wrapped both my hands around his throat, and I pressed the entire weight of my body against his, pinning him. He tried struggling, but he seemed so stunned that he didn't give me much of a fight.

I held him to that wall and watched his eyes bulge even bigger than they normally did, and heard him gasp for breath. I was prepared to kill him. I really was. I didn't care what happened to me. I was going to kill this Mike, squeeze the life out of him. He had it coming.

My gaming partners—which included a couple of girls—struggled hard to pull me off of him. Eventually, someone convinced me to let go. "He's not worth it! He's not worth it! Let go!"

As I let go of Mike, he wriggled out from under me, insulted me again, and ran off. I think he may have even told the vice principal (the irony of that makes me laugh), because I ended up in his office again. But I wasn't suspended.

What I remember most is what nearly strangling Mike to death accomplished. He now stayed clear of me. And every time he looked at me, there was fear in his eyes. I don't like it when people are afraid of me, but this Mike, he *needed* to be afraid. He needed to live with the fear that I might hurt him again. That I could do worse. And even this didn't really stop him. It just meant that whenever he felt the need to insult me, he did it from just outside my reach, so he could scurry away (I still couldn't outrun anyone). And he did this well into high school, an occasional reflex action from a day long gone. By then, however, Mike was no longer a member of the most powerful mob in school but was himself an outcast, consigned to a distant and unimportant place.

But in his eyes was always a little mote of fear. Good.

There weren't many other fights or altercations, if there were any at all. I had a group of "friends" who could also be pretty cruel at times, and one of them got the better of me one afternoon, throwing the only punch after a long, tense standoff (over what, I don't recall) and making me back down.

Self-respect and *dignity*. These are important words. It wasn't so much that I won fights, because I didn't. It was that I fought in the first place, that I'd overcome my fear of physical pain and whatever punishment might come, and in fighting had shown some people who were paying attention that there would be a cost involved in bothering me. I could claw back some sense of self—that I was a person who mattered—only with my fists, my willingness to inflict and endure violence. Because it was clear that I didn't matter to anyone else. No one else was going to "fight my battles." That had been made perfectly clear. Only I could. And so only I would.

It helped that I had many fewer tormentors. The social structure of Upland Junior High School was not so arrayed against me as it had been at Citrus, and there was no institutional or social memory of my abuse as "the way things ought to be." I was not quite so alone (though I was still very lonely), and anyone my age who might try to make my life miserable on purpose tended to be more alone as well. I didn't face an angry, organized mob. Mike had a few friends from Citrus at Upland Junior High, but if he told them what I had done, they weren't willing to help him.

I suspect that had I seriously fought back at Citrus, I would have faced a fairly united and brutal gang of boys. I was far too afraid of them to fight back. But if I'd been willing to struggle, to take that beating, I might have eventually figured out how to fight. I was too afraid of the fastball to hit it, but in my last couple of baseball games, I screwed up my courage (partly in disgust at myself and my fear) and started swinging. And regularly hit triples. So, who knows.

Because of this, though, I was no longer so afraid. I even gained the courage to use the bathroom at times I knew it would have other boys in it. By the end of seventh grade, I stopped peeing my pants. I'm not sure this could have happened if I hadn't at least been willing to throw a punch or choke a tormentor. Dignity and self-respect are things that can be ripped away from a person. They were taken from me, on a daily basis, for several years, as vicious students and indifferent or cruel adults either actively bullied me or sat by and let it happen, unwilling to challenge things or to let me fight for myself. But they can never be handed back. They are not gifts you receive. So, any dignity and self-respect I would have, I would earn. I would have to fight for it, take it by force. There could be no other way.

This is why, years later, the Palestinians and African American Muslims made so much sense to me. Because some people will never be taken seriously or treated with any respect unless they are willing to fight back.

And then there was something odd that happened at Upland Junior High, something I still cannot make sense of today. There was a Mexican street gang at UJHS, the Upland Los Olivos. They don't sound terribly threatening, "the olives," but to most of us middle-class white kids they were terrifying, and we steered clear of them as best we could. Theirs was a truly foreign culture. Not just the language difference, but it was impossible to understand the boys who wore hairnets, white T-shirts, flannel work shirts buttoned only at the collar, and the girls with their garish makeup. Some of the boys were bigger than junior high school boys should have been, and a few had crude, blue tattoos on their hands. Long before respectable people got inked.

Mostly, the Los Olivos kept to themselves. If you left them alone, they left you alone.

And I followed that rule. They were too frightening. But they didn't leave me alone. No, a few of them would smile at me in the hallway and say hello, or "Yo, wassup homeboy?" Sure, they'd laugh with each other when they did this, and I couldn't tell how serious any of it was. I didn't even know what *homeboy* meant. Was that a good thing or a bad thing? I knew what teasing was, or at least I thought I did, and this didn't seem to be it. The ULO kids didn't seem to do this kind of thing to anyone else, but I couldn't be sure. And I didn't cross paths with them often enough to know if this was them making fun of me or what.

But it was interesting. People who looked like me called me names and said I was stupid. People who didn't look like me said hello and called me homeboy.

I found myself halfway through high school with some time on my hands. So I decided to teach myself how to play the guitar. It was not an entirely original choice. My friend Franklin Bruno—who has over the years made something of a name for himself as a songwriter, musician, and writer— had picked up the guitar some months earlier. We were friends, and it was something to do.

I'm not the most skilled musician, and I've always envied friends of mine like Franklin who have real chops. But playing music, and writing songs, quickly became important to me. Songwriting eventually became how I dealt with, and worked out, my feelings about what was happening to me. Some people journal, I wrote songs. The goal was not to communicate, but primarily to express myself. A few years after I graduated from high school, I managed to get an interview with singer and songwriter Scott Miller for a radio show I was doing at the Claremont colleges as Miller's band, Game Theory, prepared to release their 1987 album *Lolita Nation*. My connection with Miller's songs was visceral; he seemed to feel much of what I felt, and it seeped through his words and his melodies. But the meaning of many his songs was not obvious, and seemed hidden, almost deliberately.

"A lot of my songs are in-jokes for one person," he told me.

Which also described a lot of what I wrote too. Even into my thirties.

My closest friend in high school was Adam. A year older than me, he was sweet, very smart, and had a dark sense of humor. Adam suffered from scoliosis and couldn't sit for any great length of time. So, sometime during his sophomore year—my freshman year—he stayed home and was educated by the school district through a special homeschooling program that allowed very sick kids to keep up with their studies. I took to calling Adam's homeschooling program "Adam Robertson Memorial High School," a name Adam happily took up.

Too bad that's not what his high school diploma says.

Adam and I spent a lot of time together, especially after I got a driver's license and, in my senior year, my own car. He lived in a big, creepy old house not far from Upland High School, and his father was a retired psychiatrist who had spent a good portion of his career working in state hospitals. Adam and I had similar interests—military history, current events—and we played lots of war games. Adam almost always beat me; he was a much better gamer than I was. He had the time and patience not only to read and master the rules but also to figure out optimal strategies. To work them out, and then inflict them on me. I learned a lot losing to Adam.

"It's not like I have anything else to do," he said, reminding me once that his illness still kept him housebound, oftentimes lying on the floor to stay comfortable.

I would love to say more about Adam, but I won't. His story is his to tell. I would learn later that Adam had suffered a great deal of horrific abuse as a child, and given some of what I'd seen in his house—big and dark, with a creepy vibe—none of what he described shocked me. Adam grew up in a real chamber of horrors. In fact, Adam would seek refuge at my house for a time.

Adam's politics were very conservative, but it wasn't a law-and-order conservatism as much as it was a reaction to a kind of thoughtless, mindless liberalism of sunshine and hope that we too often found ourselves dealing with, a view of the world that believed people were inherently good and the world inherently reformable ("People are bad because systems are bad"). Such a view, held by a couple of my favorite high school teachers, failed to appreciate the depths of human brutality and cruelty. Systems were bad because people were bad. And that you couldn't change.

What we shared, Adam and I, was a cynical and wary (to the point of paranoia at times) worldview that saw power as cruel, capricious and brutal, something wielded against us. People in power could simply not be trusted. And few could be expected to understand.

Most of my closest friendships have been with people who have been, in some way, abused. There is a chasm, a profound gap, between those who have lived in a world where they can expect to be loved and accepted and even cared for, and those who have found themselves brutalized, molested, or abused. Negotiating that chasm is difficult under the best of conditions, and virtually impossible under the worst. It's like you live an another world, just slightly off-center from the one everyone else around you lives in, in which colors are just different enough that you cannot agree on simple things, like the hue of the sky or the tint of the grass. It is to hear sounds no one else can hear, and not hear sounds others hear clearly. It is to constantly have that difference held against you, and to know that it will be held against you whenever possible. That what you see, and hear, and feel don't amount to anything.

To find someone who sees the same colors as you, who smells the same smells, hears all the same sounds, who has grown to assume many of the same things you do, that's exhilarating! A kindred spirit in a cruel world! Suddenly not so alone! I don't know how I've found so many such people, or how they have found me, or how we even know.

We just do.

And after the nightmare of elementary school, there were actually some kind teachers.

My seventh-grade year, there was Geneva Miller. Geneva taught the gifted class, and as I recall, the actual class itself was of very little value. (Actually, that's not fair. I don't remember if the actual class itself was of much value or not. By this point I'd more or less given up on school.) But she understood me, and she took me seriously and treated me with the stern kindness that I have always responded well to. She expected much of me and, when I fell short or failed, told me I could do better. But she did so in a way that showed she actually cared. There wasn't a hint of cruelty in anything she did, at least not to me. My mind mattered to her, and I think my soul did too.

My freshman year of high school, there was Chris Perkins, my world history teacher, who told me she admired the fact that I learned things simply to learn them. She didn't give me extra credit for that kind of thing. She did better than that—she talked to me about it, took joy in it, and let me take joy in being smart, in knowing something just for the sake of knowing it. I enjoyed her class thoroughly. And there was Marie Copeland, who taught freshman advanced English. I did terribly in that class. I was defiant and refused to do the work or even take much of it seriously. I did so badly that I was knocked down to remedial English my sophomore year—and I had to work hard to get back into the advanced placement English program. But I think she saw something in me, and made me write. And write. And write.

My junior year, there was Jon Wenrick—my American history teacher—and Calvin French, the advanced placement English instructor. The most important part of junior honors English was the tiny library in the back of the room, where I devoured all the Max Shulman that French had (he'd read a Shulman essay on prom that was so funny I decided I needed to read whatever else he wrote) and where I discovered Aleksandr Solzhenitsyn.

Calvin French even drafted me to be on the school's academic decathalon team my senior year. He didn't ask me, he told me: "You will do this and it will be good for you." I was one of the B students, or maybe the C student (I don't entirely remember), and I earned a mess of first place, second place, and sweepstakes trophies at the county competition and took Upland High School to the statewide competition that year, where I placed third in economics.

But the most important teacher I had in high school was Bill Turner. He was the first, and most important, of my several surrogate fathers. Turner was a gruff, no-nonsense Korean War veteran; he taught wood shop and a class called aviation (basically, a version of the FAA's ground school for private pilots), and he ran the auditorium. After quitting marching band, I joined the stage crew, and that quickly filled up my time.

**Me and the baritone saxophone I marched with in
the Upland High School band, fall of 1982.**

I loved the work. It engaged both my head and my hands—building
things, hanging and aiming lights, running sound and recording equipment. I threw myself into it, and Turner came to trust me as something close
to a right hand for the two years I did it. He was patient but demanding,
and while he would always reprimand me for whatever it was I did wrong,
he never held anything against me. Which was important, because not long
after starting on the Upland High School stage crew, I crossed the positive
and negative wires on one of our ancient tube amplifiers and blew it out,

filling the sound booth with that wonderful smell of burning rubber and electronics. I was terrified that he would be angry with me, but he wasn't. It was something to learn from, and he made sure I learned it.

"You are smarter than the average bear," he'd constantly remind me, either to prod me to think more clearly or as a gentle reprimand if I'd just done something stupid or careless.

Turner taught me how to work. This was a big deal, given that about all I'd heard from my father since the last year of junior high was how lazy and incompetent I was, that I would never amount to much because I refused to work hard. (At what I was never certain, given I was only thirteen when this started.) Take the work seriously, give it your undivided attention, he told me. There is honor in doing what you do well and right. Treat the equipment you use as well as you would treat your own. And clean up after yourself, so that no one knows you've been there in the first place.

That's an old shop teacher's instructions to make sure you put all the tools you use back where you found them. So no one has to come in Monday morning and stumble over your mess. I spent a lot of time in the auditorium, fooling with the even then ancient 3M open-reel audio and video recording gear, making many lousy recordings of my awful music. It was wonderful. And I always tried to make sure I cleaned up after myself when I was done. I wasn't always good at that—and Bill Turner would remind me, gently but sternly, every time I wasn't—but I worked on it. I truly did. And I tried never to make the same mistake twice.

A private pilot and very active in the Civil Air Patrol, Turner took me up in his plane a couple of times. I'd been doing a self-guided ground school course, and once, while we were five thousand feet over Rancho Cucamonga, Turner let go of his control stick and said, "Now you fly it." It was terrifying, having this little machine—and our lives—in my hands.

He did a couple of touch-and-go landings that day at Cable Airport in Upland in an attempt to show me how to land. I couldn't get the hang of it.

I have never been one to get into trouble. Not on purpose. Certainly not for attention. That saying used to describe troublemakers, "they only want attention," makes no sense to me, because I'd learned by high school it's better to get no attention at all then it is to be on the wrong end of popular opinion and official sanction.

At the same time, I was almost constitutionally incapable of keeping a low profile, and very occasionally I would do things so utterly and publicly stupid as to boggle the imagination.

It was an early spring day, I think, in my junior year. I was, for some reason, in the band room. There was no reason for me to be there, since I'd given up on band, but the Upland High School band room was connected to the auditorium, and I'd gotten to know the band director some. I'm not sure where the discussion was going, or why, but to make some point, I grabbed the marching band's American flag (which was on a short staff so it could be carried by a color guard), flipped it over, and pretended to mop the floor with it. I have no idea what I was trying to prove; that point is lost to me now. At sixteen, I was full of obnoxious and indignant and angry self-righteousness. The deed was done, I put the flag back, and didn't think about it again.

But someone else did. A senior penned an angry letter to the high school newspaper. I was not named, but as I recall, the letter writer was outraged that the action had gone unpunished, that such an act could even happen. It was a short letter, and while what I had done had clearly gotten around, no one seemed to be investigating or asking. I probably could have let this go and been no worse for wear.

However, even if I could have escaped the whole mess with some measure of anonymity, I decided I had a point to prove. I'd been reading a lot about U.S. foreign policy, mostly from a left-wing perspective—books that were very critical of the United States, books that spoke to me. I knew who bullies were and what they did. And in these books, I saw a bully: my country and my government. My country was hard for me to like. I wanted to love my country, and in some ways I did. But it was hard for me to separate the abstract ideals of America from the brutal reality I'd lived in since I was nine.

So, like the hot-headed and self-righteous young man I was, I responded to the student newspaper full force, writing one incredibly long, angry, and sanctimonious letter, a wall of words that attempted to rhetorically prove, beyond anyone's doubt, that I was right. In dragging the flag on the ground, in making it a mop, in writing and writing and writing in my own defense. Somewhere along the line I became "The Mad Flag-Dragger," and I may have even made that one up myself. I don't recall.

Bill Turner gave me a fairly stern lecture on the matter one morning. Mostly, he couldn't understand—what I'd done made no sense to him. But I don't think it changed how he thought of me. And his lecture, mercifully short, ended on a more serious note than most of his lectures did: "You should know better than this. You should know better."

I don't recall how long any of this went on. Weeks, I suppose. And mainly because I would not let up. I had to respond to every letter to the school newspaper. More words. More argument. I thought it mattered. I even think this was the subject of a special PTA meeting at some point. I do remember my mother in particular in a panic over this.

"What will people think?!" That was panic for her. I could hear it in her voice.

I wanted to tell her, "I don't care what people think, because nobody likes me anyway!"

Thankfully, there were no official consequences for all this—no punishment, no sanction, nothing. There was a group of kids who would sometimes taunt me, but they weren't many, and I didn't run into them often. As I look back, I clearly led something of a charmed life in high school. I'm not sure why.

One day, when I was fourteen, I suddenly found myself interested in God. Wanting to go look for God.

Living in suburban Southern California in the early 1980s, the only religion you were likely to bump into by accident was a conservative, happy-face dispensationalist Christianity. It was everywhere. (Jack Chick of the garish pamphlet fame hails from the Inland Empire, and I think he lived in Upland for a time.) I got involved because I met Keith, and he was a fervent believer at the time. He slowly worked on me, getting me involved with a Bible study that would meet informally at lunch under one of the trees at the high school. And then there was a Friday evening youth Bible study associated with a little church in north Upland I remember being called Upland Bible Church.

It was a very awkward beginning. I had a religious experience of some kind, and for a time, I did call it "being born again." There was something, in particular, one morning walk to school when the sky was bluer and the flowers far more colorful and the grass much greener than it had ever been before. Something happened. In the mysterious ways God has worked in my life, I was slowly being shown the road I would travel. And if I didn't have a proper guide, well, from time to time, guides would find me, and I would be led a least a little bit of the way.

But there was also belonging. I ached to belong, and to an extent, I was welcomed into this group. And yes, there were girls. For the brief span of a week during my freshman year, a junior by the name of Kristin who was part of the lunchtime Bible study decided to be my girlfriend. It didn't last very long, because it turned out she was interested in Keith and not me. In fact, she never told me we were done, she just told Keith, who then told me. The end of that more or less ended my involvement in that Bible study group. It was just too awkward. (Later that year, in early summer, Keith called me up to ask if I still had any feelings for Kristin. I told him it hardly mattered if I did. He then proceeded to tell me all about the sex they'd just had, in more detail than I wanted. I never really spoke to Keith after that either.)

I attended the Friday evening Bible studies for a good bit longer with Adam and his sister Liz. It was one more way for Adam to get out of the house. And one more thing I could belong to, another place where I was taken seriously as a human being with something to contribute.

Honestly, I find the whole thing pretty embarrassing. I was never a particularly good Christian in high school, and by my junior year I would give it up all together. But I did believe for a time, even in much of the nonsense theology of dispensationalism. (A group of us decided to write "rapture letters," explaining to people what had happened to us when we disappeared. My mother found mine in my typewriter, mistook it for a suicide note, and had a meltdown.) In fact, if you're a teenager who is obsessed with history and current events and who has something of a cynical view of the world, dispensationalism is a perfect theology. It takes you seriously, takes what you know seriously, and your knowledge is no longer simply a strange collection of facts and stories that fascinate you (and perplex everyone else) but suddenly has cosmic import. You know the signs of the coming of the end and can read those signs with a subtlety most others cannot. You're valued, even if your faith is rough and needs forming. For a time, I was very impressed by the youth pastor and Bible study leader, Wally. He was a young-earth creationist, a biblical literalist, and deeply committed to the belief in an imminent rapture of the saints followed by a horrific tribulation. He was also smart, and he took our faith and our questions seriously.

But this faith, as intellectually interesting as it was for a bit, couldn't do much me for otherwise. It could not give meaning to my suffering. It could not deal well with the suffering of the world. It was, near as I could tell, the faith of comfortable people, people who had never struggled. It looked for one thing and one thing only—the coming end of the world. Everything was about signs and portents, wars and rumors of wars, nations fighting nations, Jesus returning on the clouds, and making preparations for all that. Nothing else seemed important. Nothing else mattered.

During a field trip my junior year to the *Los Angeles Times* (I think this was a high school newspaper trip led by Jon Wenrick), I found myself face to face with homelessness in downtown Los Angeles. And I found myself wondering—what does faith in God have to do with any of this? I had no answers, just questions I had no way of answering.

One day, I found some answers. Entirely by accident.

In the back of Calvin French's advanced placement English class was a tiny library, two or three small stacks of books. Things you wouldn't find in the school library. We could check them out, for as long as we wanted. I'd read through all of the Max Shulman in that little collection and taken a stab at Tolstoy, and because of that had become fascinated with Russian authors.

So, when I came across a fat, silver volume with its title in bright blue across the cover—*The Gulag Archipelago*—I was intrigued. It was a thick book, but that hadn't stopped me before. That just meant it was a challenge.

Gulag is Aleksandr Solzhenitsyn's epic literary investigation into the Soviet Union's criminal justice system, from just after the Bolshevik seizure of power in late 1917 to the late 1950s. As history, it's impressive and distressing reading. As anticommunist polemic, it's a powerful indictment of a social and political system that had relied on mass terror almost from the very beginning.

But what I found in Solzhenitsyn's book was meaning. As absurd as it may sound, his book on the Soviet prison system gave me a way to make sense of my life in grade school and high school. It was intoxicating, as the Qur'an would be. As Malcolm X would be.

First and foremost was the matter of suffering and power. Inflicting suffering was just something that power did. It couldn't help it. Because of that, there was no inherent meaning to the infliction of suffering. "Why, O Lord?" is a question asked of the silent darkness:

> If you are arrested, can anything else remain unshattered by this cataclysm?
>
> But the darkened mind is incapable of embracing these displacements in our universe, and both the most sophisticated and the veriest simpleton among us, drawing on all life's experience, can gasp out only: "Me? What for?"
>
> And this is a question which, though repeated millions and millions of times before, has yet to receive an answer.

Because there is no answer.

Our thinking about suffering tends toward "why does suffering happen?" It usually interrogates God, and often quite harshly. But it always does this presuming that the one suffering is the only one who matters to the question, as if God and the sufferer are the only things in the equation. As if suffering is merely a passive verb, with an object but no subject. But Solzhenitsyn flips this. Suffering is an active verb with a subject, something human beings very purposefully inflict upon other human beings. In his understanding, the people who matter, morally, are those who inflict the suffering, and not those on the wrong end of their laws, their clubs, their guns. The people who torment and oppress are the ones who need to be questioned.

> And what would one then have to say about our so evident torturers: Why does not fate punish them? Why do they prosper?
> (And the only solution to this would be that the meaning of earthly existence lies not, as we have grown used to thinking, in prospering, but . . . in the development of the soul. From that point of view our torturers have been punished most horribly of all: they are turning into swine, they are departing downward from humanity. From that point of view punishment is inflicted on those whose development . . . holds out hope.)

Suffering is rarely, if ever, deserved. But once you are targeted by power, it will not let go. Because it is not in the nature of power to let go of those it has grasped hold of and swallowed. The only salvation that can come is reached by accepting suffering.

> But—there is nothing that we can do. And nothing is going to save us! . . . And the conclusion is: Survive to reach it! Survive! At any price! This is simply a turn of phrase, a sort of habit of speech: "at any price."
> But then the words swell up with their full meaning, and an awesome vow takes shape: to survive at any price. . . .
> But simply "to survive" does not yet mean "at any price." "At any price" means: at the price of someone else.

You can accept that your lot, your life, your conditions will be hard and your path long. But you won't take from others. You will lay down whatever privileges you think you should be entitled to, and do the hardest work. And take toughest path.

A very good friend at seminary once told me she found me oddly fatalistic. And I think I am. I take to heart a concept not much used in our mass democratic modernity: lot. It was my lot in life to suffer. Because of this, I have never been an activist (just a loudmouthed malcontent), and I'm willing to accept a great deal of what many people would call injustice.

Because I never lived, as a child, as a young person, with any sense that the world could be changed. Little would work in my favor. There was no cavalry, no knight in shining armor, no guardian angel waiting to save me. That never happened. There was no justice. Just loneliness, shame, fear, and violence. The world was a fundamentally unjust place, and it had to be endured. Because surviving in the face of the brutality, the indifference, the loneliness—and not becoming part of it, not succumbing to power and privilege and the cruelty that necessarily came with it, and all without resorting to cruelty or violence—well, that was what counted.

And a life of suffering could bear witness to the world. Of what, at the age of sixteen, I wasn't sure. Perhaps my soul was being refined for a purpose, though that purpose wasn't clear either. All I had was a very rough faith in something I couldn't even begin to see.

Solzhenitsyn helped me understand there could be dignity in enduring suffering. I devoured all three volumes of *Gulag*—eighteen hundred pages—twice during high school. And twice more in the next few years. My copies are tattered, in pieces, marked up, highlighted, and water damaged. But I have carried them virtually everywhere I have gone.

I was fifteen the last time my father hit me. It was an afternoon when my mother wasn't home, and I'd failed to clean the bathroom to his satisfaction. (Yes, I'd really done a half-assed job.) He slapped me hard in the face. And I realized at that moment that I hated him. I swore I would never let him hit me again. I didn't care what it took, he wouldn't be able to do that to me ever again.

We weren't much of a family. My parents' marriage, their relationship, never made much sense to me. For several years, they slept in separate bedrooms (which is why my father and I shared a bathroom). Much of the time, it was my mother and me against my father. She and I were close. Too close, I think. My mother used me as something of a buffer between the two of them. It was an uncomfortable place to be, but it was better than the alternatives. And I still wasn't in much of a position to choose my circumstances. If the choice was between being hit and not being hit, that was an easy one.

While my mother and I were close, we also argued, mostly over my grades. I didn't care how well I did in school, and I could get straight B's with almost no effort. So, I expended almost no effort. My parents tried cajoling, bribery, even punishment to get me to work harder. They were both straight-A students in high school, and I suspect their anger was mixed with some shame at how I was probably squandering my talents and intelligence.

There were few things I could choose, but I could damn well choose this. I would not be moved—not by bribes, not by losing access to my car, not by anything. I hated school so much I'd given serious thought to dropping out at sixteen. But what would I have done? That's all that kept me in.

Besides, there was no upside to doing well. My parents busted themselves getting good grades in high school because it was a way out for them. For my father, that meant his ROTC scholarship (after West Point was no longer an option), and for my mother, it meant leaving the farm. But my father had made it clear—I would receive no help for college, financial or otherwise. I was entirely on my own. And I wasn't all that welcome at home after I graduated, either.

I had no idea what to do. I had no idea where I could go, what I was good at, or whether I was even good at anything.

I was determined to leave Upland. Somehow. I was going to get out of this miserable city if it was the last thing I did. Because there was no belonging in Upland. No place, and no group of people, who would really want me. I brought nothing of value to this community; it would accept no part of me. Conformity in this place was entirely about meeting community expectations and demands. There was no meeting anyone halfway. It was just being what was expected and demanded of you. Individual human beings were widgets, interchangeable parts, molded and shaped to fit into a machine. How much force you had to use to make the pieces fit all depended on how much the pieces resisted, or how oddly shaped they were.

Some parts could just be thrown away. They clearly were not worth the effort.

What was even worse, after all this, after eight years of brutality and abuse, this community could turn around and demand my love and loyalty. And act as if somehow they were the injured party when I was something other than fervently in love with them.

They got neither my love nor my loyalty. They hadn't earned it.

At seventeen, I had three great questions of the world. Would anyone ever want me? Would anyone ever love me? Would I belong anywhere? I had no idea what the answers to those questions would be. I had the vague hope, thanks to that voice I had heard in fifth grade, that there was a "yes" out there. Somewhere. But really, I had no idea where I was going. Or how to get there.

I ached to be loved, for the affirmation that I mattered to just one human being. After Kristin, there was no one. Oh, a girl a year behind me named Jennifer (not my wife; this Jennifer is currently a bigwig at Genentech) asked me to a dance, but I couldn't tell how interested she was, and while we went to the dance, and later to a movie, nothing else came of it. The night of the senior trip to Disneyland (this was, after all, Southern California), Ed Lyon, a fairly popular senior and football player, had a particularly nasty spat with his girlfriend and decided to share a bus seat with me. Now, Ed was always fairly nice to me. I just got the sense that like lots of people, he never really knew what to think of me or how to act toward me.

But that night, he decided to be my company. And he talked at length about his girl troubles.

"You should feel lucky you don't have to worry about girls. Nothing but trouble," he said. Was he being honest, or merely patronizing? I couldn't tell.

I looked into the darkness.

"You don't tell a starving man the food is bad, Ed. You just don't."

I don't know if anyone else has emerged in the world as uncertain of themselves or as incompetent as I was. For so long, I had felt so alone that I was convinced no one could possibly feel as alone, as unloved, and as angry as I was.

The day I turned seventeen, a couple of weeks before my senior year started, I signed delayed enlistment papers for the U.S. Army. I would start basic training the following July. I'd grown up in the army, and it was not a foreign institution to me. It meant leaving home, and maybe things would be different. Because of my age, my parents had to cosign. I suspect they had reservations, but they signed the papers anyway. I know my father had concerns, but by this point I wasn't listening to him. It was not a good decision, but what else could I have done? (I almost enlisted in the Marine Corps, and that would have been *much* worse.) I'd like to think I would have listened to good counsel at that age, but I'm not sure I would have. Because I'm not sure what good counsel would have looked like.

6

Disneyland

You could set your clock by the rains in Panama.

In the rainy season, the rain would come about five times a day—a little before sunrise, mid-morning, early afternoon, suppertime, and about an hour after sunset. It would rain for about half an hour, and the fifteen minutes after a regular downpour were the only comfortable times of day.

This meant that when the soldiers of Headquarters Company, Law Enforcement Activity, did our physical training during the hour before breakfast, the ground was usually still soggy.

"Good training!" someone, typically a sergeant, would say of the wet and the muck.

Panama was a country of heat and humidity, and I still remember how it smelled when I arrived in the fall of 1986, the air heavy and wet with the sharp aroma of mildew. It didn't get any better in the dry season, when the rains stopped altogether, and Panamanians took to setting the jungle on fire. The only smell worse than mildew is that of burning mildew.

The soldiers of Headquarters Company, Law Enforcement Activity, didn't do PT every day. We only had to peel ourselves out of bed three days a week to run, do push-ups and sit-ups and whatever other physical exertions were found for us to do.

And even then, we didn't do *that* all the time either. Some days we practiced riot-control techniques. Those mornings involved showing up early to formation with our Kevlar helmets (complete with a plexiglass face shield), flak jackets, and long wooden batons about an inch thick. Dog handlers showed up with their attack dogs. We would get into formations of blocks and wedges and practice advancing into a crowd and the proper use of the baton (two-handed, not one). Sometimes smoke grenades would be used to simulate tear gas. And we learned to march using the "stomp and drag" technique, stepping forward with one foot and then dragging the other foot up behind it.

We were supposed to be more menacing that way, and tougher to fight, grouped in a wedge, stomping and dragging.

It was Panama in the mid-1980s. Our relations with Manuel Noriega's government were very strained. Panamanians just barely tolerated the U.S. military, and there was a strong national memory of the riots in the mid-1970s that had led to the Panama Canal Treaty. One Saturday I was wandering around Panama City and stumbled across a huge mural depicting the late Panamanian dictator Omar Torrijos as a golden-haired Adonis leading the valiant people of Panama against anonymous American soldiers who all looked like pigs in their black gas masks (the same kind of mask I'd been issued and sometimes wore during riot-control training). The Reagan administration's Nicaragua policy—opposing the Sandinista government that came to power in the 1979 revolution by, among other things, supporting a motley group of rebels called the Contras—was not well liked by most Panamanians. So we trained for what some saw as inevitable. War with Nicaragua, if it came, would mean conflict in Panama.

For a time, we did this training once a week. And it bothered me. It bothered me a lot, learning to beat people. I hadn't signed up for that.

So, one morning, I showed up to riot-control training without my helmet, without my vest and club. The first sergeant, who didn't like me much anyway, was livid.

"Private Featherstone, where's your gear?!"

"In the barracks, First Sergeant."

"Why don't you have it?"

"I don't want to do this anymore, First Sergeant."

A man who had lost all patience, he glowered at me. Even under the best of circumstances he was frightening—tall, skinny, and very pale, with a face that looked like a skull on a pirate flag.

"You had better go and get your goddamned gear and be back in one minute or I will throw you in the stockade!"

He meant it. He could do it. I was surrounded by military police, there was nowhere to hide. So, I got my things. And stomped and dragged with the best of them that morning.

I had picked a very strange time to finally find the courage to up and defy, to finally say "fuck you" and truly not care what happened. The power arrayed against me was real. Far more real than any power I'd ever dealt with before.

I may not have been the world's worst soldier, or the saddest sack who ever donned woodland camouflage or olive drab jungle fatigues, but I was very, very close.

My time in the army had begun well. It's not that anyone likes basic training—I certainly didn't—but at the same time I found it exhilarating. For eight summer weeks in the middle of Missouri, I was pushed as hard as I've ever been pushed physically. I got to be a pretty good shot. And I had an eight-week vacation from worrying or even thinking about myself. We were all in the same situation, though I wasn't anywhere near as whiny as those missing their girlfriends and wives. I was too busy learning how to tear down and clean my rifle and trying to memorize all the information in my "Army Smart Book" so that I could tell my colonels from my chief warrant officers, know how to respond to a chemical weapons attack and how best to roll my socks and be ready for inspection.

But then, anything that lasts only eight weeks can be lived through. It's what comes after that's the hard part.

I had done very well on the ASVAB, the Armed Services Vocational Aptitude Battery, the test the military gives to potential recruits to help figure out what they should do. So well, in fact, the recruiting sergeant told me I could do whatever I wanted to do. (I've long been told this, and it isn't as helpful as you might think to someone lacking direction.) So, I decided I wanted to be a linguist. That involved taking another test to let the military determine which language I would be "best suited" to study. I don't remember the name of that test, but it was an all-afternoon affair full of logic puzzles and the like. The exam even made up a language that you had to try to make sense of, and working through that section was the only time in my life diagramming sentences ever came in handy.

The language test form included a section where you chose which languages you were interested in learning, and I selected Russian, Arabic, and Chinese. It was, after all, 1985, and I figured I had a very good shot at Russian. I knew nothing about either Arabic or Chinese, but they were exotic and therefore probably hard. A challenge sounded fun.

However, the computer in the Pentagon had something entirely different in mind for me, and enrolled me in Czech. I was scheduled to start at the Defense Language Institute in Monterey, California, in late September of 1985.

I remember the afternoon at Ft. Leonard Wood when our drill sergeant handed out the advanced training orders. Most of the recruits in my basic training unit were simply moving across the street to the combat engineer course. Some were assigned to mechanic schools. A few had opted to become infantrymen. Three of us were off to DLI.

"That's not the army," he said. "That's goddamned college."

The Czech classes at DLI were located in a row of very old barracks buildings—dating maybe to the First World War—that housed the rest of the Eastern European language programs: Polish, Bulgarian, Hungarian, Serbo-Croatian. (There used to be an Albanian course, but it hadn't been offered for years.) All of us soldiers studying the minor Eastern European languages lived together in a big and fairly modern barracks building up the hill from our classrooms.

There were a few airmen (we called them "zoomies"), sailors and Marines in the Eastern European program. (An inordinate number of Marines were studying Bulgarian when I was there.) But they lived in their own barracks according to their own rules. The Marine cantonment at DLI, for example, was beautifully kept and somewhat terrifying. It helped, I think, that the Marines punished their miscreants and wrongdoers by having them scrub the sidewalk with toothbrushes.

I showed up a day or two early, signed in, and happily presented myself.

"I am here to learn Czechoslovakian!" I said.

"There's no such thing," the sergeant on duty told me, handing me room keys, sheets, blankets, pillowcases, a heavy stack of newly printed language textbooks and a thick little volume with a then-unreadable title, "Český-Anglický/Anglický-Česky Slovník."

We studied Czech for six or seven hours a day (Slovak was saved for a couple of weeks toward the end of the course), in addition to homework—memorizing vocabulary, writing essays (that got longer as our studies advanced), dealing with the rather complicated grammar of Czech, preparing for exams. We also had military duties we had to tend to, such as daily PT. So, we were busy.

Our instructors were a collection of defectors, almost none of whom had ever taught back in their home country. They all had stories, some more interesting than others. My primary teacher was a soft-spoken man named Peter Bednařik. He had been a mountain climber, and I think—if I remember his story right—he had been a commando in the Czechoslovak Army. Part of his service had involved training Palestinian militants in the use of high explosives. He had managed to smuggle his family out of the country in something akin to the Von Trapp family's escape from Nazi-occupied Austria.

My class was all soldiers—a combination of new recruits, one sergeant who had taken Polish a few years earlier, and a few Special Forces NCOs from Ft. Devens, Massachusetts. Most of us were training to be linguists or interrogators. My job would have involved many more weeks of training with very sophisticated electronic equipment, sitting in West Germany and listening to the Czechoslovak Army. Or wandering around Texas practicing listening to the Czechoslovak Army and painting things when we weren't busy.

It was a difficult class, and not everyone made it. Some people couldn't cope with the study—Czech is a hard language—and some people simply broke because they combined the intensity of the schoolwork with other life complications.

Ah yes, complications.

Not long after I arrived, I met Anna. She was in the class ahead of me. She was small and curvy, five-foot two, with big brown eyes and an utterly enticing smile. Her skin was pale and a little freckled, and her almost-shoulder-length hair was a little wavy and a little wild. I found her captivating. I had fallen in "love" before and knew from experience that nothing was ever going to come of it. I was willing to accept this with Anna, too. It seemed my lot. So I lived with my feelings toward her and kept them to myself. For a while.

But I saw her every day. And it was agony. So I worked up the courage to talk to her. She was funny and seemed to appreciate my sense of humor. We became friends.

It turned out, however, that she was married. And that wasn't going to change. I sunk into despair. I wrote lots of songs about her, about the pointlessness of being in love with her. I even played her some.

Something interesting had happened in basic training. Running fifteen miles a day while chanting about some scoundrel named Jody had taught me how to sing. I didn't quite know what to do with my voice the first time I sang after basic training. It still needed some work, but it wasn't the out-of-tune mess I'd sung with only a few months earlier.

One day, I decided to tell her how I felt.

"I love you," I said.

She looked back at me. Her eyes could melt me.

"What am I supposed to do with that?" she asked.

We figured it out.

Anna and I carried on for a few months—four, maybe five. At first, it was amazing—to be in love, to have someone in love with me. To be with someone, to be a part of her, to have her be a part of me. I hadn't been entirely sure this would ever happen.

But Anna didn't want to choose between her husband and me. And that was awful. I wanted her to choose, but I wasn't going to ask her. I knew there was no point in that. And so I grew increasingly desperate and anxious. I wanted her, and couldn't have her the way I really, really wanted her. She wasn't mine. She gave herself to me, but she wasn't mine.

It was hard to end our relationship, though, and it took a couple of attempts. None of it was easy on her either. Eventually she chose, and it wasn't me. In the midst of this, overwhelmed by sadness and despair, one day I was found curled up underneath a table in one of the Czech classrooms, weeping. And someone, I have no idea who, decided enough was enough. I was done studying Czech.

I felt broken.

During the next two months, while the army tried to figure what to do with me, I was put on casual work, which meant picking up trash, mowing grass, even painting yellow lines down the middle of the streets of the Presidio of Monterey. There was a crew of us, it changed slowly as soldiers circulated on and off casual status, and the work wasn't hard. Eventually, someone asked me: Do you still want to be a soldier? Sure, I said. Why not?

So, I was given a little time to find a new job. Which meant new training.

I was in a fairly black mood. I thought about the hardest job I could find and was immediately drawn to cavalry scout, a choice several of the Green Berets I knew heartily approved of. I wanted a job that involved lots of risk and danger, the crossing of borders, the patrolling of demilitarized zones and being way out in front.

"And then send me to Korea, so when war breaks out there, I'll be among the first who are killed," I said.

Oorah! We may make a soldier out of you yet, one Special Forces corporal told me.

When I told Anna this, she just looked at me and laughed. "You don't want to go to Korea."

She was right. I didn't want to go to Korea. I can see now how that could have gone. The moment I ended up on the wrong side of a commanding officer or first sergeant, I suspect I would have been sorely tempted to follow Private James Joseph Dresnok's 1962 dash across the DMZ. And soon come to regret that particularly dumb and impulsive choice as I sat in Pyongyang's semi-darkness studying the works of Kim Il Sung. Some things you can talk your way out of, but I suspect the Democratic People's Republic of Korea is not one of them.

So I chose something far more sedate—legal clerk. Which meant a few weeks of advanced training at the Soldier Support Institute at Ft. Benjamin Harrison in Indianapolis. Our classes were in an old elementary school the Pentagon had, at some point, acquired from a school district. As we marched to class, we'd end our cadences with "hoo, rah, sue somebody!"

I was now equipped with a thick binder containing the entire Uniform Code of Military Justice, and instructions for properly filling out forms. The same Pentagon computer that had assigned me to study Czech sent me, and Rodney, another legal clerk in my class, to Panama.

After a long flight on an airline I'd never heard of, I arrived at Albrook Air Force Base, was in-processed (so much of what the military does to people also sounds like it could be done to lunch meat), and then sent to an ancient temporary barracks to await final assignment. Rodney was assigned to the Judge Advocate General's office, the military's lawyers, while I was sent to the Military Police battalion—Law Enforcement Activity. They had been agitating for some months to get a legal clerk of their very own, and now they finally had one.

Law Enforcement Activity. It strikes me as so bureaucratic, so impersonal, so procedural. A banal glove to hide a fist. The colonel in charge was also the provost marshal—the senior U.S. military policeman—for everything south of the Rio Grande. The battalion consisted of three companies: a headquarters company and a combat MP company, both located at Ft. Clayton on the Pacific side, and an MP company on the Atlantic side. I was assigned to the headquarters company, and my job was supposed to involve handling all the legal paperwork for MPs who got into trouble.

There was precious little for me to actually do once I got settled in, however. So they set me to work on other things—helping the supply sergeant (who took to calling me Perry Mason and gave me a long lecture one afternoon about the price of dog food, our single biggest budget item, as bomb-sniffing dogs and drug-sniffing dogs needed a special and very expensive diet), filling in as the colonel's receptionist, getting mail, copying things, and shredding documents scheduled to be shredded. There was talk of qualifying me to be a driver.

Most documents I shredded were mundane things that had reached their "terminal date," the end of the length of time the unit was required to keep them. Important documents were stored elsewhere, sometimes for decades or even centuries. The most interesting thing I ran through our shredder was a three-year-old court martial of a female MP lieutenant for having a lesbian relationship with a Navy petty officer. All I had was the transcript of the court martial, but it described the exhibits in great detail—still pictures, film, video, audio. Clearly, someone in the criminal investigations department had great fun investigating this. It was difficult to believe that the military would have spent even a quarter this much time, effort or resources investigating a couple of suspected gay men.

About a third of the military police officers in the headquarters company were women. At the time, in the mid-1980s, military police was the closest women could get to combat arms in the U.S. Army. They often had to bear the brunt of our incredibly tense relations with Manuel Noriega's government and his army, the Panamanian Defense Forces (PDF).

When the Panama Canal Zone disappeared in 1979, it was replaced by a complex patchwork of American, Panamanian, and joint control areas, where American and Panamanian patrols were supposed to work together. I was in the dayroom one evening when an agitated female MP sergeant came in. Apparently, the PDF corporal assigned to patrol with her at Gorgas Army Hospital showed up drunk, and decided to try and take some liberties with her. She pulled her weapon on him and forced him out of their car, then sped away as quickly as she could to Ft. Clayton. She was shipped stateside two days later.

Our relations with the Panamanians were so difficult that we were all told upon arriving in Panama that under no conditions were we to allow ourselves to fall into Panamanian custody. There was a status of forces agreement that supposedly covered such things, but the Panamanians had long ago stopped keeping their end of the deal. If they got ahold of you, we were told, there was no guarantee anyone would ever see you again.

The PDF had a horrific reputation. I remember one of my first trips into Panama City, seeing a giant driftwood, plastic and corrugated metal shantytown built on a crescent of beach between Ft. Amador and Panama City, the poorest and most miserable place I'd ever seen. Someone told me Noriega recruited some of his fiercest and most loyal soldiers from these slums, and Noriega himself had begun his military career as a torturer for Omar Torrijos. I remember one afternoon seeing a convoy of PDF trucks skulking menacingly through the streets of the capitol, the unit logo stenciled on the side of each truck—a garish painting of a dog holding a severed human arm dripping blood.

Knowing all this, one afternoon, Rodney and I went into Panama City, got off at the main bus terminal, and walked around. We walked for a while, taking in the sights, sounds and smells of the city, window-shopping in electronics stores. But the neighborhood we were walking in got a little less commercial as we went, and suddenly we found ourselves in a place of shabby apartment buildings and shuttered stores.

"You gringos shouldn't be here. It's not safe for you," an elderly black man sitting on a corner stoop warned us.

Rodney and I turned the corner and saw three PDF soldiers—two privates and a sergeant—walking a patrol. They carried clubs and submachine guns, and the sergeant motioned to us. "Come here," he yelled. I looked at Rodney, and we didn't have to think about it. We turned and ran. One of the PDF soldiers yelled at us to stop, and we could hear them running after us.

We ran all the way back to the bus station, got on the first bus we could, which happened to be going past Balboa, the old Canal Zone capital, to Ft. Clayton. When I got back to my barracks, I told the sergeant on duty what had just happened.

"Welcome to Panama," she replied.

Rodney was about the only friend I had in Panama. I had too much time on my hands, too much time to think about myself, too much time to wallow in my misery and loneliness. I wanted to love and be loved, and there was no love in Panama. There was sex, drugs, drink, all manner of pleasure-seeking to dull the pain, but there was no love. So I made do. Every Friday afternoon, after work, I'd grab a four-pack of wine coolers (the drinking age in Panama was sixteen, and our barracks had vending machines that dispensed cans of beer for twenty-five cents) and the latest issue of *The Economist* at the local shoppette. That, and writing songs, was what I did for fun. I was an overly serious young man, and I didn't quite understand or know what to do with the world around me.

I had a couple of roommates who tried to loosen me up a bit. Specialist Jerry, who worked as a contraband investigator, decided one night, "I'm going to get you laid!" The evening at the enlisted club involved a great deal of alcohol, and at some point a very cute little Panamanian girl was sitting on my lap, running her fingers through my closely cropped hair, cooing, "Oh, Carlos!" Jerry was confident. "She's gonna fuck you, dude!" he happily proclaimed. But the girls disappeared, and Jerry and I drunkenly stumbled and crawled back to our barracks through the mud without them.

And there was Sergeant Valdez, who took me into Panama City one afternoon. He knew the city, at least parts of it, and out on the street in the late afternoon we ran into a woman he apparently knew well—a Panamanian prostitute. He introduced me, and as they talked, she groped me. To see if I was interested. And when she discovered I wasn't, she tried to make me interested. I'm not the publicly excitable type, and she eventually gave up.

One night in December 1986, I was listening to the BBC. The top report dealt with an incursion of Nicaraguan army units into Honduras following a Contra attack, and a clash between Nicaraguan and Honduran forces. As we prepared to go to sleep, Valdez looked at me.

"Don't expect to sleep much tonight."

We didn't. There was a pounding on the door at a little before three in the morning. We were on alert, and everyone needed to suit up and draw their weapons. A friend in Korea told me they were on alert all the time; it was a natural state of affairs. But alerts were very rare in Panama, and we took it very seriously. Ft. Clayton was alive in the predawn darkness with the sound of trucks and helicopters. We sat for several hours, in our helmets, holding our rifles, wondering if we were going to be at war.

The alert was called off at about eight that morning. It would be just another workday.

Sometimes, I would sit in my barracks room and watch out the window as the ships transited the Panama Canal. This big muddy ditch was not worth a single human life. Not one.

Rodney and I would frequently go drinking, and I'd watch while he tried to pick up girls. But we got a little too loose one weekend evening, and as we walked back to our respective barracks, talking and laughing as we went, Rodney kissed me on the cheek. I turned around kissed him on the nose. It wouldn't have amounted to anything if the first sergeant from the combat MP company hadn't been watching. He was frequently described as "thinking he has the biggest dick in Panama." The following Monday morning found me in the company commander's office, explaining to an embarrassed captain and first sergeant (and answering formal charges) that I was not, in fact, a homosexual.

"Don't do it again," the first sergeant said as he dismissed me.

I did become friends of a sort with one of the dog handlers, a sensitive young man from somewhere in the South. We'd started chatting one afternoon when, bored, I walked over to the front gate to talk to some of the MPs. I bent over to say hello to his dog. "Don't," he told me. "She's on duty, and she can't be distracted."

Some weeks later, he and his dog got orders to go to Honduras. And he was scared.

"People don't come back from Honduras," he said, struggling to fight back tears.

That was the moral swamp that was Panama. Soldiers went to Honduras and got killed, all too often under "mysterious circumstances." There were constant rumors that U.S. military supplies and equipment were being diverted to the Nicaraguan rebels. There was also whispered talk that the US military was actively complicit in shipping drugs, mostly cocaine, to fund those same rebels. I have no idea if any of that is true, and it mostly involved conversations with people who said, "I heard someone say . . ." I do remember hearing the MP captain in my administrative section saying that we barely had enough ammunition for proper training, much less several days of action if things got bad, and blamed it on the diversion of our munitions to the Contras. I know that the afternoon Congress passed a bill funding the Nicaraguan rebels, we were suddenly told we could keep our OD green jungle fatigues and our jungle boots. Previously, soldiers had to turn them in when they left the country. And no American was ever issued used fatigues or boots.

I'm not sure exactly when I figured out how to get out. In December 1986, I had not been sleeping well, and I met with an army psychiatrist who quickly determined I had no business being in the army. I wasn't adjusting to army life, and I never would. "You ought to be eligible for a trainee discharge," he said, noting most of my military "career" up to that point had been training. "But you've been in too long for that." So we started the process of getting me out of the army for having a "personality disorder."

My first sergeant was not happy, but rather than threaten me, or even yell at me, he asked me to reconsider.

"What if you want to run for governor? What if you want to run for Congress? You'll never be able to now," he said.

I didn't know what to make of this comment. Was this his typical speech to every soldier seeking an early out?

For several weeks, I was watched very closely, told that if I broke the rules in any way he would court-martial me faster than I could take my next breath. I toed a very, very thin line.

"I will send you to Leavenworth if I can!" one senior sergeant, who spent the better part of ten minutes dressing me down one afternoon, yelled at me.

But to everyone's shock, it worked. I received an honorable discharge. I had managed to wriggle out of the army. My last few days as a soldier were spent filling out papers in the out-processing center at Ft. Jackson, South Carolina. I wasn't sure what would happen next, but I'd figure that out somehow.

One evening in the dining center at Ft. Jackson, I sat with a group of soon-to-be ex-soldiers, swapping stories, talking about what we might do next. I didn't notice the blonde girl sitting across from me. She'd been very quiet, but she had definitely noticed me. As she got up to leave, she tossed me a folded up piece of paper.

"Lauren," it said, with a phone number in the 714 area code—Southern California. "Call me in a week."

"I was so afraid you wouldn't call," she said. I could hear every bit of nervous excitement in her voice. "I wanted so much to talk to you that day at Ft. Jackson, but I was afraid I would get in trouble."

Lauren didn't own a car. In fact, she couldn't drive, so I agreed to meet her at the small apartment she shared with her mother and stepfather in Stanton, right next to Anaheim. It was a bit of a drive. But it sounded like it would be worth it.

She greeted me at the door wearing a pink and white sweater dress that clung to every curve. We went to Disneyland.

Lauren had a beautiful, happy smile, and her round cheeks and shiny blue eyes made her look like a 1940s pin-up girl or something out of an Alberto Vargas painting. She was inordinately cheerful, and told me everybody called her Sunshine. It fit, that name. She sparkled. She was a year older than me, I think.

But she also had a sad story to tell. Lauren had been discharged from the army for medical reasons. She'd grown up mostly in California, though at some point I remember her saying she spent a couple of high school years somewhere in Washington State. I don't think she ever had a father in her life, not really. At sixteen, she had a boyfriend who was eighteen. When she got pregnant, he left her. So, she got an abortion. She was not going to raise a child alone.

Lauren enlisted in the army when she graduated from high school. Like me, she saw it as a way to leave home. She met a soldier, married him, and got pregnant. What no one knew at the time is that the abortion she had at sixteen had been badly done, and several months into her pregnancy, she miscarried. And nearly bled to death in an operating room. Her husband, when called and told his wife was in serious condition and could very well die, responded by saying he was busy and had other things to do.

She never went back to him (though she hadn't yet divorced him when we met).

Lauren was an astoundingly sweet girl. She bore the hardships in her life with an amazing grace. She too wanted nothing more than to love and to be loved. She adored me, and gave herself to me utterly and completely. She got a part-time job at a small lingerie shop, and there were some nice benefits to that. She looked exquisite in white lace. Lauren talked about all of the things we would do together, and the places we would go.

When I suggested camping, she laughed. And drew a line: "I'm not going anywhere I can't plug in a curling iron."

Even under the best of circumstances, Lauren and I would never have been compatible. We were tossed together, and it was fun for a time, but we just didn't fit well with each other. Lauren was a sweet, simple girl, and there were times she began to suspect I looked down upon her because I thought she was dumb. And, sad to say, she was right.

"I'm smarter than you think I am," she angrily told me once.

Up to this point, I thought it would be enough if someone simply loved me. That nothing would matter more than that. Lonely and abused, I had believed just about everything everyone told me, and thought that if someone rejected me (or accepted me), that it was all about *me*. It never occurred to me that what someone felt about me, or how someone acted toward me, might be just as much about them. Or that they might even have their own problems. None of that had ever really entered my mind. It was a strange kind of self-centeredness, created by abuse and neglect, which left me convinced that I was the only person in the world who had ever suffered, felt pain, and ached to be loved. I would slowly learn I wasn't. But that's a hard thing to learn, especially when you spent so much time—as I had—marinating in your own loneliness and sorrow.

So it never occurred to me that someone might love me and I might not love them back. And it soon became clear to me that I did not and could not love Lauren anywhere near as much as she loved me.

But sex is a hard thing to say no to. When you feel so unloved, and so unlovable, that kind of contact with someone—to lose yourself in them, to become part of them, to have them become part of you, to touch, to feel, to hold, to play, to be wanted by them—is a powerful affirmation. Sex and love were intertwined and inseparable. It must be love if someone wanted me this way.

I would later learn that's the kind of understanding that leaves a lot of people open and vulnerable to being abused and exploited.

And I began to really struggle with what I was doing. I needed to have feelings for Lauren. And I was not feeling much for this sweet little girl who loved me.

During one particularly passionate evening, Lauren looked at me.

"I want to have your baby," she said.

Because of her miscarriage, Lauren had broken down and cried a couple of times, wondering if anyone would ever love her if she couldn't bear children. Would I ever really love her if she couldn't have my children? And I held her heaving, sobbing body, stroking her, saying little.

What I said: "Are you sure? Are you really, really sure?"

What I thought: "I can't do this anymore. I can't take this girl seriously, the way she needs to be taken."

I had no idea how to say no to Lauren. The drive from Upland to Orange County became a miserable chore, something I dreaded. I never imagined I would have to say no to someone, someone so sweet and beautiful who loved me so intensely. I'd never even really expected to be loved like this in the first place. I didn't want to hurt her. But I had to. I had to end it.

This not expecting to be loved, and then not knowing how to respond to it when it came, would hit me upside the head several times in life. It's been a hard lesson to learn.

One day, we'd had an argument. Or, more to the point, Lauren had been angry with me. I don't remember what it was about. But she called me the next day, apologized profusely, and I accepted. Not long after, I'd drearily made the long drive down I-10 and then the 57 freeway, swearing wherever the traffic was heavy. We spent several hours together.

"When do I get to see you next?" she asked.

I turned to walk out without saying anything. She started screaming at me. She followed me out of the apartment, down the stairs, all the way out to my car, yelling—desperate, angry, frightened. I said nothing in response, didn't talk back. I felt awful. I was a horrible human being. I hated what I was doing. But I didn't know what else to do.

"I hope you remember one day when you are old and lonely that someone loved you once!" It was the last thing she yelled at me.

I drove away. She called me the next day, apologizing for all she'd said. I told her no, she was right, I was everything she said I was. She was right to be angry.

"Okay," she said, her voice trembling. And hung up.

I don't regret much about my life. But every day I draw breath, I feel some sorrow and shame for how I treated Lauren.

Lauren was there with me and my mother the day the phone rang to tell us Grammie had died. It came as a shock, out of nowhere, and my mother broke down. Mom, Dad, and I went up for Grammie's funeral. I was there for several days, then came back. While my mother stayed for another week, Lauren stayed with me.

My parents' marriage was in a shambles at this point. Dad had left, but then he came back. And then he left again. Eventually, they would get divorced.

After Lauren and I were done, I moved into the garage. To earn a little money, I worked at a Chevron station pumping gas and fixing flat tires, I delivered pizzas for Domino's, I was even a security guard at a factory in Rancho Cucamonga. Franklin Bruno also asked me to do some fill-in work as a DJ at KSPC, the Claremont College radio station. That was a lot of fun, but it didn't pay.

I made a little music with some friends, and in the fall of 1987, I took a French class and sang in the choir at Chaffey Community College. It wasn't much of a life, but it wasn't high school either.

Grammie left me $10,000 in her will. It was enough to go to school somewhere. Somewhere far away. So I decided to go to San Francisco State University and major in journalism.

7

Bus Stop

I DON'T REMEMBER THE day I met Abdel Malik Ali. As the ombudsman at San Francisco State University, he was a fairly important person on campus. He being an African American Muslim, we probably met at prayer. Abdel Malik became one of my early mentors.

He said he'd lived the Malcolm X story. He'd been a young thug on the streets of Oakland, bound for a bad end. After fathering several children with several women, he'd been rescued from a life of crime and prison by the Nation of Islam, and from there eventually became a proper Muslim, got a university degree and a job a SF State, and married.

In fact, when he became Muslim, Abdel Malik said he went to all the women he'd had children with and told them he now had a moral and religious obligation to care for them and their children. And he did just that. So, he married one woman civilly—his wife Khadijah, an African American Muslim herself who also worked at SF State—and two other women, I think, under Islamic law.

The Palestinians and others could tell me a lot about being Muslim, but only someone like Abdel Malik could really help me figure out what being an American Muslim meant. We didn't become close friends, but Abdel Malik was always there to help when I had questions I needed answered or had issues to deal with.

One day, not long after we met, he handed me a book. It was Alex Haley's *The Autobiography of Malcolm X*, and he told me I needed to read it.

"This will strengthen your faith," he said.

I think Abdel Malik wanted me to see Malcolm's journey from angry young criminal, to articulate Nation of Islam spokesman, to someone who appreciated that everybody, white or black, snores the same. What he hoped

I would understand, I think, was how little race mattered in Islam, and how Malcolm X had come to see that.

And I did, but I got something much more important about the nature of life from Haley's book. I found it in the way Malcolm narrates his young life and his time growing up in Detroit and Boston and as a young hoodlum in Harlem, the frequent no-win situations he found himself in with white authority. Strangely enough, I saw in this something from my own life. And I could finally give it a name: *The Box*. This was an epiphany, a stunning *Allahu Akbar!*—God is greater!—moment.

The Box has three simple rules.

First, you will be punished for everything you are caught doing wrong. Or it will be held against you.

Second, you will rarely if ever be congratulated or praised for behaving yourself, complying with or following the rules. You have to obey the rules—punishment awaits if you don't—but you never get any points for doing so.

Third, punishment will simply be meted out randomly sometimes, whether you earned it or not. Just so you won't get too comfortable. Or think the world has changed.

Needless to say, the whole concept of "right" and "wrong" is rigged to begin with. It's less about what you do than who you are—your very existence is a problem that needs to be regulated or dealt with. Or it quickly becomes about that.

We live in a world in which people—individuals, whole communities and even nations—are put in boxes. People with power often do this without thinking. Because that's one of the advantages of power—not having to think about these kinds of things. Palestinians are a people living in a box. African Americans lived, and in many ways still live, in a box.

This resonated so intensely with me because I saw myself growing up in a box. And there is no winning when you live in a box.

In becoming Muslim, I had found that parts of the African American experience were useful in explaining both my life and my experience of living in America. This is akin to what Norman Mailer wrote in his 1957 essay "The White Negro." Though Mailer is speaking of 1950s hipsters, with their existential cynicism, I think what he says can also describe some white Americans who, like myself, found themselves growing up on the wrong side of America, in which whiteness conferred no social advantage because the people abusing us were also white:

> Any Negro who wishes to live must live with danger from his first
> day, and no experience can ever be casual to him, no Negro can

saunter down a street with any real certainty that violence will
not visit him on his walk. The cameos of security for the average
white: mother and the home, job and the family, are not even a
mockery to millions of Negroes; they are impossible. The Negro
has the simplest of alternatives: live a life of constant humility
or ever-threatening danger.

In this essay Mailer speaks of physicality, the "in the moment" enjoyment of the illicit and the sensual that portions of black American life
opened up for some whites. That wasn't what interested me. Rather, what
spoke to me was the experience of social power and state power as a constant, almost existential threat that African Americans like Malcolm X wrote
about. That a "life of constant humility or ever-threatening danger"—think
Citrus Elementary School—could also lead to other responses—to separat-
ism, because "if you don't want me, then I don't want you either."

Or violence. Because that can be a legitimate response to being put in a
box as well. Certain parts of the African American experience—particularly
the experience of the brutality of America, and the country's long unwillingness to accept black people as Americans, much less as social and political equals—told me things about my life the mainstream story of America
didn't or couldn't. I wasn't drawn to reform. I didn't want to make America
work better—I wanted to damn it and burn it down. Because of that, I was
drawn to radical, even revolutionary, critiques of power and society, and
sometimes, the more radical and revolutionary, the better. It was revolution
simply for the sake of revolution, and not to change the world.

I am not pretending to be anything or anyone I am not—I am not
claiming blackness. But the story Malcolm X told of how he experienced
America made sense to me. It made an awful lot of sense. It was an America
I experienced and understood.

I do not know if I am the only white person who has felt this way. This
isn't something I have ever talked about much, because I've never assumed
anyone would begin to understand, much less share, any of this.

San Francisco State University has a reputation as a hotbed of radicalism,
mostly dating from the student strike of 1968. And there was a fascinating
collection of radical groups on campus in the late 1980s. They weren't everywhere. It just seemed like it. Especially if you paid attention.

And what a motley group they were, too. Socialists, communists, Sandinistas, Maoists, even a few Stalinists. (I don't remember any Kim Il Sungists!) There was usually something going on somewhere—antiapartheid demonstrations, protests on behalf of the Farabundo Martí National Liberation Front (El Salvador's rebels), or various and sundry actions by black nationalists. Most students, in fact, probably never gave the agglomeration of aspiring activists and revolutionaries much thought, much less their time. They had studies to worry about.

My feelings about them were mixed, however. I was drawn to revolutionary critiques of power and will always remember something I saw printed in a copy of *Workers Vanguard*, the newspaper of the International Communist League. (It was tough keeping the various groups and their publications straight.) The newspaper's masthead stuck with me—"For the Communism of Lenin, Liebknecht and Luxemburg!"—and the editors fielded a question from an anxious reader. "Why do you pick on Democrats so much? At least they try to help working people."

Workers Vanguard responded with vigor, something along the lines of "We don't bother criticizing Republicans because they know they are the enemy of the workers. Democrats, however, only pretend to be friends, but work just as hard against the interests of the workers as Republicans do. Do not be misled!"

That was something I could heartily agree with. Reforming power was beguiling, because it made nice-sounding promises, all while still being power. And doing all the evil things power does.

But I had no patience for anyone's bright, shiny new tomorrow. I bought into no one's revolution. All I wanted was a corner of the world where I could live without being bothered, without having who and what I was constantly held against me. I went to a couple of educational lectures hosted by some socialist party somewhere in the Mission District and got a basic primer in Marxist-Leninist revolutionary theory. It sounded a lot like premillennial dispensationalism to me, except that global revolution by the working class replaced rapture and tribulation and the withering away of the state replaced the thousand-year reign of Christ.

The whole point of the revolution, the lecturer said, was to end the struggle of "man versus man" and return humanity to a condition of "man versus nature," where a united humanity would struggle to master the natural world.

After the lecturer explained the exploitation of the proletariat, and how the workers would seize power from the bourgeoisie, I asked what would prevent the newly empowered proletariat from exploiting the newly subjugated bourgeoisie.

He laughed. "Exploiting and subjugating the bourgeoisie is the whole point of the revolution," he explained.

I did not go back.

What was I looking for? What did I want? Some kind of justification for the urge to do violence, some way to legitimize my rage at the world I lived in. That's what I wanted. I had a nihilistic urge seeking a pretense, some sort of idea, some mess of words to cover the naked desire to simply burn everything down.

I wasn't looking to change the world—that simply did not seem possible to me. To believe in change is to believe that the world and its ways should, somehow, be accountable. When was anyone or anything *ever* accountable to me? I had no faith in change, not the change of the reformers, not the change of the revolutionaries. (And I still don't. Not really.) Besides, everything I'd read in history told me that attempts to change the world simply increased the pain, suffering, and death. I didn't want to simply rearrange things, to flip who was doing what to whom. Not so long as the what remained the same. I am far too empathetic to wield a club for very long. I wanted no more pain and suffering, no more cruelty and callousness, and figured the only way that could happen is if everything, everywhere simply came to an end.

I didn't want a better world. What I really wanted was a kinder one. Perhaps that makes me the ultimate naïve utopian. But no one's dreams, no one's programs, no one's platforms, no one's rewriting the occasional rule, promised kindness. Not so long as what was sought was power, the ability and willingness to dominate others. In power, all the callousness and cruelty human beings are capable of could be justified as righteous means to a glorious end.

My nihilistic desires struggled mightily with this wanting a kinder world. And lost. And thank God. Somehow, in the midst of all of this, I realized that I could do the kindness I sought in the world. Islam, with its emphasis on good deeds, helped guide me to this place. Maybe my kindness would matter and maybe it wouldn't. I wasn't always good at it. But even angry as I was, it honestly struck me as the only thing that made real sense. I have no idea why.

This, however, did not happen all at once. And there were days when the anger could get the best of me. One morning, in the SF State Student Union's east courtyard, there was a memorial service for a group of Israeli tourists who had been killed in Egypt by Islamist militants. At the time, Egypt was dealing with significant violence, and tourists were a particular target. A female rabbi was leading the service, and a fair number of people had gathered. I'd stumbled upon the service after it had started, and stood in back with a couple of young African American men I'd seen around but did not know. They were half-heartedly and rather ineffectively heckling her.

As I stood listening to the rabbi, I got angrier and angrier. It was a good, liberal, and inclusive speech, noting that all sorts of people, especially Muslims, had suffered from the violence in Egypt. Which was certainly true. But the fact that she was there, that day, marking the deaths of Israelis (and not, say, non-Jewish Americans or Egyptians), also gave the lie to her liberalism. The lives of other people—non-Jews—did not matter enough to mourn directly, but only in passing. Only the lives of Jews, and Israelis at that, were valuable enough to publicly mark. No one else mattered.

Certainly not the people the Israelis were killing on a regular basis in the West Bank, in Gaza, and in Lebanon.

This is one of the hardest things American Muslims have to deal with—their attitudes toward Jews. To be Muslim in America is to secede from the widely shared narrative of Jewish victimhood, existential dread and any sense of Jewish chosenness or even specialness. It is to know and worship God with Palestinians and Lebanese, people who have suffered under Jewish power, have been occupied and bombed, have lost loved ones and family. Writ small and highlighted very brightly, all that was wrong with Israel was everything that was wrong with America—it was the power to take whatever you wanted, hurt whomever you wanted, and kill whomever you wanted. And call it righteousness.

And that made me angry. Very, very angry.

Sometime during the rabbi's speech, my anger got the best of me.

"*Allahu Akbar!*" I shouted. As loud as I could.

The effect on the disaffected elements in the crowd was electric. The two African American men behind me had not been able to get any traction with their heckling, but my shouting the *takbir* changed the situation. Those who were opposed—and it turned out there were more than I thought— suddenly found a voice. The heckling grew louder and more organized. The rabbi was no longer able to be heard above the noise, and people in the crowd began shouting at each other. I had provoked a disturbance, and it appeared to be careening out of control.

I'm not sure what exactly it was I wanted to accomplish when I shouted "*Allahu Akbar!*" I hadn't given the matter any thought. I merely wanted to voice my anger. I never imagined my words would have that kind of power. I've never wanted that kind of power, not even in opposition. I wasn't particularly bothered that the rabbi was silenced. But I was bothered that I had been the cause of the silencing.

I slunk away to the journalism department. It was cowardly, but honestly, if things got really out of hand, I didn't want to be there when the authorities showed up.

"You probably ought to send someone to the student union. There's a riot going on there right now," I told the editor of the student newspaper.

He looked at me.

"You were there? You should be covering it!"

"Well, I can't," I responded honestly. "I kind of started it."

I got the chewing out I deserved. And I never did that again. The SF State student newspaper had enough trouble with activists and revolutionaries posing as journalists (we may have been the only college newspaper in the United States with a staff of reporters and photographers covering the 1990 Nicaraguan elections). I wasn't going to contribute further to the problem.

I would participate in demonstrations later, in 1990 and 1991, to protest the military buildup in Saudi Arabia following Iraq's invasion and annexation of Kuwait. I would march with Veterans for Peace, though I never joined the group. I was probably the youngest former member of the military (I am uncomfortable with calling myself a veteran, as I'm not sure I earned the title) to march with them in the big demonstration in San Francisco the day after Operation Desert Storm began in January 1991. (I had been invited to join a group of the more militantly inclined who would briefly shut down the Bay Area's two main bridges and break into a military recruiting center. But I was not interested in risking arrest.) Joan Baez was there, and made a point of saying hello, chatting with me, thanking me for being there, and linking her arm in mine and marching with me for a couple of blocks.

She kissed me too.

My studies at SF State weren't all riots, prayers, and revolutionary theory. For the first time in my life I actually loved school and found that school could actually love me back. SF State was a big urban campus, full of all kinds of people. Evening classes were the best, because then I found myself in classrooms with such an immense variety of people with all kinds of life experiences, many with families and full-time jobs struggling to make life work. The conversations, and the different views that were brought to these classes, were a wonderful thing to be a part of.

I took my studies seriously, and I did learn something of the craft of journalism. Several professors took enough interest in me to mentor me. Aguibou Yansane was a French-educated economist from Guinea who had finished a PhD at Stanford just as a coup in Guinea made returning home an impossibility. He remained in the United States and taught economics and African studies courses at SF State. I took three classes on Africa from him, and he had me help him organize a major symposium on economic development and neocolonialism in Africa.

"Charles is a brilliant student!" Yansane would say in his lilting and heavily accented English—a beautiful weaving together of French and Mandinka—to everyone he introduced me to.

Tom Johnson was a journalism professor who also covered Latin America—especially El Salvador—for a couple of major U.S. news magazines. He also had a tremendous interest in data crunching as a tool for reporting. I took three classes from him as well (at the start of the third one, he looked at me and said, "Back again? Are you sure? I'm a one-trick pony and I've taught you all I know"), and his interest in my career continues to this day.

Me overseeing the SF State Journalism Department computer network, late 1988 or early 1989.

After my first semester at SF State, I sublet an apartment for the summer near San Pablo and University in Berkeley. I was still living off the largesse I inherited from my grandmother. I bought a bicycle and rode everywhere I could. I had a part-time job in the Mission District of San

Francisco, working as the receptionist (yes, me) at a small chiropractic clinic run by a friend of one of my Russian teachers. I looked up *masjids*—Muslim houses of prayer—wherever I could. I played music at a few places.

It was a Monday morning, August 1, 1988, when the phone rang unexpectedly. It was the person from SF State who handled the math exam waivers. I could come in and get mine taken care of today, he said, if I wanted to.

"Okay, I'll be in today," I said. "But I thought you were on vacation."

There was an angry silence on the other end of the phone. I wasn't supposed to get this phone call for another week.

"I was."

I walked to the nearest BART station, got on the train, appreciated the light, mid-morning crowd, and got off at what was then the final stop, in Daly City. I stood there, waiting for the Number 28 Muni bus. I wasn't alone but I hadn't really paid attention to whoever else was there.

The 28 Muni bus, which follows 19th Ave. from the Daly City BART station all the way to the Golden Gate Bridge in the Presidio, was at the time the only way you could get to SF State from the Daly City BART. The 28 dropped riders off and picked them up at different platforms. Sometimes, a bus dropping people off would stop to pick passengers up, and other times an arriving bus would zip on past after letting people off without picking anyone up. There didn't seem to be a pattern to it.

That morning, a bus let people off, and then whizzed right past. It was always discouraging when this happened. It meant more waiting. And that was annoying.

"It must be cigarette break time," I said to no one in particular. It's a habit I have, speaking to the air sometimes.

"I guess it must be."

I'd never been answered before. I turned around.

What I saw first were her eyes. Two beautiful, sparkly blue eyes. In fact, I was struck by just how beautiful the girl was who'd answered my comment to the air.

"I thought you deserved an answer," she said.

We talked. Her name was Jennifer, and she too had an appointment at SF State that had been rescheduled at the last minute. Eventually, a 28 bus stopped, and we got on. We talked, and I could see as she stuttered and stammered and struggled with her shyness just how much work Jennifer was putting into this conversation.

Into this conversation with me.

Once, on a streetcar coming back to SF State, I'd had a long talk with a young lady about school, and prospects, and careers, and the future. On the one hand, it was gratifying to be the focus of that kind of attention. On the other hand, it felt very much like I was being sized up, interviewed for a job, or possibly even fitted for a suit. She could have been having that conversation with anyone. At least that's how it felt.

But not Jennifer. She struggled a lot to talk to me, stammering and pausing awkwardly to find more words to say. She was interested in me. *In me.* Not some possibility. Not some idea. Not some prospect. But the person in front of her. And this beautiful, sweet, shy girl was fighting every urge in her body in order to make eye contact and talk with me. It was charming, all her effort. I was captivated.

We went to our respective appointments and then met afterwards in the student union, over tea and coffee. I had to go to work, but we met again that evening in Berkeley, at Wolf House, where she was staying with her sister. We talked—okay, I did much of the talking—for hours. She said she found me fascinating. It got late, and I had to leave. Another day of work, and I had to ride home in the dark. We agreed to meet the following morning for breakfast, at a La Petite Boulangerie on Telegraph Ave.

I wasn't sure what to do next.

But she was. She got up on her tiptoes, wrapped her arms around my neck, and kissed me. In that moment, it was as if the universe had been breathed into existence again.

"I had to let you know how I felt about you," she told me later.

She had left little doubt about that.

I'm not sure at this point what I can or should say about Jennifer. Her story is hers to tell, and she is very protective of it, but I need to say some things here. When we met, she was bouncing between her sister's place and her oldest brother's, staying as long as she could until she wore out her welcome. Jennifer was the oldest of four, and at twenty-five was five years older than me.

Her father was a pastor in the Lutheran Church Missouri Synod and had been on the wrong side of that church's political struggles in the early 1970s, even being run out by one particular congregation. Jennifer had found school unpleasant and abusive, and life at home cruel and loveless. Like me, she ached to be both loved and taken seriously. It was the kind of ache that a predator took advantage of during her first year of university. And Jennifer told me that she never really felt like a part of her family after her parents blamed her for the loss of her "virtue."

In fact, that encounter with her parents left her feeling terrified and cornered. What little safety she'd had at home had been ripped away.

And she concluded: "Fine. If you're going to treat me like a bad girl, then I'm going to be a *bad girl.*"

With many of the terrible consequences you can imagine.

What impressed me most about this young woman as I got to know her was her courage. It takes a lot of courage to live a hard life, to wake up every morning and face abuse and abusers knowing that things would likely be awful today and much the same tomorrow. That there was little chance or even hope that anything would ever get any better. Jennifer had never had the advantage of a voice inside telling her to hold on for the day when it stopped hurting. Jennifer just got up and lived, even when it made no sense to do so. Even when it was clear to her no one really wanted her. She lived.

That is an act of profound courage.

It was very nearly love at first sight. I say "very nearly" because I wasn't sure at first just how committed I should be to Jennifer. Yes, I wanted to love and be loved. But at SF State, I discovered I could get and keep the attention of the opposite sex, something I could only dream of in high school and that only got me into trouble in the army. I was just turning twenty-one, and how was I to know that Jennifer would be the one? What if she wasn't?

Because as much as Lauren had said she loved me, she hadn't been.

The matter was settled one November afternoon in 1988. Jennifer was finishing up her last semester at SF State, and we were both living in the same dorm building. So, we saw a lot of each other. There was a knock on my door, and there she was, agitated and crying.

"I think I'm pregnant," she told me. She was terrified.

We sat on the side of the bed and I held her. I asked her what she wanted to do and she said she wasn't sure.

But as I held her, I thought: I have to be a great deal more serious about this girl than I have been. Because I want to be. Because she's worth it.

She wasn't pregnant, though, a fact that relieved both of us to no end. But I was a little saddened by that as well.

We have been almost inseparable ever since. We cling together, to each other, for dear life. Our relationship has worked so well because we both see the world in the same way, as a cruel and brutal place, and our love is the only real refuge we have from that world. We are unconditional, unearned, unmerited love for each other. We both learned that love from each other and taught that love to each other.

Jennifer and me, our first picture together, September or October 1988.

"Preach the Gospel, and if necessary, use words." A saying often attributed to St. Francis of Assisi, and a good one, too, though there's no proof he actually said it.

When John's Gospel tells us, "In the beginning was the Word, and the Word was with God, and the Word was God. . . . And the Word became flesh and dwelt among us, and we have seen his glory, glory as of the only Son from the Father, full of grace and truth," we are hearing something very important about God. God is not simply a distant, abstract presence, on high or somewhere else, but is here among us, in our midst, as one of us.

A presence we encounter in each other.

And that makes how we act important. In fact, how we act toward each other better confesses our faith than any words we use.

When Jesus speaks, it is less to tell his disciples what we should believe or know than it is to tell us what we should do and how we should act. The question "Who is my neighbor?" is answered with a description of what a neighbor *does*—he cares for a stranger, a foreigner, an enemy, and an injured one at that—and the risks taken in being a neighbor. The very evocative description of the final judgment in Matthew 25 suggests that on some level, the world will be judged on the basis of small acts of kindness and generosity. "When did we do these things?" both the righteous and the cursed will ask, and they will be told, "As you did it, or not, to one of the least of these my brothers, you did it to me."

Love can be an abstraction or an ideal only for those fortunate enough to take its presence in the world—its fleshiness, it goodness, its generosity—for granted. To ache to be loved, as Jennifer and I both did when we were young, is to ache to know God. To touch and hold, to be touched and held, to belong to someone, is to know something of the promise of God, that we are not alone. If that sounds physical, even carnal, well, we are not simply spirit and mind, we are bodies too.

The same is true of life in community. We oftentimes treat the rules as a door or a gate—obey the rules and come in, refuse or fail and find yourself on the outside. But that's not how God acts. God gathers Israel together *first*, in the wilderness at the foot of Mt. Sinai, and only then gives Israel the rules. Jesus calls disciples *first*, and then he teaches us what it means to be disciples. Again and again. Because we can never fully follow the teaching, never really obey the rules. Now, I am not opposed to rules, but I have found that too many people concerned with the rules are also willing to tolerate (or even practice) the casual cruelty that frequently betrays the words of love we speak. The rules become more important than the love they are supposed to foster.

In this, Paul is correct when he writes to the church at Corinth, "If I speak in the tongues of men and of angels, but have not love, I am a noisy gong or clanging cymbal. . . . If I give away all I have, and if I deliver up my body to be burned, but have not love, I gain nothing."

Because love is a relationship, and it's meaningless to claim to love someone if there's no chance she will understand or experience the doing as love. And the people who most need to know that they are not alone, that God really, truly loves them, are those who have been cast aside, discarded, left behind. Wounded, broken, and alone.

8

Muhammad Speaks

EVENTUALLY, IN THE SPRING of 1991, my grandmother's inheritance ran out, and there was no more money for school. And I wasn't going to borrow any. So this left us with no options. Jennifer had graduated with a literature degree in 1989, but her dyslexia—diagnosed only toward the end of her university studies—made finding work difficult. (At an early age, Jennifer decided reading was important, so she taught herself a form of speed reading that involves taking in whole paragraphs and pages at a time. Her dyslexia manifests itself largely in her difficulty with numbers—"They just won't stay still"—and poor hand-eye coordination that makes using machines very, very difficult for her. She doesn't know how to drive, for example.)

With half a college education, and little formal experience (I had helped run the journalism department's computer network, but that didn't amount to much), I simply could not find a job. There was nothing to be had. It was my first bout of extended unemployment, and like a lot of people facing that monster for the very first time, I thought it was all my fault. If I just worked harder, I could get a job. Anything, so Jennifer and I could get settled long enough and I could go back to school.

I stopped beating myself up one afternoon when I overheard a lawyer and an architect on a Muni streetcar lamenting the lack of work. The lawyer wasn't sure what he was going to do.

The economy was really bad if a lawyer—a lawyer in California— couldn't find work.

The best I could do were a couple of good, multiweek assignments through a temporary agency. The longest was five weeks doing various desktop publishing tasks for Pacific Gas & Electric. It paid well, though the job wasn't as busy as I would have liked. But even temp work was hard to come by at that point.

I'd been working with a temp agent I'd gotten to know over the phone (and only over the phone—we'd never actually met) named Larry. He'd landed me some good assignments, so I called one Monday morning only to be told Larry no longer worked there.

There were no more assignments either.

A couple of weeks later, the phone rang. It was Larry.

"Are you still looking for work?" he asked.

"I thought you didn't work at the agency anymore?"

"I don't," he said. "I have a friend who is looking for someone who can do exactly what you do. Are you interested?"

Of course I was interested. Larry gave me the address and phone number of a small newspaper located in the Bayview-Hunter's Point neighborhood of San Francisco. It was far from where we were living, but I could get there by transit. I had no idea about the neighborhood's character, but I didn't care if it meant work.

"He's a friend of mine. His name is Muhammad al-Kareem."

That really piqued my interest.

"You mean he's a Muslim?" I asked.

"Yes, he's a brother!" Larry replied.

I think about that exchange a lot. It is carved deeply into my memory as an example of what happens when you think you understand what someone has just said but, really, you're not even speaking the same language.

What I imagined was an Egyptian, Pakistani or Palestinian businessman, struggling but honest, sincere in his faith but a little profane because, well, sometimes the world demands a little profanity. It would be a place where I could be a Muslim, where prayers would be kept, where that would matter.

What I got, after two busses and a streetcar ride, was the Bayview-Hunter's Point—the largest and poorest African American neighborhood in the city.

The New Bayview was a small community newspaper located in a storefront very close to the corner of 3rd Ave. and Oakdale. Muhammad ran a print and graphic design shop, and as I stepped in I noticed some Afrocentric prints on the walls, a large collage of old photos titled "Heroes of Black History," and an elegantly framed photo of Elijah Muhammad, the founder and first leader of the Nation of Islam.

The Nation of Islam. That possibility hadn't occurred to me.

The air inside was heavy, and the smell was a combination of sandalwood and synthetic strawberry that evoked just about every taxi ride I took in Panama. A short black man in a simple suit and a sparkly fez gazed at me with a somewhat incredulous look on his face.

"Larry sent you?" he asked, not sure if he could believe who was in front of him.

"Um, yeah," I said, not sure if I could believe where I was.

He came out from behind the counter and stood in front of me. He looked up at me, and then down at my feet, and up again, and shook his head, a look of disgust on his face. He started to walk away, shook his head again, and then looked at me.

"As long as you're here, I might as well put you to work," he said.

I spent several hours on his little Macintosh computer that afternoon, laying out the week's issue and working on copy problems. And then helping Muhammad with a few other things. At the end of the afternoon, when there was no more for me to do, Muhammad said I could go.

Before I could ask about being paid, Muhammad looked at me.

"The job is yours if you want it."

Of course I wanted it. I had no other prospects. And Muhammad's print shop, with all the people who came and went, was fascinating. I might not get another chance to work in a place like this.

Muhammad didn't talk much about his past, at least not to me. Not that I recall. I had no idea how long he'd been in the Nation, only that he had a black-and-white photo of himself as a young man in the uniform of the Fruit of Islam, sometimes described as the Nation's security service. He was also very proud of two photos prominently displayed in his office, one with Nation leader Louis Farrakhan and the other with the then-Libyan leader Muammar Qadhafiy.

In fact, Muhammad told me he'd been in Libya on the night in 1986 when the U.S. Air Force bombed Tripoli. As he described that night, there was anger in his voice. Anger tinged with just a little bit of fear.

If there were a religion built upon the foundation of righteous rage, it would be the Nation of Islam. Originating in the 1930s, at a time when various black nationalist and afrocentric religious movements percolated in America (many claiming to draw inspiration from Islam), the Nation offered meaning to many black Americans seeking to figure out their place in a violently racist society that had both forcibly brought their ancestors here and compelled their labor but at the same time didn't want them in its midst. The black man was God's chosen race, and a day would come when God would save His chosen people from the demonic whites who oppressed and enslaved them. Until then, it was the job of black men and women to build a self-sufficient community that could support and protect its people as well as promote self-respect and racial pride.

"Do for self!" That was the Nation of Islam's refrain. Whether the Nation was able to accomplish anything remotely resembling what they preached, I have no idea. But what they preached—dignity, self-reliance, effective secession from American society—made a lot of sense to me. The Nation's actual religious and racial beliefs were foolish, though I was half inclined to agree that white people were generally evil. (In a nod to the Nation's theory that white people were created by an evil African scientist forty thousand years ago, my high school friend Adam and I once talked about getting T-shirts made that read, "I'm Yacub's Fault.") But their political and social views, at least many of those publicly stated, struck a chord in my soul.

Because anything other than a confident or even violent assertion of self felt like groveling to me. And there was no dignity in groveling, no pride in asking, "Pretty please, may I be a part of your society now?" Especially humiliating was the idea of asking America for a place, for the right to be treated decently, to be taken seriously, to not be humiliated or brutalized. That anyone would have to ask for such "favors" put the lie to any promises of freedom, justice, equality, fairness, and decency that American society makes to itself. The promises of America—the story it told itself—were either true or they weren't. They weren't something you worked toward.

While I was introduced to Muhammad as "Charles Featherstone," he soon learned that I was Muslim. I don't remember if this surprised him or not—he said he knew other "orthodox" Muslims, and had heard stories of people like me. He was also a lot more comfortable calling me "Brother Umar" than calling me by my given, legal name.

I quickly felt relatively safe working in and walking around the Bayview-Hunter's Point, and I explored the place a bit. I was especially fond of the little barbecue place on 3rd Ave. in the same block where Muhammad had the newspaper. The owner was very proud of his restaurant, and told Jennifer and me one day how he had the oven transported brick by brick from his family home in North Carolina. It took a bit, but I even acquired a taste for greens in his little restaurant.

Next door was a little *taqueria* that was always well stocked with copies of the English-language newspaper published by North American supporters of the Sendero Luminoso, Peru's communist rebels.

One of the first things I noticed about the Bayview was how it was policed. In most of San Francisco, the police patrolled two to a car, or walked a beat. But not in the Bayview. The police tore around the neighborhood in windowless Chevrolet Astro vans, six heavily armed cops to a van. And the vans were everywhere.

The folks I met in the Bayview—most were black, those who weren't were Latino—wanted the police to succeed. They didn't want to live with the drug trade and gang violence, and all the temptations those things posed for their children, any more than anyone else does. But they also feared the police and didn't like that they acted more like an occupying army than a police department. The Bayview-Hunter's Point reminded me a little of the images of the First Intifada from Gaza and the West Bank.

Now, the Bayview had its problems, largely gang and drug related. Gunfights between gang members were apparently common enough, though they mostly happened at night. I never heard gunfire—not even during the nights I stayed over—but these things happened often enough that they weren't talked about with any shock. The older Bayview residents would shake their heads in resignation, and the younger ones were either excited—and wanted to be a part of the action—or they hid as best they could.

Something interesting happened the very first time a police officer—a white police officer—noticed me in the neighborhood. On my second day there.

"Hello," he said. "Can I help you? Are you lost?"

"No sir, but thank you," I said. "I work here."

Two days later, the same officer was not so friendly.

"You work here, huh? You're sure you're not here to buy drugs?" he asked while another officer patted me down.

"No sir, I work right there, at *The New Bayview*. You can ask my boss, the publisher."

"Okay," one of the officers said. "But if you need help, don't call us. Ask your 'friends' here to help you."

After that second encounter, the SFPD didn't bother me again. I'd become invisible, a part of the landscape.

As Muhammad got more comfortable with me, he gave me more responsibility. He always picked the stories—*The New Bayview* was hugely interested in the ongoing court case of an African American religious leader by the name of Yahweh Ben Yahweh—but he let me edit them, and generally put things where I thought they should go. Or where they fit best.

Muhammad also did a lot of the in-house printing for the San Francisco Black Chamber of Commerce, so I spent a lot of time with him on the road going to the printer or doing errands. One afternoon, he left me with his friend the printer, who carefully explained and showed me how his offset lithography press worked. We even talked a little bit about the possibility of my coming to work for him—Muhammad had trouble paying me on time—and learning how to run a press. It was still a bad economy out there, and that would be a useful skill.

But occasionally, I would get glimpses of Muhammad's bigger life, and of his past. One afternoon, he left me alone in the newspaper office while he was off doing something, and I came across a huge archive of Black Panther Party newspapers from the late 1960s. We got a lot of African American newspapers from across the country—my two favorites were *The Chicago Defender* and the now-defunct *Big Red News*, which I think was published by Al Sharpton—but I'd never seen anything quite like the Black Panther newspaper. I read through a few, and they were fascinating.

One afternoon, a well-dressed man who was clearly an old friend of Muhammad's walked in. I rarely saw Muhammad smile—he wasn't that kind of man—but he did that afternoon as they said hello. They talked a bit, and then Muhammad asked me to come over.

"Brother Umar, this is Brother Eldridge Cleaver. You may have heard of him."

Heard of him? Eldridge Cleaver *was* the Black Panthers in all their gun-toting, militant glory. His book *Soul on Ice* was still essential reading in some places. When the evening news in California wanted to frighten white suburbanites, all they had to do was show pictures of Assembly Speaker Willie Brown or Eldridge Cleaver. They were everything we were supposed to be afraid of.

Cleaver smiled widely and shook my hand.

"Brother Umar, it's good to meet you!"

"I've asked Brother Eldridge to write for us, and I want you to work with him. As his editor," Muhammad said.

The Eldridge Cleaver I talked with was not the fear-inspiring revolutionary he had once been. By this time he'd become a Mormon and had dabbled in Republican politics. But that wasn't much of a third act to his life. He had a somewhat dissipated look to him, and was trying to make a living peddling a liquid vitamin supplement. He clearly believed in the product, but he wasn't happy with the promotional material, which showed a happy, white, middle-aged couple cavorting awkwardly in reasonably beautiful settings, clearly the result of using this company's product.

"Black people need to see black people using things, otherwise they won't buy them," Cleaver told me.

I wouldn't have bought them either. The woman in the photos looked too much like my mother. And the vitamins—Cleaver had given me a sample—tasted funny.

To live and work in the Bayview meant that both Jennifer and I had to wear a uniform of sorts. I always, or almost always, wore a crocheted Muslim skullcap and Jennifer always wore a headscarf, things that made us identifiable as Muslims. Most of the adults in the neighborhood knew Muslims and how they dressed, so while they may have found us odd at first, they knew how to make sense of us.

The only trouble I had was with a group of kids who cornered me one morning, thinking I might be an undercover police officer. One of the older kids in the group eventually thought his way out of the situation—what cover was I under, exactly?—and they didn't bother me after that.

Aside from small things like that, I had discovered that in becoming a white American Muslim, I had abandoned some of my whiteness. I had done so not with a proclamation, but by my willingness to learn and live in the midst of people whose lives I could have otherwise bypassed or ignored. I was clearly an outsider—that was obvious—but I was attempting to learn and live by the rules of the people I found myself in the midst of. And that was respected.

This insider-outsider position is an incredibly comfortable one for me. I have a gift for negotiating and living in cross-cultural relationships, and being neither in nor out actually feels safe to me. I've had no choice; I've had to cultivate this. I was used to being an outsider, and in places like this—in learning to be Muslim, in working for Muhammad in the Bayview—I could use that to my advantage. If I violated a social or cultural (or religious) rule, I could always plead ignorance. Because that was usually true.

I knew had I arrived when a few years later an African American Muslim asked me, "Brother Umar, what's your 'slave name'?"

I think Muhammad liked having a young white man to boss around. After that first day, when he seemed so disgusted that it was I who showed up at his doorstep, my race was simply not an issue. But he also never censored himself, especially when friends of his from the Nation came into the shop to talk, and the discussion came around to "the white man." If he thought of me as white, he generally kept that to himself.

Not always, though. One afternoon, Muhammad and I were working. And we'd been joined by two of Muhammad's other part-time employees, Lynn and Roger, both young African American men in their twenties. Lynn was an artist and illustrator, and I forget exactly what Roger did.

Lynn had just finished a drawing of some kind, for an advertisement, I think. He showed it to Muhammad.

"Well, what do you think?"

"It needs work," Muhammad said bluntly.

Lynn had been working on that drawing all afternoon. As he got up, he looked at me.

"Brother Umar, take a look at this and tell me what you think."

Muhammad intervened.

"A black man tells you that you need to do more work, and so you go running to the white man for approval! What's wrong with you? Remember who you are! Have some self-respect!"

With that, Roger stepped in.

"Whoa, whoa, wait a minute! So, he's 'Brother Umar' when it's convenient for you, but then he suddenly gets to be the 'white man' when you feel like it?"

There have been many times in my life when I've just sat around and watched when maybe I should have said or done something. But that day I knew there was absolutely nothing I could do but keep my mouth shut and let these three men hash this out. Because there was nothing—*absolutely nothing*—I could add to this conversation.

And they did hash it out. I don't remember much of what was said after that, but two things became clear—Muhammad seemed to realize he was wrong, but he also would not back down. The conversation quickly died out, Lynn never showed me his drawing, and we all got back to work.

From then on, Muhammad was a little more careful. He seemed to think a bit more before he'd say things. But not always. One afternoon, after coming back from Marin County with a truckload of newspapers, Muhammad stopped by a restaurant where the Black Chamber of Commerce was having a luncheon. As we walked in, he pointed to a chair near the entrance. "Sit there and don't move. I'll be back in about ten minutes."

So I sat there. And I didn't move.

The chamber president, a man I recognized—we ran his column every month—saw me sitting and said hello.

"You work for Muhammad, right?"

"Yes sir, I do," I said.

"Well, please, feel free to have something to drink. It's okay. You have my permission."

"Are you sure?" I asked.

He smiled and nodded, and went back to the luncheon. I grabbed a can of Coke. And was still sipping on that can when Muhammad came back. He took one look at me and shook his head.

"You white people, you always walk into a place and act you like you own it."

I thought about trying to explain things to Muhammad but decided it wasn't worth the effort. For some reason, I found his crankiness to be part of his charm.

But one day, Muhammad asked me, "Would you like to come to a Nation of Islam worship service? Because I can arrange that."

"I would love to! Are white people allowed?" I asked.

"Of course white people are allowed," he said. "But they have to be invited first."

I had to leave before I could take Muhammad up on that offer. Which is too bad. I really wanted to see how the brothers and sisters of the Nation worshiped God.

I worked for Muhammad for only three months. As interesting as it was, Muhammad wasn't the best businessman, and I think I maybe got paid for six weeks of work. The months of not having steady work had taken a toll; Jennifer and I no longer had a place to live. We stayed with friends when we could but wore out our welcome quickly, and began scoping out abandoned buildings for a place to stay.

We slept where we could—at an Islamic prison ministry we were volunteering at, in the Student Union at SF State. Muhammad was even kind enough to let us sleep in his business for several nights.

"Don't let anyone know you're in here. And don't open the door," he said.

Eventually, an Egyptian businessman I'd met at the San Francisco Islamic Center offered me a job cleaning his warehouse in exchange for a small salary and a room for my wife and I to sleep in. It was all there was, and we were prepared to take it. And then my mother's boyfriend, Chuck Braswell, who owned several nursing homes in Southern California, offered Jennifer a job. We decided to take that. "I bet you Muhammad's going to ask me to stay," I told Jennifer.

Which he did. He tried appealing to my masculinity, to my sense of religious duty, even to a bit of solidarity, saying that I belonged there with him. I was moved by his appeal, but not enough to leave Jennifer on her own. We packed ourselves onto a junkyard motorcycle and headed south.

The motorcycle exploded on Highway 99 just outside Merced. We holed up there for a week at a small, spider-infested *masjid* owned by a group of Yemeni families, waiting for the motorcycle to be repaired. And when it gave up the ghost completely, we waited for my mother's boyfriend to pick us up outside Bakersfield.

I saw Muhammad again some months later, when Adam and I came up to San Francisco to pick up some of our things. I had told Adam all about Muhammad, and as we pulled in front of his business, said, "You watch, he's going to put us to work doing something."

We walked in, and Muhammad said hello as if I'd never left. As if two giant white men weren't standing in front of him.

"I'm glad you're here. I have something I need you to help me with," he said.

And we helped him move someone's pigeon coop.

The Islamic Center of San Francisco was, in 1991, a shabby little building on the corner of Crescent and Andover in the city's Bernal Heights neighborhood. If memory serves, it used to be an Elks Club, or something similar, before Muslims turned it into a *masjid* in 1959.

I was there a lot at the time, both for regular prayers and for special evening things. Especially if communal meals were served. Jennifer never had an enjoyable experience at any of the *masjids* we went to, was never made to feel welcome—her thin, wispy hair always got out of control and emerged from under whatever head covering she wore, and that would arouse someone's ire—but she put up with it all, for my sake. I'd made some connections with some people at the *masjid*, spent some time memorizing my prayers and bits of the Qur'an I needed to be able to recite when I prayed.

One afternoon, we stopped by. I needed to make up the midday prayer, and the Islamic Center was always open in the afternoon for people who wanted to come and pray or study for a while. So, I went in on my own to pray.

I was being torn up by anger. Some months earlier, Jen and I had gone south to be part of my father's second wedding, and when he fell short in paying the catering bill, I rather stupidly offered to pay the remainder—$2,000—with a credit card, on the promise that he would pay me back. And he hadn't. And I was furious with him. In the midst of unemployment and homelessness, I was also furious with my father. Everything he had ever done, ever been, and ever failed to be seemed to be summed up in this.

The center's main room was brown—the walls were covered in cheap wood paneling, the carpet was the color of heavily creamed coffee, and the afternoon light filtering through the colored glass windows was yellow and orange. I was alone, and I began my prayer. *Bismilah ar-rahman ar-rahim . . .*

Sometime during my second prostration—when I bent down to touch my head to the ground, to "grovel before God," as a future employer would put it—something like a massive spark of electricity hit me right smack in the middle of my head. Everything was suddenly bright, and blue, and I was breathless. And exhausted.

And the words appeared, fully formed in my head: *You do not need to be so angry.*

They weren't my words. I hadn't thought them. They came from outside of me. I had to stop praying and catch my breath. I rolled over on my back. What had just happened? Had God just spoken to me?

There was no question in my mind. And no doubt whatsoever. God had spoken to me. God had reached inside, put this thought in my head, this thought that wasn't mine and that I needed so much to hear, to feel, to become a part of me. It was a tiny moment—it happened in an instant—and yet it was utterly overwhelming. It engulfed me from the inside, left me gasping and in shock. It was as if I'd been momentarily annihilated, as if I'd ceased to be an individual human being, ceased to be anything other than an appendage of the infinite.

The whole of infinity. Bound solely by my flesh.

That's the thing with getting God inside you. There's no piece of the infinite that isn't itself infinite, no small portion that touches gently and carefully. When you get God inside you, you get all of God, every bit of universe-creating, "says be and it is" infinity. All crammed inside a tiny, finite mess of flesh, bone, and blood. It cannot be gentle, or kind, or pleasant. It can be nothing other than utterly, completely and absolutely overwhelming. It can do nothing but verge on obliterating.

I'd not asked for this. Or wanted it. And I did not want it to ever happen again.

When I came out, I must have looked like I was in shock. Jennifer asked me, "What happened?" I'm not sure how much I explained. She noticed something over the next several days, however. I was, in fact, a lot less angry. That's when I told her what happened.

She looked at me with a mixture of awe and disbelief.

"I'm jealous," she said.

9

Blue Eyes

"STRAIGHTEN YOUR LINES AND fill in the gaps. Feet to feet, and shoulder to shoulder . . ."

The imam's voice was soft but insistent. Men jostled and moved up where there was enough space for them to fit in. Those with glasses took them and placed them on the carpeted floor in front of them. The closer you got to the front, so we had been told, the more likely God would hear and credit your prayer. There was whispering, then some shushing, and then relative silence.

All you could hear was the whir of the ceiling fans. *Bismilah ar-rahman ar-rahim*, the imam chanted.

We all raised our hands, and then folded them over our chests. Mouths moved in time with the imam's words as he rhythmically recited the first surah of the Qur'an, *surat al-fateha*, "The Opening." And when he was done, when he hung on that second-to-last syllable, *wa la doh-leen*, the entire congregation matched his tone and chanted the word *Ameen*.

It would oftentimes feel to me like a word chanted in time with the breath of God.

And we stood silently as the imam waited for a moment, and then began reciting another passage from the Qur'an. Sometimes it would be a long recitation, a small part of the some of the very early *surahs* of the Qur'an, and sometimes it would be one of the shorter *surahs* toward the end. I had memorized a few of those, and it was always nice to hear someone who had memorized the Qur'an—a *hafez al-qur'an*, a "guardian of the recitation," someone who has committed the whole book to memory—and who could recite it well.

This was a typical Friday prayer at the Umar ibn al-Khatab Masjid in Columbus, Ohio. That miserable little *masjid* had once been a Jehovah's Witness Kingdom Hall but was now run by the Muslim Student Association. Prayer was awkward in that little building, since it hadn't been built as a Muslim house of worship and was not oriented correctly toward the Saudi city of Makka. So we all lined up diagonally behind the *imam*, who stood in the northeast corner. The stage in front of the hall meant some space was wasted. And all our arrangements to have a proper place to wash before prayer, or segregate the genders, were ad hoc, and done about well as could be expected.

Somewhere between a half and a third of us worshiping there were students, mostly at Ohio State. Some were students elsewhere. The rest were a combination of immigrant professionals—physicians, engineers, and a few relatively successful businessmen—and refugees. We all prayed together, but socializing generally broke down along ethnic group—Kurds, Indians, Pakistanis, Bangladeshis, Palestinians and Egyptians, Saudis, Algerians and Moroccans, Afghans. The number of languages spoken in that place on a typical Friday—Arabic, Kurdish, Dari, Pashtu, Urdu, Bengali, even a handful of Turkish dialects from Central Asia—was amazing.

We were held together by English and Arabic.

It was typical for the men who wore glasses to take them off and put them on the carpet in front of them as they prayed—glasses easily slip off the noses of those who grovel before God. This particular afternoon, Khaled's son, a precocious three-year-old, wandered between the lines picking up all of the glasses he could find.

Clink! Clink! Clink! It was distracting, and funny. And it felt a little sinful, being distracted. A prayer leader once told us such distractions were temptations from Satan, who wanted nothing more than to have us wasting our time going through the motions praying prayers God would never hear because we weren't focused.

After the prayer was over, Khaled got up. He had corralled his son, and a pile of eyeglasses sat on a corner of the carpeted stage.

"If you are missing a pair of glasses, see me," he said, unable to restrain an embarrassed laugh. "I probably have them."

I didn't have glasses to pick up. But I did want to say hello to Khaled. He held his son in his arms as people picked through the pile. I shook his hand, we spoke briefly, but before we could finish, his little boy looked at my face, smiled wide, and grasped my ears with his hands.

"Your eyes!" he said with wild excitement. "They're blue!"

Like he'd never seen blue eyes before.

And maybe he hadn't.

In this place, that made me different.

I'd ended up at The Ohio State University almost entirely by accident. We'd moved back to Southern California after Chuck Braswell, my mother's boyfriend at the time, offered Jennifer a job in one of his nursing homes. He also gave us a car, a 1967 Plymouth Valiant, on the condition that we get it running. It sort of ran, well enough to drive home. Adam and I went to work, tuning the vehicle up, changing the oil, gapping the spark plugs, and changing the distributor cap. I remember turning it over for the first time after we tuned it up, and how good that engine sounded.

"I've never heard a car sound so much better after a simple tune up," Adam said.

I loved that car, built the same year I was born. I learned to fix cars on that Valiant, doing everything from replacing the shock absorbers to the rear wheel bearings, which I sat and carefully greased for the better part of an hour the day I changed them.

Not long after Jennifer had found a job, I got hired by a psychiatrist in Pomona, Joel Dreyer, who ran a worker's comp clinic. I was one of several people typing up his notes into coherent medical reports so Dr. Dreyer could bill the state. Dreyer was something of a charming rogue, a larger-than-life figure who had court artist drawings of him testifying at a trial in Michigan up on his office wall. It didn't take long for Jennifer and me to get back on our feet, and I began to consider where I would go and finish my university education.

I had two and a half years of a journalism degree under my belt. But I really wanted to study Arabic, possibly even major in it. My first two choices were the University of California's flagship schools, UCLA and Berkeley. I got applications from both schools, and actually visited UCLA.

At the time, the folks at UCLA admitted that they didn't really have much of an Arabic language program and that I would probably be better off someplace else. I noticed that several of the Arabic textbooks they used had been created by Ohio State, and it occurred to me that if UCLA was using OSU's Arabic program, it was probably fairly good. So, I called Columbus, got an application, and filled it out.

I was a little shocked at how much shorter and simpler that application was compared to the University of California.

My grades were not good enough to transfer to either UCLA or Berkeley from a California State University school—I think I would have needed a 3.8 or 3.7 GPA, and my grades from SF State were solidly in the 3.3 range.

So, all my hopes hinged on whether or not the folks in Columbus would let me in. I had no idea how this worked, and the waiting was anxious.

I need not have worried. I had a pulse and at least a C average, which it seems was all one needed to get accepted to Ohio State at the time.

So, Jennifer and I bought a proper motorcycle—not one from a junk dealer—and rode across the country with just about all our worldly possessions strapped on front or hanging off the side. Along the way, we stopped in Las Vegas and got married. It was about time.

After doing a little work with the course catalogues and looking over the requirements, I discovered I could finish up in two years if I continued pursuing a journalism degree and took as much Arabic as I could without majoring or minoring in it. I'd be one class short of an Arabic minor, but I'd be done in two years. After a chance encounter in a laundromat with a Veterans Administration benefits counselor, I discovered I actually had exactly twenty months of VA education benefits. That, and nothing else, set the deadline for my studies.

I remember the day I first showed up at the Ohio State journalism department and introduced myself.

"I'm transferring here from San Francisco State," I said.

"Why?" the professor overseeing the program said. "They're a much better j-school than we are. Why would you want to come here?"

"Because OSU has a much better Arabic program," I said.

I took to Arabic easily. In fact, I found it a simpler and more elegant language than either Russian or Czech. It helped that I had a place—the *masjid*—to hear and speak Arabic every day.

I took being Muslim very seriously while I was in Columbus. We lived as close as we could to the little Muslim Student Association *masjid* so I could walk to prayers. I tried to get up every morning early for prayer, sometimes trudging through awful weather—rain, bitter cold—to get there. The angels bless every footstep of someone making their way to *salat al-fajr*, the early morning prayer, according to the Prophet Muhammad.

I tried to orient my life around the five daily prayers. I went to the *masjid* whenever I could, and my Fridays were set aside so that I could pray with my brothers (and a few sisters, always secluded in a back room) and then enjoy some fellowship with them afterwards. Prayer time was sacred, a moment when the world came to a halt and we, as a community of believers, were suddenly there as the Qur'an itself was first revealed through Muham-mad to his gathered followers. This felt good. It felt right to stop what we were doing and pray as a community to God.

In fact, it felt good to give myself over to God. I wanted nothing more for my life than to serve God and be what God wanted me to be.

For Muslims, the Qur'an is not just a book. It is the very speech of God. It is God incarnate in the world, and Muslims have argued about the createdness of the Qur'an in much the same way that Christians have ar-gued about the divinity and humanity (and how those mixed) of Jesus. Is it eternal? Or was there a time when these words of God did not exist? I was inclined toward believing the Qur'an was "created," in that what we have is an articulation, an incarnation if you will, of the words God spoke. It exists in time and space, came to us in history. There was a time when the physical book we call the Qur'an—a *nuskhat al-qur'an*, or copy of the Qur'an—did not exist. And the recitation itself refers to many events and people in his-tory: Adam, Moses, Abraham. They are no more, and there was a time when they were not yet.

But as God says in *surat an-nahl*,

> Verily, Our Word unto a thing when We intend it, is only that
> We say unto it: "Be!"—and it is. (16:40)

Perhaps, in telling the stories of Moses, Abraham, Joseph, and all the others, God is breathing them into existence and writing their history as we listen and recite. The idea intrigues me, but this is also more speculation than I want to engage in here.

Now, I wasn't always successful in making prayer as central to my life as I wanted. Sometimes I was unmotivated. Sometimes I was lazy. And some-times I was just plain distracted or busy. There was always a little guilt and anxiety attached to that, since good, pious Muslims are required to make up any prayers they miss. Sometimes I did this, and sometimes I didn't.

And sometimes, I simply forgot which prayers I'd missed.

Islam is a religion of deeds and actions, and there is no great argument among Muslims about the distinction between faith and practice, at least not among the Sunnis I worshiped with. I had always found the Protestant argu-ments about faith and works to be both smug and pointless, especially since the formulation most Protestants used—saved by faith in grace apart from works—always seemed to make the faith that saves the believer's faith. If I'm saved by my faith in God, then I'm saved by something I do, and not by God's action. Isn't that faith a work in and of itself? It certainly seemed that way to me.

Believing in God, trusting the revelation given to the Prophet Muhammad, praying and fasting and giving to the poor—all of these things mattered to God, and God would keep track of whether and how we do them. The most important deed we could do was to believe, to confess *la ilaha ila allah muhammad rasul allah*: No gods but God (literally, "The God"), and Muhammad (literally, "the one who is praised") is the messenger of God. This was as much of a confession of faith as any Muslim ever needed, and it was not only a confession of the ultimate reality—that there is only one, indivisible God—but it is also a confession of allegiance and loyalty to the "praised one" who is God's messenger. This confession was not just about what we believed, but who we follow. And for us, it was simple. There is no god but God, and Muhammad is the messenger of God. It said all there was to say.

Of course, nothing really is that simple. To be fair to the complexities of Muslim history, whole volumes have been written about what exactly those few and simple words of the *shahadah*—testimony or witness—mean. And Muslims themselves have long argued over what exactly loyalty to the messenger of God means.

In fact, at the Umar ibn al-Khatab *masjid* there in Columbus, we argued about that a lot as well.

We didn't argue about the very basic things, what the Qur'an itself clearly attests to and those things the *hadith* literature—the collected sayings and doings of Muhammad and his companions—agree about most broadly. The "righteous good deeds" the Quran and the *sunnah*—practice, or habits, a word that comes from a verb that can mean to sharpen, or to mold, or to enact—were in broadest agreement about were faith in God, the five daily prayers, fasting during the month of Ramadan, giving charity to the poor, and making the pilgrimage to the *ka'aba*, the House of God at the center of the *haram ash-sharif* in Makka, at least once in a lifetime.

I was most drawn to those passages of the Qur'an and the *hadith* that commanded believers to care for the poor and their neighbors. Surah 90—*surat al-balad,* or "The City"—states it most simply:

> I swear by this city;
> And you are free in this city.
> And by the begetter and that which he begot;
> Verily, We have created man in toil.
> Thinks he that none can overcome him?
> He says, "I have wasted wealth in abundance!"
> Thinks he that none sees him?
> Have We not made for him a pair of eyes?
> And a tongue and a pair of lips?
> And shown him the two ways?

But he has not attempted to [take] the path that is steep.
And what will make you know the path that is steep?
Freeing a neck.
Or giving food in a day of hunger,
To an orphan near of kin.
Or to the impoverished afflicted with misery.
Then he became one of those who believed, and recommended
one another to perseverance and patience, and recommended
one another to pity and compassion.
They are those on the Right Hand.
But those who disbelieved in Our signs, they are those on the
    Left Hand.
The Fire will be shut over them.

There is a lot to consider in this short *surah*. The accountability of human beings in the face of their arrogance and sense of self-sufficiency. And the call for believers to follow a "steep path." Feeding the poor. Caring for orphans. (God is constantly commanding Muslims to care for orphans, widows and wayfarers—people who have no one to stand up for them, no one to seek vengeance or redress if they have been wronged.) "Freeing a neck" is almost always taken to refer to freeing slaves, and freeing slaves is considered an act of great mercy and is sometimes required in order to repent of a sin.

At the end of all of this is the promise of eternity, of Paradise for those on "the right hand" and the Fire for those on "the left hand." For the point of all this exhortation is to get on the right side of God, because human choices have cosmic importance. And determine ultimate fate.

So, whoever does good equal to the weight of an atom shall see
it. And whoever does evil equal to the weight of an atom shall
see it. (99:7–8)

Unlike the Bible, the Qur'an is very explicit in its descriptions of heaven and hell. Paradise, *al-jannat*, is literally "The Garden" underneath which rivers flow. It is a place of shade, couches to recline on, good food to eat, wine and cool spring water, beautiful wives, lots of servants, eternal peace, security, joy, and the everlasting presence of God. Hell, *al-jahennam* (from *gahenna*, the garbage dump outside Jerusalem), is a photo negative of the Garden. It is an eternal fire "whose fuel is men and stones" (2:24), a place where there will be neither shade nor relief, where the food is painful thorns, and where the only thing to drink is scalding water that is like either boiling oil or molten brass, depending on whose translation you read. God is not there, but only because it was created to be a place where God is not.

(Whether hell was an eternal abode, or merely a temporary purifying one, was a matter for much debate, since there are Qur'anic passages and *hadith* that testify to both positions. I was inclined to believe hell was temporary.)

The depictions of Paradise and the Fire are very physical, very tangible, very corporeal, even almost carnal. They are places of great pleasure and enjoyment or great pain and suffering. That's because they aren't abstractions where disembodied souls will float around. They are places where human bodies—resurrected human bodies, remade from the dust—will find themselves after the Day of Judgment, or *yaum al-qiyamah*, "the day of standing," an event the Qur'an describes in great detail. A trumpet will sound, the mountains will fall to dust, the earth will be rolled up like a scroll, the stars will fall and the sun will fail. All humanity will be gathered together under this failing sun and these falling stars, under these crumbling mountains and upon this flattened, rolled up earth. It will be a day when no human being will have the ability to do anything for anyone else. Again, the Qur'an says it best in *surat al-ghafir* ("The One Who Forgives"), also titled *al-mu'min* ("The Believer"):

> This Day shall every person be recompensed for what he earned. This Day [there is no injustice]. Truly, [God] is swift in reckoning.
>
> And warn them of the Day that is drawing near, when the hearts will be choking the throats, and they can neither return them to their chests nor can throw them out. There will be no friend, not an intercessor for the wrongdoers who could be given heed to.
>
> [God] knows best the fraud of the eyes, and all that breasts conceal.
>
> And [God] judges with truth, while those to whom they invoke besides Him cannot judge anything. Certainly, [God]! He is All-Hearer, the All-Seer. (40:17–20)

These images of the judgment day, especially the importance of human accountability—"every person shall be recompensed for what he earned"— were essential to me. They would stay with me. Not because I wanted to damn some portion of the world to hell. The afterlife, as essential as it was to many Muslims, was still not that important to me. I found some of the tales I was told about what Paradise would be like—we would have seventy-foot-tall, physically perfect bodies and God would show himself to us on Friday afternoons when we would have prayed the *salat al-jumuah*—to be quaint but uninteresting. What mattered to me was the world, the here and now. I wanted kindness, decency, mercy, and compassion to matter and, somehow, to win. I wanted God to judge the world, and judge it harshly. But I was now beginning to experience a God of mercy, who would judge the world with justice *and* mercy. I wanted to believe that even hell itself, filled with the unbelievers and the wicked, would someday be empty. Every sinner, every wrongdoer, would find his or her way to paradise, even if took it a million years of fire, boiling water and molten brass.

There is a *hadith qudsi*—words God spoke directly to Muhammad but not included in the Qur'an—in which a group of believers on Judgment Day ask Adam, Moses, and Jesus to intercede on their behalf. Each refuses, and finally Jesus tells the believers to ask Muhammad, and he makes several tips to hell to fetch out believers, finally leaving in the fire only those the Qur'an itself has imprisoned (whatever that means). Muhammad is then reported to say,

> There shall come out of Hell-fire he who has said: There is no god but Allah and who has in his heart goodness weighing a barley-corn; then there shall come out of Hell-fire he who has said: There is no god but Allah and who has in his heart goodness weighing a grain of wheat; then there shall come out of Hell-fire he who has said: There is no god but Allah and who has in his heart goodness weighing an atom. (Hadith Qudsi 36)

I pinned my hope on God's mercy.

Islam can be a very exacting faith, and there were times when it seemed that God was merely a great cosmic accountant, keeping a ledger, tabulating good and bad deeds meticulously. Indeed, I knew some very pious Sunnis who acted as if what mattered was the accounting itself, and that if you kept proper track of all your good and bad deeds you could keep a separate set of books. This was definitely a minority view, but it became clear, at least in the way they talked: if you kept your own books, what need was there for God?

In fact, I once met an Egyptian Muslim who had worked himself into a state of near-permanent despair. "I've missed too many prayers and can never make them up, I've been too bad, committed too many sins, I can never do enough, and God will never forgive me. I'm doomed, I'm hell-bound, and there's nothing I can do," he told me once. Weeping.

Most Muslims, however, including me, lived neither in the lands of despair nor with the self-assurance of accurate accounting. Rather, we trusted in a kind of rough grace, a grace in which good deeds are given extra value:

> Whosoever brings good, he shall have the better thereof; and whosoever brings evil, then those who do evil deeds will only be requited for what they used to do. (28:84)

There was a scale, an accurate balance, a judgment in which each person would receive recompense for everything—good and ill—that they ever did. But we also had the promise from the one who would judge us that a thumb was on the scale, giving extra weight, extra value, to the good we have done. Rigging the judgment in favor of even the atom's weight of good, the mustard seed of faith we had. That's what I believed. And that's what I trusted.

Or as God told the Prophet Muhammad, "My mercy outweighs My wrath."

Religions aren't simply pure ideas, nice words, and volumes of books, however. They are products of history, of time, place, and circumstance. They are believed in and lived out by beating hearts wrapped in flesh, incarnate as cultures and communities of people. Because of this, the white American convert to Islam is posed with an interesting problem—which Muslim culture will he or she adapt or conform to? Because unlike African American Muslims, we don't have a Muslim culture of our own to embrace us and to tell us what being Muslim means.

And we only share so much with our African American sisters and brothers. As I learned, I could voluntarily shed a fair amount of whiteness. But only so much.

This intertwining of religion as a set of universal ideas with a particular cultural articulation is very pronounced in Islam. Islam is tied to the Arabic language (which is said to be not merely the language of the revelation but also the language of God, the language everyone will speak in Paradise), to the time and place of sixth- and seventh-century Makka, to many of the cultural norms and practices of the Prophet Muhammad and his tiny but also rapidly growing community (and the interpreters of those habits several centuries later). Islam's universal proclamations—the brotherhood of humanity, the prophetic calling of Muhammad to reveal God's message to all humanity—are interwoven with a language and custom that make becoming Muslim an exercise in adopting and conforming to a very different and at times very foreign culture.

Western Christians—especially Americans—can much more easily pretend that the universals proclaimed by the Christian faith are not so wound up with culture. In part, this is because the culture that gave birth to Christianity—partly Hellenized but frequently resistant Judaism in

first-century Roman Palestine, Greece, and Asia Minor—no longer exists. I
know a tiny handful of Christians, mostly scholars, who can effectively read
Koine Greek, but it's not a spoken language anymore. Western Christendom
has been so thoroughly filtered that anything resembling a founding culture
or community has long disappeared. What replaced it were convert communities, including Europeans who over the centuries slowly grafted their
pre-Christian pagan ways of doing things and understanding the world
onto whatever form of Christianity they embraced (or were compelled to
embrace).

The same is true of Islam, of course. There are as many Muslim practices and traditions as there are Muslim communities in the world, even
as the essentials remain the same from Morocco to Malaysia. The difference is, no Swedish Lutheran or American Baptist has to measure her faith
against that of a living, breathing, vibrant Greek-speaking Christian community in what is today Palestine. Makka and Madina are Muslim cities,
and while they haven't always been the center of intellectual gravity in the
Islamic world, they are where the faith began—and are currently inhabited
by people who can credibly claim continuity with the original founders of
the faith fourteen hundred years ago.

So, everyone lives in a little bit of a tension with the Saudis, who won't
say they're the best and most authentic Muslims, but will sometimes act like it.

For some Muslims, marriage or other family relationships dictate the
matter. In Columbus, I got to know a white American like me who married
a Tunisian Muslim. The Islamic culture he was slowly embracing, and that
was embracing him, was the Sufi-flavored Islam of his wife's extended family. The Arabic he was learning was the Arabic of Tunisia.

No such luck for me. My wife was a Lutheran pastor's daughter who,
despite her best efforts, simply could not become Muslim. Her simple
Christian faith was permanently pressed onto her heart. That she tried, despite everything, was impressive. I never held it against her that she didn't
become Muslim. I loved her, and she was the wonderful little girl who loved
me without condition. That we couldn't worship God together disappointed
her, but her own experiences with church life, and growing up as a pastor's
daughter in a conservative church riven with conflict, also made the whole
subject a difficult one for her to deal with. She wasn't much inclined to at-
tend church at that point in her life anyway, and certainly not by herself.

(That I couldn't worship God with my wife didn't bother me in the
least. I actually appreciated Islam's segregation of the genders, since the
last thing I wanted to deal with were the sensibilities of women. Notions of
social power were still wrapped up with my experience of personal power,
and many of the women I'd met in institutional settings—school and the

army—did not appear to lack for power or the willingness to use it. My mother has an incredibly strong personality and never seemed to shrink from imposing her will on the men around her. And I'd been abused by an incredibly cruel fifth-grade female teacher. No, women had not appeared to lack power in the world in which I lived. So I was very grateful to have only men to deal with. Having been afraid of men for so long, and not really liking men very much, it was something I very much needed to learn how to do.)

If culture and tradition can't guide your religious journey, then finding that path is quite a task. The Islamic culture that would shape me would largely be dependent on the friends I made—like the African Americans and Palestinians I knew at San Francisco State University—and the Muslim groups I gravitated to.

I don't remember how I met Tarek. He was a tall, blue-eyed Egyptian, an officer in the Egyptian army from a prominent family. He was working on a PhD in aeronautical engineering, and he told me he spent his days playing with ballistic re-entry vehicles—missile warheads and capsules—in a wind tunnel, studying their properties, concocting new designs.

He was a charming man, Tarek, with a mischievous smile and a very commanding personality. He told me his blue eyes were an inheritance from the Crusades, that some of his ancestors had been soldiers in a French army that had landed somewhere in the Nile Delta and then was never heard from again. He could be a bit cruel at times, poking and pushing me, asking pointed questions, and Jennifer sometimes complained about how he spoke to me.

Tarek would frequently greet me by grasping my right hand hard and kneading it, so that my knuckles snapped and popped. He had powerful hands and took no small joy in doing this to me.

"You need to toughen up!" he'd tell me.

Sometime during his stay in the United States, Tarek had been radicalized. I was never clear quite what it was—some combination of U.S. support for Israel, what he saw as a fairly libertine American culture (life at Ohio State troubled a lot of Muslim men, especially the young single ones, who never quite knew what to do or how to feel about the way many American girls dressed, especially in the spring and summer), and outrage at how so many Muslims across the world were oppressed or the victims of violence.

He was also increasingly angry and outspoken regarding his government, especially Egypt's dependence on the United States and its unwillingness to do anything about the Palestinians. This was probably not a wise
move given that the government was paying for at least part of his doctorate
as well as his salary as a senior officer in the Egyptian Army.

But Tarek was more a passionate man than a wise one.

He let his anger take a political and theological form by embracing the
idea of *jihad*, of God-sanctioned war on behalf of the faith and beleaguered
Muslims. There was a lot to be angry about in the early 1990s—wars and
struggles in Chechnya, Kashmir, Algeria, Afghanistan, the beginning of
Iraq's suffering under sanctions, and the never-ending misery of the Palestinians living under Israeli military occupation. Not a Friday went by that
the *khatib*, the preacher, didn't either mention all these places directly or
invoke God's aid for the Muslims of these places in their struggles in the
supplications after the sermon.

"But what can we do about it?" some would ask in despair. "We are
powerless, and there's nothing we can do."

"We can do what *Allah subhana wata'ala* has commanded us to do,"
Tarek once said. "We can fight. We can make *jihad*."

There was a tiny group of aspiring jihadis at the *masjid*, and I joined
them. It seemed to be one way to follow my call and give myself fully and
completely to God. We read and discussed Sayed Qutb's book *Milestones*, his
ideological and theological justification for revolution and war. We also read
another important figure, Maulana A'la Maududi, a Pakistani journalist and
Islamic thinker who invented many of the ideas embraced by Islamists and
revolutionaries around the world, including the very modern notion of an
"Islamic State." Maududi's commentary on the Qur'an was important, as
were some of his other books. Sudanese Islamist leader Hassan al-Turabi
also fascinated us. We studied, and talked, and prayed, and considered.

What many people call "fundamentalist Islam" I have taken to calling "Revolutionary Islam." It is a thoroughly modern idea, one born in the
twentieth century by disaffected Muslim intellectuals like Qutb and Maududi who struggled to balance what they understood were God's promises to
the Muslims—power and importance, a calling to order the world on behalf
of God—with the experience of powerlessness in colonialism, secularism,
military defeat and occupation, and the hit-and-miss promises of modernity, which seemed incomplete for so many. It is a modern idea because it
looks to modern political forms—electoral democracy, violent revolution,
the nation-state—to order Muslim society along the lines God and His
Prophet commanded.

A properly Islamic society would be one that maximized the ability of people to do good and minimized their ability to do evil. That's what we believed.

We studied the times of the Prophet and his immediate companions, believing that they were the most authentic Muslims, theirs the most authentic Islamic community. A handful of deeply faithful Muslims took on two powerful empires—Byzantium and Persia—and conquered them. In fact, within a couple generations of the Prophet's death, most of the "civilized" world of antiquity had come under Muslim rule.

If men with faith could do that, then what could we do if we had that faith?

"No Muslim has any business emigrating to the United States for anything other than education," Tarek said. More than once. "If a Muslim has the chance, he should leave the non-Muslim place he is living and migrate to a Muslim society."

For Tarek, that wasn't Egypt. He talked a bit about Afghanistan, especially those parts of the country under the control of Gulbuddin Hekmatyar. But that wasn't his ideal Muslim society either.

"The only place where Islam truly rules is Sudan," he said. "And that is where we should go."

I found myself trying to imagine living in Khartoum, in Hassan al-Turabi's Islamic "paradise." It did not appeal. I certainly couldn't imagine taking Jennifer there.

One afternoon, we were having a discussion on Islamic finance, on what tools an Islamic state might have to mobilize resources to build large projects, because without debt, the modern state, or modern corporations, could do little. The idea of strangling the state, and all its projects, appealed to me. But somehow, whatever conversation we were having always seemed to come back to enforcing the law and sending people to prison for either a lack of faith or simply disobeying the rules.

Police and prisons. That's what too many of those I studied with wanted. They didn't object to the gun and cudgel—just being on the wrong side of them.

It was at this point that I realized: I'm still not a real revolutionary. I still don't want to change the world. I'm just an angry young man with some vague idea of vengeance. I just want to blow stuff up. And not even that so much anymore. I'm not sure I can do this, I said to myself.

Not that I gave up the idea of *jihad*. Just the justification that in fighting, we were fighting for a better world. That was nonsense, and not something I cared about anyway.

Around that time, the Bosnian War broke out. It made a lot of us, in-cluding Tarek and me, very angry. As a *masjid*, we raised a lot of money for the Bosnians, filled up a couple of shipping containers with food, clothes, and medical supplies (including a crudely equipped surgical suite). We hosted a Bosnian refugee family, and a minister from the Bosnian govern-ment spent a week with us.

Everything about the Bosnian War pushed my buttons. Mostly, though, what made me angriest were the French and British peacekeepers sitting ar-rogantly on white armored vehicles in their blue helmets and berets, lectur-ing the Bosnians for having the temerity to fight and defend themselves. It was also disheartening to see the European and North American Left twist itself into knots because somehow the Bosnians, for fighting back, were no longer "proper" victims.

In addition to the wannabes, we actually had a real *mujahed*—one who fights *jihad*—or two in our little *masjid*. Ali was an African American convert to Islam, and he had fought in Afghanistan for a few years. (He got to be good friends with an Uzbek working on a doctorate in economics who had fought with the Soviet Special Forces in Afghanistan, and occasionally they would sit and swap war stories.) Ali went to Bosnia, spent a year fighting there.

And I wanted to go too.

I cornered Ali one afternoon after he came back. He'd never been ter-ribly friendly with me, but he seemed impressed that I was interested in going to Bosnia.

"You want to go make *jihad*, huh?" he asked. "Well, don't talk to me unless you're serious. If you are serious, I know who you can talk to. But," he added, with both suspicion and sternness in his voice, "don't talk to me about this again if you aren't serious."

I was serious. At least I thought I was serious. But there was the mat-ter of Jennifer. If I wandered off to southern Europe to fight in a war, what would happen to her? Who would take care of her? Where would she go? I prayed. I contemplated. I listened. People kept telling me that God would provide for her if I went. But I knew caring for her was my responsibil-ity—marriage was half the faith for a good Muslim man! So eventually, I decided couldn't go fight in Bosnia. I had to take care of Jennifer. She was more important.

A couple of weeks later, Ali came up to me.

"So, are you still serious?"

"No. I've decided not to. No one to take care of Jennifer."

"Well, trust God," he said. Which was everyone's answer. He then looked at me and smiled. "But I didn't think you were serious."

Tarek, however, was. His anger over Bosnia ate him up. It hadn't helped that he'd reached an impasse with his academic advisor, a Jewish professor he could say some of the foulest things about. Or that his government had started pressing the State Department to cancel his visa and deport him so that he could be tried for sedition and antigovernment activity in Egypt. His wife and daughter were protected by his family connections, but Tarek himself was not. His life was quickly becoming disconnected from just about everyone and everything around him.

Jennifer and I saw him nearly every day. Jen had gotten a job at a day care center in Dublin, Ohio. But then our car broke down. Tarek had done the very kind thing of offering to take Jennifer (with me present, of course) to work. And picking her up (again, with me present) every afternoon. He did this for several weeks.

It was an incredibly kind thing for this man—this sometimes cruel, oftentimes angry man—to do.

One morning in the spring of 1993, Tarek arrived a little early. I'd invited him into our apartment while Jennifer was getting ready. He looked around. We had no furniture, just bare carpeted floors and some pillows to sit on.

"Where are the musical instruments? I expected to see guitars and a keyboard," he said.

The question stunned me. This was not something I expected from Tarek. We'd talked a little bit about music, but not much. Like a lot of converts to Islam, I struggled with music and decided that in order to be a good Muslim, I couldn't do music anymore. I gave that part of me up. It was *haram*—forbidden. The Prophet Muhammad himself had said so.

"I didn't think it was allowed," I told him.

He smiled that bright, mischievous grin of his.

"Brother Umar, you are a musician. I see it in your soul. And besides, what else is *tajweed*"—the formal recitation of the Qur'an—"but a type of music anyway? Get your instruments. You need them. They are part of you."

Sometime before I graduated in 1994, Tarek sent his wife and daughter home. He was looking for a way to get to Bosnia that didn't involve the risk of arrest at an airport.

One of the last things he said to me: "All I want to do is fight and die in the cause of Allah."

I hope God granted Tarek what he wanted. I truly do.

I remember the day the Columbine High School shooting happened.

It was after class at Georgetown, where I was working on a master's in Arab Studies. Some classmates of mine stood underneath a giant television, gawking up at the images flowing live on CNN; they were incredulous.

"How could this happen?" they gasped.

I've never asked that question. I've always wondered, "How come this doesn't happen more often?"

Because when I was fourteen, a freshman in high school, for a time I wondered where I might get guns and how I might build bombs, and I fantasized about getting even with the world in an explosive spasm of violence.

And yet, on that same television, we saw daily images of NATO planes bombing bridges and buildings across Serbia. Some shook their heads in angry disbelief. But no one was stunned.

No one asked, "How could this happen?"

Columbine was several hours one afternoon in the midst of a nearly three-month war.

As Americans, and as Western Christians, we have an odd stance toward violence. On the one hand, we abhor individual violence. It shocks and repulses us. How could one or two or even a handful of people do such things? And yet we celebrate, we sanctify, we apologize for and justify state violence. Even if we are opposed to it. It's necessary, for order and justice. So that evil and sin can be restrained and punished.

Lutherans can be the worst when it comes to theologically justifying "the sword," as Martin Luther constantly referred to it. We do so as if it never cut a wider swath than promised, never shed more blood than expected, as if somehow the only thing keeping us from utter chaos and absolute mayhem is the constant threat of pain, suffering, and death included in the law. As if there should never, ever be consequences for state violence.

As Christians, we have invented great doctrines out of tiny Bible passages to justify our positions on violence, whether we support the state or oppose the war. People should render unto Caesar and be subject to governing authorities, who rule not for their own benefit but for ours, at the behest of God. We have even been told that God too "is a man of war" (Exod 15:3). Conversely, we proclaim a world in which everyone should turn the other cheek, in which swords are beaten into plowshares and war is studied no more.

What if in seeking moral guidance for how we should act, we have made an absolute of something that simply is not? What if the Bible has no opinion on the morality of violence and war? Or who does it?

This is one reason I really like David. As a soldier in Saul's army, he does a lot of what we might call "officially sanctioned state violence," beginning with the rock he embeds in Goliath's head (which he then cuts off with a sword). His dowry for Saul's daughter Michal was two hundred Philistine foreskins, and he didn't get them by asking pretty please. "Saul struck down his thousands," women sing, but "David his ten thousands." In doing all this, David gains the love and adoration of Israel.

However, not all that much later, David is a fugitive, the leader of a band of angry, alienated, and disaffected young men. (And quite possibly a woman or two.) He flees from Saul, finds refuge among the Philistines, and becomes what we might call a *terrorist*. "David would strike the land and would leave neither man nor woman alive, but would take away the sheep, the oxen, the donkeys, the camels, and the garments," the Bible tells us. The Philistine king whom David serves, Achish, is pleased with this: "He has made himself such an utter stench to his people Israel; therefore he shall always be my servant," Achish says.

You would think scripture—or at least Israel—would condemn David's genocidal raids. But neither is true. Because war and violence are facts of the human condition, whether waged by kings, bandit captains, nation-states, or terrorists. These things are realities that go unquestioned. That scripture simply records something is not a sign of approval.

Scripture does two things, however. First, in the story of Israel, it clearly marks the difference between war waged by God on behalf of God's people—to save them—and war merely waged by God's people. God frequently saves God's people through acts of horrific violence—the drowning of the Egyptian army at the Red Sea, for example, or the selection of Gideon's army of three hundred to defeat the Midianites. "The LORD will fight for you, and you have only to be silent," God says, reminding Israel who really saves them. That God's people are fighting doesn't make a conflict sacred. Jeremiah's constant unpatriotic warnings to Judah that defeat is immanent and everyone would do well to surrender or flee are proof of that.

Second, though, is what Jesus does. He doesn't so much condemn violence as he does rob it of its power and its finality. And Christ does this by surrendering willingly and completely to *our* violence. We do violence because whatever else we seek, we want the last word. And killing our enemies, or our oppressors, seems pretty final to us. We killed Jesus—yes, *we* did—in the hope that we would shut him up and make him go away, that we would stop having to hear how difficult love and forgiveness and living as God's people really are. But Jesus would not stay dead. He rose to show us that love and forgiveness, and not death and terror, have the final word. That we should not trust in the death we can deal. Or fear it, either.

10

Refugees

THERE WEREN'T THAT MANY *jihadis*—aspiring or otherwise—at the *masjid* in Columbus, Ohio, in the mid-1990s. While the appeal of *jihad* was fairly broad, it was also fairly shallow, and in the end, few wanted to risk life or limb.

Most of the Muslims there were students and so were busy with their studies, more concerned about passing qualifying exams, raising their families, and, for those from abroad, going back to their home countries. They might be angry over Palestine, Iraq, Kashmir, Chechnya, and Bosnia—and willing to pray prayers and give a little money to help—but they weren't willing to commit their lives "in the path of Allah." They took another kind of piety as important: the piety of marriage as half of faith, of obligations to children and kin, of finding a moral purpose and the presence of God in day-to-day life.

And there were some at the little *masjid* in Columbus who were tired of war. Because they'd been fighting nearly their entire lives.

There was a group of Iraqi Kurds who had been settled in Columbus in 1991 and 1992. Nearly all were Iraqi soldiers who had been captured or had surrendered to Coalition forces at some point during the Kuwait War in 1991, had claimed refugee status and been offered the opportunity by the United Nations to resettle anywhere in the world that would take them. Anywhere except Israel and Saudi Arabia.

One such refugee was Ibrahim, whom I got to know fairly well. I helped him with English and he helped me with Arabic. Ibrahim was in his mid-thirties, a Kurd from the Iraqi town of Khanaqin, and was fairly typical of most of the Kurdish refugees. His Iraqi passport said he was a "farmer." But Ibrahim had the misfortune of turning sixteen the year Saddam Hussein

ordered his army to invade Iran, and he'd been drafted. He spent the entirety
of the war with Iran in the Iraqi Army, had been fortunate enough not to be
wounded, and was demobilized in the months following the 1988 ceasefire.

But his time as a civilian was short-lived. All of the Iraqis told me that
about eight weeks before the invasion of Kuwait, they were called up.

"We knew war was coming," Ibrahim told me. "We knew it would not
go well."

Ibrahim was assigned to an Iraqi division dug in deep in southern Kuwait, and he spent almost the entire six weeks of Operation Desert Storm
cowering in a bunker, hiding from the U.S. Air Force. He surrendered the
first chance he got, along with a hundred other Iraqi conscripts, to a pair of
American soldiers on patrol.

He still lived with those six weeks. Once, Ibrahim and I were walking
across the Ohio State campus, and an airliner came in lower than normal
on its approach to Port Columbus. Ibrahim panicked at the sound of the
jet, dropped to the ground, got as flat as possible, and then, realizing where
he was, started slowly to get up. I took his hand and helped him to his feet.
He was embarrassed.

"Sorry," he said in English. "Kuwait."

"*Ya sheikh, afhamu*," I said in Arabic, adding in English, "Do not
apologize."

Ibrahim taught me how to make yogurt, and he made amazing coffee
by brewing Folgers—Folgers!—in a pot of milk on the stove. He spoke Arabic, Kurdish, Farsi, and Dari, and his English slowly got better too, though
we talked mostly in Arabic. Most of the Kurds I've known could speak at
least four languages.

There was Ahmed, who was about Ibrahim's age and, like him, had
spent his entire adult life in the Iraqi Army, at war. Unlike Ibrahim, he'd
been shot five times during the war with Iran and had the most amazing
collection of scars on his body to prove it—entrance and exit scars. That he
survived one was amazing. But five? I couldn't help thinking of Ahmed as
blessed, which sounds strange. It hardly sounds like a blessing to be shot five
times, especially during a long and miserable war.

"This is where I was shot the first time," he said one Friday after prayer
in the *masjid*, pulling up his shirt to show me a twisted mess of scars on his
stomach. "This is where it went in"—and turning around, he showed me the
mess of scars on his lower back. "This is where it came out."

Ahmed was an amazingly cheerful man. He'd spent some portion of
the war with Iran working with Soviet engineers advising the Iraqi Army
and had picked up passable Russian. Better than mine.

"*Zdravstvuyte, tovarich! Kak dyelat?*" Ahmed would eventually say to me whenever he saw me at prayers.

And there was Khaled, the only non-Kurd in the group of Iraqis. His life had been as different from theirs as mine had. His father, an Iraqi national, had been a senior engineer of some kind for Kuwait's state oil company. So Khaled had been born, raised, and educated in Kuwait. He'd gone to university, and his English was impeccable. His father had gone missing, and was likely killed, during the initial Iraqi invasion, probably defending an offshore oil platform from attacking Iraqi soldiers. It's what he'd heard. But Khaled wasn't entirely sure.

Khaled had gone into hiding for part of the occupation, and even helped the Kuwaiti resistance for a time. But because he was Iraqi, he was expelled from Kuwait following the war. And he had opted to become a refugee rather than "return" to a country he'd never lived in.

He arranged for just about all the refugees to meet with me one afternoon. "We want to tell you our stories," Khaled said. And he was our translator, since I was only just beginning my Arabic studies. I recognized most of the Iraqis because they prayed regularly.

But not everyone. There was a man who looked much older than his years. He walked with a hunch, had a haunted look on his face, and rarely talked. And he almost never came to prayers.

"He survived the gas attack on Halabja," Khaled told me.

Students and refugees. Columbus was only a way station for most of us, a temporary community. As Ibrahim's English improved, he began to disappear for long stretches as he followed work and training. Eventually, he moved away, taking a job doing some kind of skilled labor in a factory near Cleveland. Same with Ahmed, who followed whatever skills he could leverage or learn to make a new life for himself. Even Khaled left at some point. They were not a permanent community and could not be a permanent part of my life.

Still, I admired these men almost more than I can say. Their lives were truly hard. Much, much harder than mine. They found themselves at the mercy of events and powers far beyond their control and were grateful for simply being alive. It was humbling. They picked themselves up every day, said their prayers, and thanked God. If any of them were angry at God, or the world, to the point of murderous rage, they didn't show it. Or talk about it.

But then, honestly, I didn't either.

The truth is, most of the people who worshiped at the Umar ibn al-Khattab Masjid in Columbus were transient. There was a lot of coming and going.

But some communities were more or less permanent. There were enough Saudis working on doctorates or studying at the American Language Institute at Ohio State that the Saudi government started a school for their children. It was among the Saudis that I came to make some of my closest friendships.

And it was the Saudis who effectively decided, "If Blue Eyes is going to become one of us, then we're going to need to teach him what he needs to know."

It began with meeting Abdullah al-Hamdan. He was working on a doctorate in agricultural engineering. Actually, he'd finished his doctoral work some years before and had written and defended his thesis. But an odd contractual arrangement prevented him from actually graduating.

Abdullah specialized in food processing and packaging technology. He had signed up with a program partly sponsored by the U.S. Department of Agriculture and a major American food processor. The goal was to create a new form of packaging for cooked food: plastic containers that would completely replace cans. (Plastic fruit cups came out of this.) This seemed easily doable when they started, Abdullah said, and so the contract with the university specified that no one could graduate until the company actually had patentable technology in hand.

So, Abdullah spent his days trying to get beans that would snap properly, just like they'd been steamed, and potatoes that would mash just right, as if they'd just been lightly boiled, when sealed in these new plastic containers. Again, everyone thought this could be done in five or six years.

But it turned out, Abdullah told me, that it couldn't. In fact, it was becoming clear after eight years that what the company wanted simply could not be done. Abdullah had done all his work, finished his degree, and yet could not leave. The Saudi government was upset—they were saving a teaching spot for him at King Saud University, and it had gone empty three years longer than expected. Officials in Riyadh were tired of paying his bills and threatened more than once to cut him off. Because this was a multinational program, with doctoral students from several countries, other governments were angry too.

When I met Abdullah, the State Department, USDA, Ohio State, and the food processing company had just started complex negotiations with representatives from China, Saudi Arabia, Turkey, and several other nations to get those nations' students out of this limbo and home with their doctorates in hand. The company still held out hope that they could get a workable technology. So, the talks were tortuous and slow. Abdullah was exasperated.

"How was it in the lab today?" I'd ask him. And he'd always respond with a joke about smashing potatoes.

Abdullah al-Hamdan was very curious about America, and we would sometimes sit in his car in the evenings after prayer, talking. He would pepper me with questions. How does the American government work? Why do Americans eat so much pork? I may have been an outsider, but I was still an American culturally, and it was, for better or worse, my home. I enjoyed those conversations a lot.

It was Abdullah who gave me my *kunya*, my honorific "father of" name. I wasn't anyone's father, of course, but childless men were often given humorous "father of" names, at least until they really became someone's father. So, one evening, Abdullah decided that I needed a *kunya* of my own.

It took him several days, but Abdullah finally came up to me one Friday evening.

"I have it. You shall be Abu Sakhr," he said.

"Abu Sakhr?" I asked. "What does it mean?"

"Well," he said, grinning, "It means 'Father of the Stone.' It's a joke on your last name."

But it wasn't only that, he explained. It was also an honorific title given to many of the young Palestinian men who had thrown stones at the Israelis during the First Intifada.

Abdullah thought himself awfully clever, and smiled for several days afterwards. But it stuck, and I was "Abu Sakhr."

My friendship with Abdullah was my entry to the Saudi community in Columbus. And it was the Saudis who taught me what being Muslim meant in everyday life. It was their Islam, and their Arabic, and their ways that I learned, and that I became comfortable with.

One afternoon, after Friday prayer, I was sitting on the floor of the *masjid*. Ibrahim al-Khuweiter, who was also working on a PhD at Ohio State, wanted to keep my attention while he was talking with someone else.

He took my hand, then laced his fingers in between mine. It was an incredibly strange sensation, having this man hold my hand. I'd seen it before, something the Saudis, the Kuwaitis, and the Iraqis did frequently with each other, a way of keeping someone's attention, of letting someone know, "I want to talk to you. I may be busy right now, but you are important to me, so don't go anywhere. You are next." But I'd never seen them do it with an outsider, someone who wasn't of their nationality. For Ibrahim to do this was a big a deal—it meant he considered me one of them.

One day, not long after I arrived in Columbus, a large man showed up at the *masjid*. He was tall, had a scraggly beard and very short hair. He spoke with a deep, loud voice and had an ease with preaching. In Arabic, of course.

Abdullah introduced him to me as his cousin, Dr. Hamdan al-Hamdan. He was a somewhat well-known scholar of Islamic law, currently teaching at King Saud University in Riyadh. Dr. Hamdan bounced between King Saud University and Imam Muhammad University, usually staying until he said something that offended the government—for example, he'd signed a post-Kuwait War petition demanding more government accountability—and was dismissed from his job. His notoriety, and family connections, kept him free, safe, and employable.

This made Dr. Hamdan al-Hamdan a member of Saudi Arabia's *ulema*, the religious scholars who preside over that country's official faith.

Dr. Hamdan was at Ohio State for a year to study English at the American Language Institute, and there were times I feared the whole point of his American sojourn was to measure out enough rope to hang him at home in Saudi Arabia.

And that Dr. Hamdan was a little too obliging in the matter.

I'm not sure how it came about, but he and I agreed to help each other. He would help me with Arabic and I would help him with English. We did a lot more talking in Arabic than we did in English, mostly in his rented townhome. His daughters—and he had a gaggle of children—were fascinated by me, and the youngest three would climb quietly down the stairs and watch me, scrambling away when they saw me looking back.

He was also truly curious about life in America, particularly how non-Muslims lived. How had I lived before I became Muslim? What was the appeal of alcohol? How did it make you feel to get drunk? Did I ever use marijuana or any other drugs? What did it feel like? Why did it feel good to lose control? He asked these questions not as a moralist, not in a stern and judgmental way, but because he was really curious. I can't imagine him ever engaging in vice, but he wanted to know the appeal, wanted to understand.

One evening, a group of Saudis sat in the *masjid* and had a very interesting discussion about marriage. On one side was Dr. Hamdan, who argued that the right of men to have four wives was not absolute, that a man could, as part of a marriage contract, waive the right to have other wives as long as he is married. Dr. Hamdan said he'd done just that in his current marriage.

On the other side was Dr. Abd al-Mohsin, another member of the Saudi *ulema* studying English at Ohio State. Dr. Abd al-Mohsin said that because the right was stated in the Qur'an, it was inalienable, and no man could sign it away in a marriage contract. (As I recall, Dr. Abd al-Mohsin had only one wife.)

It got to be quite a heated discussion, and it went on for a couple of hours before we all broke to pray and then have coffee and sweets. It was entirely in Arabic, and my ability to understand was limited. But with some help, I was able to understand a fair amount.

But the most stunning encounter I had with the Arabic language happened during an early night one Ramadan. It happened one evening during the *taraweeh* prayers, the special prayers during which Muslims recite the whole of the Qur'an during the fasting month. The Qur'an is divided in a couple of different ways—into thirty relatively equal parts (*juz*) that allow the Qur'an to be read or recited over the course of a month, and also into seven equal parts (*manzil*) that allow the entire scripture to be recited or read over a week.

It was the second or third day of Ramadan, as I recall, and I hadn't been there for the previous nights. Abdullah al-Hamdan had been particularly eager to have me come and pray, so I found some time in my studies to go to the *masjid*.

We broke the fast with dates and buttermilk, shared a small meal (something with rice, it was always something with rice), and then people gathered for the prayer. It's just like a normal prayer, except that it goes for a couple of hours—as long as the *imam* needs to recite whatever *juz* of the Qur'an he is reciting.

It's physically taxing, standing for long prayers, trying to focus on the tones and rhythms of a language you don't understand very well. My mind always found it easy to wander.

But that evening something else entirely happened. I stood there, in my row, the sides of my feet pressed hard against those next to me, hands folded over my chest, eyes closed, hearing the *imam*, and it seemed that the Arabic just flowed into me, whole. It was as if I'd been opened up, and the breath of God was being breathed through me. The words suddenly found their way not to my mind but to my heart, where they rested, completely comprehended. It was overwhelming, like just about every other encounter with the divine I have had in my life. As I was being filled with Arabic, with the word of God, with the divine breath, it seemed that every bit of what was being recited made deep, intuitive sense to me.

It became hard to breathe, even to stand. I focused, let it all just flow in and through me, and was able to finish that portion of the prayer. But once it was done, I got out of line and sat down against one of the *masjid* walls while the prayer continued.

I needed to catch my breath. Abdullah sat down next to me.

"Abu Sakhr, why aren't you praying?" he asked.

"It was . . . too much. I had to stop. I understood . . . everything. In here," tapping on my chest. "I understood everything, and it was too much. I had to stop."

He smiled. He had been praying earlier and was taking a break too.

"*Ma sha'allah*," he said. "A gift from *Allah subhana wata'ala*. You have been blessed."

Jennifer has never enjoyed any of the jobs she's ever had. She is dyslexic, and because of that has a great deal of difficulty manipulating objects, such as tools and machines. (She's a tremendous reader, having taught herself a kind of speed reading that involves ingesting whole blocks of text at a time.) We suspect she's also borderline Asperger's, and she's always had a great deal of difficulty seeing and dealing with social cues. And this has caused its fair share of problems.

So, childcare work has been the only kind of work she's been able to reliably get. It's not work she enjoys very much, though she has been able to find joy in it—especially in dealing with the kids she's cared for. We took to calling some of the more corporate childcare outfits she worked for "Kinder Kennels."

And I've never much liked the stresses work puts her through. I've always told Jennifer, "If you don't want to work, and you don't have to, then don't. Let me do that."

Again, it would be one thing if she found something to do that was intellectually challenging and emotionally rewarding. But nothing she has done has ever been either. So, Jennifer hasn't always worked. At times, she can be quite resentful about it—about not finding a vocation that respects her intelligence and her capabilities, about being relegated to doing miserable work that no one really appreciates, in places where no one is treated with any dignity.

For a time, Jennifer herself considered a call to ministry. So we made a trip to Trinity Lutheran Seminary in Columbus, but could find no one who was willing or able to talk to us. So, after getting an interesting introductory offer of $400 for a full semester's worth of classes, she enrolled at the Pontifical College Josephinum, a Catholic seminary on the north side of Columbus. She worked part time in the seminary library, was distressed at the ethics of the seminarians (especially how poorly many of them treated the staff), and enjoyed her studies, though not enough to want to continue.

Mostly, Jennifer came to classes with me. We love being together and would rather not be separated, not ever, if we can help it. Sometimes she would hang out in the Ohio State library and read, especially when I took Arabic—she found my language classes boring.

At first, we weren't sure what instructors would think. After all, she was in class without paying for it. No one ever objected, and a few asked her if she wanted to do the work and write the papers. (Her answer was always no.) Mostly, she'd just sit there, listening.

Jennifer pays attention to everything.

One of my classes at Ohio State was "The Qur'an in Translation" with Dr. Michael Zwettler, a specialist in medieval Arabic whose great project was an update of A. J. Arberry's translation of the Qur'an. Zwettler was a stocky man with a big smile, a shaved head, and a giant handlebar mustache. His voice wasn't soft—he could be quite loud when he wanted to—but it had a soft and very melodic feel to it.

His command of Arabic was impressive, and he truly appreciated the beauty of the language. He was not Muslim, and some of his academic understandings of the Classical Arabic of the Qur'an—a language called *fushah*, or "the most eloquent"—clashed significantly with what some of the Muslim scholars I knew believed.

We had class in a long, narrow room. There were only about a half-dozen students taking the course, many of whom were Muslim but didn't have Arabic as a first language. We sat facing the chalkboard on one of the long sides, sitting in one long row. Jennifer and I would often sit to the side, near the window.

Late one morning, after class, we walked with Dr. Zwettler a bit, chatting.

"Where are you from?" I asked him.

"Oh, you've probably never heard of the place. I'm from a town in Southern California called Upland," he replied.

"Heard of it? I'm from there too!" I said.

"I'm sorry," he replied.

We commiserated about Southern California. He had graduated from Upland High School's first graduating class—1960, I think. And he left just as soon as he possibly could. And never went back.

"But when I was in high school, I spent as much time as I could in Claremont. That made high school livable."

True enough. Claremont had the colleges, and if you didn't fit in Upland—a city with a very narrow understanding of what it meant to fit—it was as close to a refuge as you could find.

"That much had not changed by the time I was at Upland High School," I said.

How funny. Here I was, studying under one of America's leading specialists in Classical Arabic, and we had attended the same miserable high school.

A couple of weeks later, we were in the midst of a fairly intense class discussion. I raised my hand, but because I was sitting off to the side, Dr. Zwettler didn't see me. He called on several other people while I sat, politely and patiently, with my hand raised.

I've never had any trouble making comments or expressing opinions in class. I'm not shy. If anything, I have learned to temper my participation at times, to give others an opportunity to speak. Because I can talk too much.

So, I was okay with waiting. I was okay even if Dr. Zwettler never saw me, and we went on.

But Jennifer wasn't. And she grew increasingly fidgety and agitated, and I noticed out of the corner of my eye that she was sitting on the edge of her seat. Which was odd, because she rarely paid this kind of attention to class discussions, and almost never participated.

I'm not sure what came next. I think Dr. Zwettler called on another student, possibly the third, without noticing my hand was up.

"Charles has a question!" Jennifer shouted.

The whole room went silent. Dr. Zwettler turned, a stunned look on his face. As if his mustache was going to fall off. Jennifer turned beet red, and slunk down into her chair. Everyone was looking at her, and she didn't want to be seen.

I put my hand down.

"Um, you have a question?" Dr. Zwettler asked me.

"I did. But I don't remember what it was now," I said.

Jennifer had seen an injustice. I was being slighted, in her eyes, and that was wrong. Something had to be done. The professor needed to know I had a question, that I needed to be heard! She would never stand up for herself that way, but she would do that for me. She can be fiercely protective of me. And I can prompt her to act boldly in ways she never would otherwise.

Like kissing me. Or standing up for me in class.

Jennifer is, at heart, a little church mouse, someone who's uncomfortable sticking out in a crowd. She has a lovely voice but only sings in choirs, because while she's happy to add to the music of the whole, she doesn't want to be heard by herself.

She knows the words to nearly all my songs. And sometimes, if I pay close attention, I can hear her singing along with me. But if I look at her while she's singing, she'll blush, sometimes even get a little angry, and stop.

In the late spring of 1993, one of the *masjid* elders approached me one Friday afternoon after prayers. There was a group from the Islamic Society of North America (ISNA) going to the United Nations Human Rights conference that summer in Vienna, Austria. ISNA was considering becoming an officially recognized nongovernmental organization, so they were going to see how the UN process worked. Was I interested in going to document the trip, and maybe write something afterwards?

"I don't have that kind of money," I said.

No problem, he replied. Your trip and accommodations will be taken care of.

"Then yes, I'm interested!"

It was an exciting prospect. Me, at a UN conference! Unfortunately, it meant leaving Jennifer behind for a week, and I didn't want to do that. I'd miss her, and she'd be lonely.

But she told me to go. It was an incredible opportunity, and one I might never get again. "I won't like it, but I'll manage," Jennifer said.

We'd traveled to Columbus with nearly all our worldly possessions strapped to our motorcycle. We didn't have much more at this point; we didn't have a lot of money, and my wardrobe was pretty rudimentary—sweatpants, army pants, and T-shirts. I didn't really have clothes for a UN conference.

On the other hand, we weren't going to be in the "official" part of the conference, where governmental delegations met. We were going to be with the nongovernmental organizations, so I supposed a little bit of shabbiness was acceptable. I was, after all, going to be hanging out with activists, and I'd seen over the years how a lot of them dressed.

My traveling companion was an Egyptian immigrant to the United States dealing with the anger and shame of what was an all too typical American problem: a pregnant, unmarried daughter. And realizing that none of the solutions to this problem offered by his culture could or would be allowed to work in America.

The trip was a little complicated: Columbus to New York, New York to Frankfurt, Frankfurt to Vienna. Long layovers in both New York and Frankfurt, but not long enough to actually go anywhere and do something interesting.

I got a fair amount of attention from the authorities in Germany. I was wearing army boots, my black army pants, a T-shirt, and an Ohio State jacket. They pulled me aside, went through my things, asked me where I was going, inspected my passport. They seemed a little surprised to find a copy of the Qur'an in my bags and went through my clothes, my camera, my notepads and my film-loading equipment, asking questions as they went.

They did this each time I passed out of the international lounge, and were quite bored with me by the fourth time, no longer bothering to ask "Was ist das?" as they made a cursory inspection of my bag.

But clearly, they were doing their duty, pulling me out of line every time and looking through my things. They didn't do it to many others that day.

Some weeks later, while listening to a Deutsche Welle shortwave program, I learned why. There was some kind of international neo-Nazi shindig in northern Germany that same week, and I fit the profile of a participant in just about every conceivable way. I found the irony of this incredibly funny.

Vienna was a bright city, a colorful city, and part of it almost looked like it had been built out of Legos. We met the rest of the ISNA delegation at our hotel and settled in.

The conference itself was both interesting and uneventful. But the aesthetics of the place was fascinating. The nongovernmental organization section was full of groups, each one trying to prove that they were the most oppressed people in the world. Sikhs, Kurds, Palestinians, Bosnian Muslims, South Korean dissidents, Tibetans, groups from everywhere and anywhere. They showed off huge photo displays of dead bodies, people who had been tortured, brutalized, beaten, boiled. The most graphic came from a South Korean group, which showed what kind of bloody mess a human head can be turned into when beaten repeatedly by rifle butts.

Each group tried to outdo the others. It was something of an atrocity carnival.

In the midst of this, a group of Bosnians had an interesting display—Sarajevo after two years of siege. Photo after photo of a modern city, buildings full of holes, once-bustling urban streets full of weeds, derailed trolley cars rusting in the middle of the street. There wasn't a dead body, or even a living human being, in any of the photos. And that made it the most moving. Here was this modern city, which looked for all the world like the San Francisco I lived in and loved, *during war*. An empty, hollow, broken city.

There was a cafe where participants could order expensive sandwiches and espresso. There was also lots of brutal and ugly art. The little cafe was it-self framed by a collection of severe paintings showing anonymous, faceless gray soldiers killing, burning, looting, and raping anonymous grey civilians, spilling blood on the brown earth while the sky glowed dark red.

I was free to go where I wanted. So I took in as many talks as I could. One day focused on the use of rape as a weapon in war, and I listened to lectures from an Algerian woman (who spoke in French) about how the Islamist militants in Algeria used rape; a Puerto Rican woman (who spoke in Spanish) talked about rape and sexual violence as a part of the U.S. military presence in Puerto Rico; and a group of Palestinian and Israeli human rights activists—all women—talked (in English) about the Israeli Defense Forces' systematic use of rape in the West Bank as a way of humiliating Palestinians and setting them against each other. (In most traditional cultures, the woman who is raped is almost always blamed, even when that rape is done as part of war or military occupation.)

Space was tight at the conference, and the Islamic Society of North America found itself sharing a room with a Dutch gay rights organization. I sat and had coffee one afternoon with a young lawyer and member of the organization who said he was busy lobbying governments across the world to consider ending, or at least limiting, the use of "he came on to me, so I had to kill him" as a defense in murder trials.

"It's depressing how often it's used," he said. "And how often it's successful. But we're trying to change that."

It was slow work, he added. But they were seeing some successes, so he was hopeful.

One afternoon, a couple of members of our delegation showed up wearing photo ID badges from the United Nations High Commission for Refugees. "Get your things, we're going somewhere," one man said to me.

"Where?"

"You'll see," he said.

I piled into a van with most of the senior members of our group, and we drove to what looked like an abandoned factory. After a conversation with a uniformed guard, and the swapping of some paperwork, a gate was unlocked and we were let in.

The factory was home to several hundred Bosnian refugees. They lived in tidy little cubicles, whole families in spaces the size of small rooms, with little to do. They were not allowed out, not allowed to work, not allowed even to have visitors. No one wanted them getting too comfortable in Austria, for fear they wouldn't go back home when the war was over.

We were the only visitors they'd had during their entire stay.

Most of the Bosnians weren't interested in us. But one family was very excited. They invited us into their cubicle, showed us their meagre belongings. The father was especially proud that his son was playing *futbol* in Austria for a professional team.

Apparently, some refugees could work and settle in Austria—if their work was deemed valuable enough.

"The Americans have come! The Marines are here!" the father said in broken English as he hugged me. "Now we go home!"

The wife escorted us to their communal kitchen, and we met the camp director, a sharp-faced, blonde-haired man from Dayton, Ohio. They made tea, gathered cookies, and demanded we sit with them.

Outside, a group of men with haunted looks huddled around a picnic table, sucking on cigarettes and staring hard at nothing. I'd seen that look before, on the young Iraqi Kurd who had survived Halabja.

"They were in Serbian prison camps," the director told me. "I wish we could do more for them, but the Austrians won't allow us to. And there's not really much to do."

I looked around at these people, at the boxes and cubicles they lived in. Their place was clean, but they had so little. And here I was, being asked to drink their tea and eat their sweets, to take from those who had almost nothing.

So I said, "No, thank you" when they offered.

The director pulled me aside.

"I know what you're doing. Now stop it. These people may have very little, but they also don't get any opportunities to have guests and be hosts. To share with others. You are their guest. So take what they have and say thank you. It's the closest thing they can have to normal human life right now," he said.

So I drank their tea, ate their cookies, and listened to the conversation. It was the most important lesson in hospitality I've ever received.

For the first few days of the weeklong UN conference, I stayed with the ISNA delegation in a small hotel. But I hadn't come all this way to Vienna, Austria, to shuttle between a hotel and the UN center, with the occasional restaurant thrown in. Having a beer was out of the question, but I wanted to see the city.

So, I went and stayed at a *masjid* somewhere close to the city center. It wasn't just a house of worship. A number of single men lived there too, and the place was constantly busy. I didn't know any German, certainly not enough to converse in, and no one there knew any English, so the only language we had in common was Arabic. I had to function for three days in Arabic, and it was the most fun I'd ever had in a foreign language in my life.

Most of the young men living in the *masjid* were from Syria or Egypt, and they made money doing odd jobs—selling newspapers and magazines (mostly pornography) at the entrances to train stations, driving delivery vans. One man, a Syrian whose name I don't remember, had just been laid off from his engineering job with Otis Elevator and was desperate to be rehired. He felt an intense loyalty to this company that had just let him go, and he hoped I would put in a good word for him when I got back to the United States.

A couple of times at the conference, I ran into a member of the German parliament who was agitating for a much more forceful NATO intervention in Bosnia. He was both charming and a little creepy, and was surrounded by a retinue of Bosnian women of all shapes, sizes, and ages. We talked a bit about the war in Bosnia, about the possibility that Croatia and Serbia were conspiring to carve up the country and leave the Bosnian Muslims with nothing but a few tiny enclaves.

I wandered around Vienna every chance I got. One night, I was out walking and, passing by a tiny restaurant, noticed the German parliamentarian and his collection of Bosnian women. He saw me and motioned me to come inside and join them.

"Please, sit down," he said. "Have you eaten yet?"

"No, not yet."

"Well, feel free to order something. Please."

"I don't have much money," I told him.

"Do not worry about that. You are my guest tonight. Please, anything you would like."

I took him up on his hospitality. Still, I didn't order anything terribly expensive, and listened to the conversation.

"What courage you Americans have," he said. "You come to our tiny Austria to see the country. Do you know how many Austrians have gone to see America? Not very many. So, what do you think of our little Austria?"

It was an odd phrasing, especially given that he was German. Had an *Anschluss* taken place that no one was aware of? Still, I told him I enjoyed what little I'd seen. Vienna is a very pretty city.

"Yes, it is," he said. "Our little Austria is a very beautiful place."

About halfway through dinner, I suddenly realized that the very pretty blonde Bosnian girl sitting across the table was staring at me. And I was staring back at her. It was an amazingly uncomfortable moment. She was an incredibly lovely young woman and she wore what looked to be a tight white Danskin top. I was uneasy.

Dinner went on for several hours, and the girl would frequently smile at me. I made an embarrassed smile back. After dinner wound down, around 10 or 11 o'clock, the German parliamentarian bid me "auf Wiedersehen" and thanked me for the meal and the conversation.

"Come back to our little Austria, American. Please come back," he said.

I was outside in the cool, nighttime air when the girl and her friend, a taller, dark-haired girl who was cute but nowhere near as stunningly beautiful as her friend. The blonde girl smiled and offered me her hand.

"Hello," she said with a sweet voice in heavily accented English. "I am Olga, and I am from Tuzla."

I don't remember whether I told her my name was Charles or Umar.

We chatted a bit. Her friend giggled and occasionally whispered in her ear. It wasn't a long conversation, and it was both awkward and frightening.

"So," she said, smiling again. "Are you busy tonight?"

And right then and there I knew: I had to run. Or I would not be going back to the *masjid* that evening.

When I look into Jennifer's eyes, I see adoration. An adoration beyond words. She trusts me with more than her life, she trusts me with her soul. And I have always known that I have to be worthy of that trust. She has to be able to trust me. I've rarely been tempted, and then never seriously. But Olga was tempting. God, was she tempting.

But as achingly beautiful as she was, I couldn't be sure—was she interested in me, or was she interested in me as an American who might give her the possibility of escaping whatever situation she was in? I remembered a trip to a shopping mall in Panama once, and noticing that all the young Panamanian girls looked at me hungrily, all big brown eyes and curly hair. "You can get me out of here," that look seemed to say.

I knew Jennifer loved me for me. And had from the day we met. What Olga wanted, I don't know. As much as I wanted to, I wasn't going to chance it. If an escape was what she wanted, I couldn't give her that. Not without betraying the most important person in my life.

"I'm sorry," I said. "I have some things I need to do. I apologize for that. Really. I'm very sorry. But thank you."

She smiled weakly and seemed very disappointed as I turned and walked away. I did not look back.

The next afternoon, I sat in the *masjid* after prayers and watched a Bosnian man teach a small group of Bosnian children. A couple of girls, headscarves pinned tightly underneath their chins, and a couple of boys, skullcaps on their heads. It was a counting lesson, and I remembered just enough Czech and Russian to be able to make sense of some of it.

"*Koliko imam?*" he asked. (How many do I have?) His voice was soft, kind, melodic.

"*Jeden, dva, tri, četeri,*" the children counted in unison. And then their teacher said something funny, and those four serious little children collapsed in a fit of squealing and giggling.

Refugees. All of us, refugees.

One of the toughest things about being a wanderer is knowing just how dependent you are on the goodwill of others. On their kindness, their patience, their understanding, their hospitality.

When Christians, especially Western Christians, think of hospitality, it's always as something we extend to others. We've taken to heart Paul's quoting Jesus in Acts 20, "It is more blessed to give than to receive." So, we are always the hosts. We possess. Whatever is needed. In abundance.

If there's a story of hospitality, it's that of Abraham in Genesis 18, when he meets the three mysterious strangers near the oaks of Mamre and fetches them water to wash their feet and quench their thirst, and then he and Sarah scramble to prepare a feast. It's a good story, and one that has Abraham and Sarah meeting the strangers as relative equals. It's our idea of Christian hospitality at its energetic best.

But we still see ourselves as the hosts in this story. Because we don't know how not to.

Compare this with Abraham's brief encounter in Genesis 14 with Melchizedek (*melek tsedeq*, or "righteous king"), king of Salem and priest of God Most High. Abraham has just been decisive in winning the war against the king of Elam and his allies. Melchizedek comes and greets Abraham with bread and wine and blesses him. It's a short story, nowhere near as detailed. But Abraham is the recipient—of a meal and of a blessing. Yes, he shares the spoils of war—and possibly more—with Melchizedek. But I don't think he's buying bread, wine and a blessing with the tenth he gives.

I'm not doubting Paul when he quotes Jesus. But it is important to remember—there can be no giving without receiving, no host without a guest. And if we, as God's people, take scripture seriously, then from creation onward, everything God gives us, all God does for us, is gift. Unearned and unmerited gift. We are the recipients of a largesse we simply cannot justify.

Maybe it will help if Christians see the Lord's Supper as the ultimate act of hospitality, an act wherein we are never the host, always the guest. For many liturgical Christians, communion is our central act of worship. It is not our table, it is the Lord's table. We are invited to this table as guests, and we come only with faithful hearts and open hands, ready to receive bread and drink wine we can never, ever earn.

So we have no business lording it over people who receive, who are guests, who wander. We, too, are beggars. We come to God with nothing.

The one thing I didn't like about The Ohio State University was the quarter system. Things went too fast, and by the time a class got interesting, it was almost over.

It also meant there was a lot less time to deal with problems when they came up.

That was my last quarter at Ohio State. I had filled out my graduation application and handed it in, and a couple of days later, I got a phone call from the registrar. Apparently, I was missing two requirements.

It seemed that San Francisco State University was far more liberal in what it did with Advanced Placement exam credits, and had taken my 4 in AP American History and 3 in English and credited me for all of the basic undergrad history and English requirements.

Ohio State, however, needed a 5 and 4, respectively, to give the same credit. The undergrad American history requirement was two quarters, and the 4 only got me out of one.

"How do we solve this?" I asked.

Well, there was an exam for the history class, I was told. I could take that. But the English department at Ohio State had pretty rigorous standards, and there was no exam to get out of basic freshman composition. I might be stuck taking a basic English writing course.

I always admired the administrative efficiency of Ohio State. It was much better run than SF State, and something that would require a day or two—or possibly three—to solve at SF State, or might never get done, took an hour or two at Ohio State. And actually got done.

So, I was not going to let a basic English writing requirement stand in my way of graduating in the same month the VA money ran out. I didn't care what the rules said.

I took the history exam cold and passed it easily. Someone in the admin office suggested that I appeal directly to the English department. Maybe something could be done. So, I explained my situation.

"We can't waive the English composition requirement," I was told. "It's just not possible."

"Are you sure there isn't something you can do?" I asked.

"Let me talk to the dean. But I can't make any promises." I prepared myself for the likelihood that we'd have to stay an extra quarter. A few days later, I got a message. I could submit some writing samples, and the dean would look them over.

Finally! I could let my work speak for itself. I handed a small stack of papers over to the English department and was told to come back in three days.

Those were three nervous days. "We have something for you," the assistant told me the day I came back. She handed me my stack of papers, a yellow post-it note stuck on the front; it read, "Don't waste anymore of this man's time. Give him credit for the composition class and let him graduate."

But what to do with myself when I graduated? I had no idea. I wanted to use the Arabic I'd spent two years learning, but journalism demanded I start by covering some tiny planning and zoning committee somewhere. I wanted more than that but had no idea how to go about it.

A friend from the United Arab Emirates had a suggestion. "There are some English-language newspapers in my country. Why don't you apply to them and see what happens."

So I did. I sent letter a few clips from my time at the SF State student newspaper to three newspapers in the UAE. And promptly forgot about it.

But I was very anxious about everything. Where was I going? What would happen? What came next? As graduation approached, it was almost all I could think about.

And then it happened again.

I'd missed the midday prayer, so I went to the *masjid* in the middle of the afternoon to say that prayer. I was alone, and the sunlight was filtering through the windows. And just as in San Francisco, as I was making *sujud*, groveling on the ground before God, I was hit. The electricity in my head, the breathlessness, the exhaustion, everything turning blue.

Unbidden, and unasked for, God was in my head and body. Again. For a moment so brief I'm not sure it could be measured. And yet so overwhelming it seemed as if the world had, in the moment, stopped. Words formed: *Everything is going exactly as it should be.* Even though they were inside my head, they were not my words. Not my thoughts.

I stopped my prayer to catch my breath. I turned to look out the window at the light.

"If this is going to be a regular part of our relationship," I asked God, "can you at least warn me when you're going to do this? Better, can you never do it again?"

Silence. God would talk to me. But never talk back.

Jennifer and I crossed the country in a beat-up old VW van that, bless its heart, couldn't help constantly breaking down. It finally gave up the ghost near Pueblo, Colorado, and we rented a U-Haul to get us to Southern California, where we were going to stay with my father for a while. My father's second marriage had collapsed, and his life had generally fallen apart. And he was beginning to deal with Vietnam. And talk about it.

Because of that, he was becoming a different man—a kinder one, a more patient one. The man who told me I was not welcome at home after I graduated from high school, and that there would be no help for college, said he was happy to have us stay with him.

One day, a letter arrived. From *Khaleej Times* in Dubai, the editor wrote to thank me for my application. In response, they were offering me a job, as a reporter. I needed to let them know whether I accepted, so that people on that end could start processing my visa and work permit.

I was going to be a Muslim living and working in a Muslim country! The prospect was incredibly exciting. I called Abdullah al-Hamdan and told him the news. He was happy, and congratulated me.

But he was also wary.

"You will be disappointed, Abu Sakhr. It will not be what you expect."

11

"Made in Belgium"

THE PARTY WAS LOUD given there weren't that many people. A karaoke machine blared Asian and Western pop. Sometimes people sang along, and sometimes they didn't.

The center of attention at this particular moment was a Filipino named William, a tall, thin man who danced while everyone watched. I'd seen William around—he'd been at a dinner I'd been invited to by a coworker who was Filipino, and it was clear he was gay.

William was wearing a red satin bustier with black lace and a pair of tight denim cut-offs. He was surrounded by Arab men who were pawing him and stuffing five and ten dirham bills in his bustier as he danced. And hooting and hollering the whole time.

Everyone was drinking, even me, and there were beer cans and booze bottles everywhere. When the Arabs, all Emiratis, weren't busy hooting at William and showering dirhams on him, they sat around a table, drank shots, and laughed themselves silly as they did Saddam Hussein impersonations.

There were women at this party, somewhere. They were just elsewhere. Occasionally, the host's wife would come in to talk to her husband, who seemed a little more sober than everyone else in the room. Because some social conventions were too important to flout.

Abdullah al-Hamdan was right. This was not the Dubai I had expected. And yes, I was disappointed.

My colleague Emilio, a longtime employee of *Khaleej Times*, had invited me to this party. He was a friend of the Filipina wife of an Emirati who worked at Dubai's Central Military Command. We were celebrating the husband's promotion, and as I arrived I saw our hosts stacking and carrying cases of beer. Someone had clearly spent some money at African + Eastern, Dubai's legal monopoly liquor store.

I have never really enjoyed parties much. And this evening was no exception. In fact, while living and working in Dubai had its moments, even prior to this night, I had sunken into a self-absorbed funk. Sometime midway through the evening, I had given in to my worst impulses and grabbed a Heineken. And wallowed deeper in self-pity.

I hated this place. It was a tawdry, commercial hub full of people wanting to do nothing more than get rich. That's all anyone seemed to care about. Since I've rarely cared about making money—I still don't—such places don't make much sense to me. And they aren't fun to be in. It didn't help that I'd arrived at *Khaleej Times* and was effectively told, "Welcome, we're glad we hired you, but there really isn't enough for you to do since no one wants to give up anything they cover. Have fun!"

It was a little like Panama. No, it was a lot like Panama. I was lonely and had far too much time to myself. Jennifer was not with me. She was back in the United States, waiting for me to get settled and apply for her residency permit.

That night I was waiting. Waiting for a word, a sign from God, anything that would convince me that I should straighten up, fly right, and live the life I was supposed to live. Because God felt distant, gone. I'd come all this way for what, exactly?

As I worked on my second beer, an Emirati soldier sat on the couch across from me. His neck and arms were a mess of burn scars, and his hands looked like claws. He was the only Arab man there not wearing traditional Arab clothes—a *thaub* and *keffiyah*. Instead, he wore black jeans and a T-shirt.

"You're probably wondering what this is all about," he said, meaning the scars on his face and hands.

I just nodded. I was not in the mood for much conversation.

"I was a sapper in the army, and a bomb I was working on during a training exercise went off prematurely," he said. "It could have been worse."

Yes, I said, I suppose it could have been.

He looked at the can of beer in my hands.

"You know, you should not be drinking that. Beer is not good for you," he said.

Finally! The voice of God—a stern rebuke that I needed to hear—telling me to pick myself up out of my crapulence. I was relieved, and grateful. God was here, speaking through this man.

He reached underneath the coffee table between us and slammed a bottle of Jack Daniels down.

"*This* is what you should be drinking," he said. "Whisky! Now this is a man's drink!"

Thanks, God.

After I had gotten the employment offer, it took me almost eight months to secure the work visa to go to the United Arab Emirates. The UAE is a federation of seven tiny hereditary monarchies—Dubai, Sharjah, Ajman, Fujairah, Um al-Quwain, Ras al-Khaimah and Abu Dhabi—that came together in the very late 1960s after Britain announced it was withdrawing from its last colonial possessions in the Middle East. Abu Dhabi, "father of the gazelle," is the largest and richest of the seven emirates. Most of the UAE's oil and gas is there, beneath Abu Dhabi's sun-scorched sands. Even though it had some oil and gas, Dubai is a trading hub, and in the 1990s was prospering mainly on "re-exporting"—taking goods and repackaging them for shipment elsewhere. And there was always talk of smuggling, money laundering, and any number of other unsavory or illegal practices.

Whatever the source, Dubai was a town stuffed full of money.

The first thing I had to do, aside from fill out the visa application form, was to get my Ohio State bachelor's degree "authenticated." That involved, according to the instructions the U.S. State Department sent me, first going to a notary public somewhere in San Bernardino County and getting a notarized copy made. After that, I had to go the California Secretary of State's office in Los Angeles and have them certify that the notary was legally and properly licensed and empowered to make that copy. And affix a statement to the notarized copy testifying to that effect, a statement that, if removed, would destroy the copy.

Then I had to send this pile of documents to the State Department in Washington, DC, where they would then further certify that the California Secretary of State was duly elected. Or some such. They affixed another document, and there were ribbons and some kind of self-destruct mechanism attached to the whole thing.

I found myself wondering: where next? Does the secretary general of the United Nations or the pope need to sign off on this?

After all that, I mailed the mess off to Dubai and waited. And waited. And waited. And sent the occasional telex message (something a few early e-mail systems could do) to *Khaleej Times* asking how things were going. And being told, each time, to hold on, immigration processes take time.

Eventually, a visa was processed. An airline ticket arrived. And after a very long flight, which involved a twenty-hour layover in Amsterdam, I arrived in Dubai.

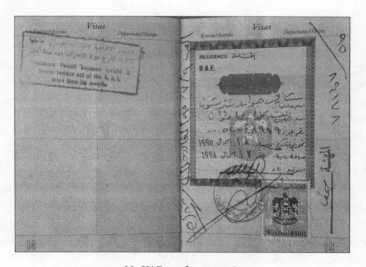

My UAE employment visa

It was clear I had arrived someplace very, very different when heavily armed soldiers boarded the plane to supervise passengers as they exited.

As I said hello to the immigration agent, I quickly discovered the power of being the giant blonde man who speaks Arabic. No one expected it, so it always resulted in pleasant surprise and conversation. So much so that whichever official I was talking to would get distracted. That evening, while my passport got stamped, the immigration officer didn't look through my bags.

It was always kind of fun to see how this would work. One morning, as I walked to work, I noticed a police officer writing a ticket for a white Mercedes that was parked on a sidewalk. I said "*as-salaam alaikum!*" to him, he looked up, closed his ticket book, dragged me inside his cousin's convenience store, ordered up mango juice, and told me all about his life for the next hour. He was from Yemen (most police officers in Dubai were Yemenis or Omanis), had a big family and was very happy to meet a Muslim like me. He wanted to know all about me—where my family was from, was I married (he seemed disappointed that I was, as he had a cousin who was looking for a husband) and what it was like to be Muslim in America. It was an exhausting conversation, and I just barely held my own.

After we were done, I walked out of the convenience store and noticed the Mercedes was gone. Someone owes me.

Dubai in 1995 was one part San Diego, one part Fresno, and one part Tijuana. All shaken vigorously. It was just beginning to become a gaudy, steel-and-glass monument to finance. But there were still examples of a much older Dubai, examples I suspect have long since been bulldozed. Like a Canada Dry bottling plant built in the 1960s along the north shore of the creek and probably abandoned sometime in the late 1970s, acacia trees growing through holes in the roof. *Khaleej Times* put me up in a hotel for a week. For my very first story I covered a shindig at Pancho Villa's, the hotel's restaurant. Their mascot was a Pakistani midget with a huge mustache who wore a serape and a giant sombrero and carried a pair of plastic six-shooters. The highlight of the evening was a jello shot contest.

And yes, I had to write a news story about this.

At the *masjid* in Nasser Square, across the street from a *Khaleej Times* bureau, I met a young Indian Muslim who was a computer programmer, Moinuddin. A soft-spoken man, Moin invited me to move in with his friends, fifteen guys who lived in a giant flat not far from Nasser Square. I took a corner of a room.

My colleagues were an interesting collection of Arabs, South Asians, and one Filipino. I would get to know Emilio the best. He told me he had sought work in the UAE after his political activism against then-Philippine

President Ferdinand Marcos made him unemployable at home. It was a government strategy, he told me, to export both skilled workers and political undesirables. (I met a lot of Filipino communists in the Arabian Gulf. In fact, some years later when I worked in Saudi Arabia, I noticed the newspaper in Jeddah not only received copies of the Filipino Islamist newspaper but also the weekly publication of what remained of the New People's Army, the armed wing of the Communist Party of the Philippines.) He'd been in Dubai for much of his career, and while the kind of journalism he did seemed to wear on him, the work allowed him to care for his family.

Something the Philippines government had, for a time, not allowed him to do.

But the real presence in the *Khaleej Times* Dubai office was Robin Arthur, who despite his name was very, very Indian. Robin was a stern but kind man, and in another time and place I would have quickly latched onto him as a surrogate father. He was round and squat, slowly balding, and sported the most immense muttonchop sideburns. I admired his intellect, his experience, and his willingness to meet the mess that was me more or less where I was. A Catholic from the Indian city of Puna, Robin had spent almost the entirety of his journalistic career writing in Dubai, and he had done very well for himself.

"I appreciate this place, Dubai, the United Arab Emirates," he told me once. "It is a very tolerant place. They have allowed me to raise my children, to worship God as I believe is right, and make a life for myself."

Robin and his family were very hospitable to me during my sojourn in Dubai, and I had dinner (and occasionally drinks) with him and his wife several times. (Jennifer and I would visit Robin Arthur after he resettled his family in Halifax a few years later.) But he was also a staunch Indian nationalist. And he could also get very angry about the discrimination he had seen during his many years in Dubai. How much you were paid in the UAE depended on a combination of the color of your skin, your nationality, and your social class.

He was particularly incensed that employers in the UAE didn't value his master's degree in literature from an Indian university nearly as much as they did bachelor's degrees from schools in the U.S. or other Western countries.

"My degree from an Indian university is every bit as good as yours," he told me once. "It is not right that someone who graduated from a Western university can draw a higher salary than someone with a higher degree from an Asian university!"

Khaleej Times paid me $1,000 a month—a very low salary for a Westerner. But that was on the high end for starting reporters, most of whom were Arab or South Asian.

English-language newspapers in the Arab Middle East are an interesting combination of chamber of commerce newsletter and community bulletin board. Not a lot of real journalism was done. But that wasn't the point. The newspaper was the mouthpiece of the Galadari Brothers conglomerate, and our job—this I had to figure out, because no one told me—was to effectively promote goods, services, and happenings sponsored by Galadari companies.

Along the line, a little journalism got done.

The Arabic-language press was a little more interesting, but only a tiny fraction of the UAE's population was actually Arab. Eight out of every ten people living in the country were from somewhere else.

Most of the stories I wrote were fluff. An interview with a Dominican master cigar roller for Davidoff Tobacco on a tour of duty-free zones across the world. (He rolled me a half-dozen cigars, and they were very good.) Parties and dances sponsored by various expatriate communities. Washed-up musical acts from the UK or up-and-coming bands from India on tour in the Gulf. Often, these "stories" simply involved rewriting press releases.

Mostly, stories involved going to gatherings, which many times doubled as press conferences. Usually, these events were community specific—Indian, Pakistani, Sri Lankan, Filipino, Iranian—and so Emiratis rarely showed.

But when the University of Wollongong in Australia held a presser to announce the opening of their Dubai campus, a fair number of Arabs attended. At some point, I found myself conversing with an erudite Emirati who wanted to know whether I was enjoying myself.

"It's okay. I'm a little lonely, but otherwise, I like Dubai."

"Good, *alhamdulillah*," he said. "You know," he added, looking kindly at me, "if you would like some company, or want to know where you can find a girlfriend, or some other kind of company, I would be glad to help you."

I was a little stunned.

"I'm . . . married."

"So?" he said. "Married men need company too."

I thanked him but didn't take him up on his offer.

I did manage to write a couple of fairly significant pieces. One involved an informal sanctuary the Dubai government had set up with the cooperation of the Philippine consulate to house Filipina maids and servants who, for whatever reason, had had to flee from their employers but couldn't leave the country because their employers still held their passports.

I wrote the story because Emilio was actually involved in the center, and I spent an afternoon interviewing women. Most had been sexually assaulted or raped, a few beaten—one woman so seriously that she had been hospitalized and, initially, not expected to live.

But one woman ran away because she won the Mercedes in the Dubai Duty Free raffle and her employer took her ticket and claimed the prize for himself.

One evening, I was sent to cover a speech by Sri Lanka's labor minister, who was touring the Gulf to talk about the poor conditions of Sri Lankan workers. So I went, did a write-up that cleared the paper's censors (our main censor was a giant and very frightening Sudanese woman), and made the paper the next day.

The minister had been very critical of the UAE government, however, and the day after the piece ran a letter arrived from the Ministry of Information in Abu Dhabi. Reporters were no longer allowed to cover any events involving officials of foreign governments without the prior approval of the information ministry.

I'd managed to make the government mad. That was something.

❦❦❦

There were some things I loved about Dubai. It was a wonderful city to walk, and I walked just about everywhere (I nearly wore out a pair of Birkenstocks that way). I walked clear across the city one evening. I loved seeing the city and meeting people.

I loved the big, open-air *souks*. I loved the smell of street food and all the shiny baubles, the bolts of bright cloth, and, again, the people. People from everywhere.

Not long after I arrived, I met Talat. A light-skinned Pakistani, Talat owned a typing and translation business. He was a serious man and a very pious Muslim, a member of the *Jama'at Tabligh*, and he was kind and very friendly.

Any convert to Islam is going to run into the *Jama'at Tabligh*, "the society for spreading the faith," at some point. They don't try to convince non-Muslims to become Muslim, at least not that I ever saw. Rather, they travel around, sleeping in *masjids*, telling other Muslims they need to spend time traveling from *masjid* to *masjid* to convince other Muslims to do the same. "Three days in the cause of God! Forty days in the cause of God!" they exhort.

They are the mendicant friars of Islam (to borrow a description from a Georgetown friend), and most Muslims I knew found them annoying but inoffensive. (And I did too, though I owe my first experience of memorizing bits of the Qur'an to an Emirati Muslim who was part of a forty-day *Jama'at* expedition that had stopped at the Islamic Center of San Francisco.) The *jihadis* I knew in Columbus found them deeply offensive, because the language they used was similar to the language of *jihad*—struggle in the cause of God—without any of the sacrifice.

Personally, I found them to be a bit circular. Go in the path of God, travel for a few days or weeks, in order to convince others to travel in the path of God. The goal, I think, was to make us all better Muslims, though I was never sure how sleeping and eating in *masjids* was supposed to do that. Aside from making it impossible to skip prayers.

At least they aren't blowing things up. That's something in their favor, I suppose.

Talat invited me one Thursday evening to come with him to a giant *masjid* complex outside of Dubai. It was some ways from the city, and it was huge. There were thousands of Muslims, all segregated by language: the Arabic speakers in one large room, the Urdu speakers—and there were lots of them—in an even larger room, and several other giant rooms for speakers of Bengali, Tagalog, and Pashtu. I'd never seen so many Muslims in one place.

The point of the segregation was to allow each group to hear the sermon translated in its own language. The preacher spoke in Arabic, but paused every few seconds so that the translators in each room could do their thing.

I sat with Talat, who sat with the Arabs. His Arabic was impeccable. I still had trouble following along.

After the sermon, we prayed. After prayer, I went outside. There were thousands of people milling about; many of the South Asians wanted to say hello to me.

It turned out one had been a student at San Francisco State University when I had been there and remembered me.

"Salaam," he said. "What an interesting place to find you! I see you have gotten fat."

Ah, Indian bluntness.

I started shaking hands. And then everyone wanted to shake my hand. I quickly found myself in the middle of a South Asian throng, bodies pressing up against me, all wanting to shake my hand.

And then I hugged someone. And everyone wanted to be hugged. Hundreds of people. I'm not sure how long this went on, but at some point, Talat waded through the crowd and yanked me out. He pulled me into a room full of Arab men who were drinking tea and chatting.

"Have some of this," one man said to me, handing me a cup of buttermilk. "We make it ourselves right here in the *masjid*."

I drank, and oh was it *good*. The men were from all over—Qatar, Saudi Arabia, the UAE, Oman, even Iraq. We talked all night, and I had several more glasses of buttermilk. Sometime after the *Isha'* prayer, Talat took me back to where I was living near Nasser Square.

And then I spent the next three days almost physically attached to the toilet, in a great deal of pain and as sick as I have ever been, unable to eat a thing.

"Are you okay?" Moin asked, softly knocking on the bathroom door.

"I'll be okay eventually. But I can't move right now. I can't stop . . . well, I can't stop. Who knew a human body could contain so much?"

"Well, if you can shift to your bedroom, the rest of us need to wash for work," he said.

"I'll see what I can do."

I imagined that in drinking the locally concocted buttermilk, my rather genteel North American gut flora met turbaned Arabian Peninsula microbes, and the resulting *jihad* made such a mess of my innards that I've never completely recovered.

Sunni Islam is the official religion of the United Arab Emirates. There is a Ministry of Islamic Affairs, and it builds and operates all the *masjids* in the country. The state pays all the preachers, scholars, prayer leaders, and *masjid* caretakers. All charity given by Muslims is supposed to go a state fund and then doled out to the needy. This didn't stop beggars from begging, of course.

There was, however, fairly broad toleration in the UAE, as Robin Arthur attested to. There were Catholic and Protestant churches, something that appeared to be a Latter-Day Saint house of worship, even a number of Shia *masjids*. (I don't know whether Hindus were allowed to worship privately or not. They were certainly not allowed to worship publicly.) But you could only talk about Islam in public; no mention of any other faith—especially

Shia Islam—was allowed. Nothing religious got past our censors, not even a cursory mention I once made of Native American religion.

I prayed faithfully at first, going to the big brick *masjid* near Nasser Square—the white-and-gold tile work on the inside was gorgeous—but it wasn't the same. I missed the community I'd had in Columbus. I missed belonging to people, people I knew and who knew me. Worship in Dubai, where there was a *masjid* on every corner, ostensibly for your ease and convenience, was impersonal. Even anonymous. A little bit like ducking into a McDonald's for a burger and fries.

It turns out that the Muslims in America are actually better Muslims. Because they have to actively *choose* to be Muslim. And so much works against their being Muslim. Those less inclined to cultivate a serious faith can simply melt away into American culture. This left me with the seriously mistaken impression that Muslims were better people.

But Dubai disabused me of that notion. Islam created the default culture, and it was a happy-face Islam that condemned sin while pretending there wasn't much sin in its midst and doing little about that sin (just one example: the cars with Saudi license plates lining up on Thursday in front of the African + Eastern to stock up on booze), except for the occasional hypocritical show of public piety.

More importantly, being Muslim didn't stop people from being cruel. It didn't stop workers from beating their employees, forcing them to work for miserable wages while being separated from their families for years at a time. It didn't stop men from raping their Sri Lankan and Filipina maids. Or from telling me where I could find a "girlfriend" if I was lonely.

Dubai wasn't just a money-hungry monster. It was also a place where basic humanity rarely mattered, where there was little real dignity and people were treated as objects, their value based solely on the color of their skin or the country they came from.

Or how much money they had.

I've never had a problem with horrific cruelty. Having fantasized myself about some very awful things, that always made sense to me. But casual cruelty, the little inhumanities we inflict upon each other when it would be just as easy to be kind—that never made sense to me. Why people abuse each other when there's no reason to has always puzzled me. It made no sense to me, hadn't since I was ten years old.

But what really bothered me, I think, was that I was no longer special. I was no longer unique. I was no longer an outsider in a way that worked for me. Almost everyone was an outsider of some kind in Dubai. (It was a white English Muslim from Yorkshire who first explained to me where my last name came from and what it meant.) I was just one more.

Oh, I was special. Just not in ways I liked.

Not long after I arrived in Dubai, I went to a state clinic to get a mandatory HIV test. The line to get to the paperwork was long but moving fairly quickly. So I found a place at the end of the line, planted myself, and waited.

Just about everyone in line, guessing from skin color, hair, and dress, was from South Asia. There were no other Westerners present that morning. An elderly Arab man, an Emirati, walked up and down the line, examining passports and paperwork, occasionally yelling in Arabic, pushing people, shoving them, and sometimes sending them to the back of the line.

He came up to me and demanded my passport and my paperwork.

"*Wainik? Amreeka? Amreeki?*" he asked.

He recognized my blue-and-gold passport.

"*Amreeka! Alhamdulilah! Georgah Bush! Alhamdulilah!*" He kissed me on the cheek, grabbed me, and yanked me out of line. He continued shouting his thanks to God for George Bush and the U.S. military.

I turned around. Hundreds of pairs of brown eyes were glowering at me. I didn't know what to do. I couldn't refuse—this was the elderly Arab man's idea of hospitality. But I didn't want this. I didn't want it at all.

At a window where a man was in the middle of filling out paperwork for his blood test, he pushed the man out of the way. He handed my paperwork to the clerk, barked an order, and pushed me in front of the window.

"*Alhamdulilah Amreeka!*" he said again, patting me on the back.

The phlebotomist who finally took my blood was a soft-spoken Pakistani. Since I was in the army, I had taken to watching as the needle is stuck in my vein. I almost never feel it, and this man was good. I didn't feel it that time either.

It turned out he had also gone to school at Ohio State. Small world.

I don't function very well without Jennifer. I fooled myself for a long time that I was independent and self-reliant. But much of the reason I wasn't enjoying Dubai was that she wasn't there.

Jennifer is five years older than I am, and I'd taken to saying that I know God loves me because, years before I was born, God took a little bit of my soul and put it inside of her. And held back a little bit of her soul and put it inside me. And our souls had been fitfully, even desperately, looking for those lost little bits, to become whole again.

That's how Jennifer always made me feel. Whole. And I was floundering without her.

The original plan had been for me to get set up in Dubai and then apply for a residence visa for Jennifer. But a couple of things happened that scuttled that plan.

First, my salary was small, and while it also came with a twenty-thousand-dirham annual housing allowance (about $5,400), I looked at what that could buy, and it wasn't much. A lot of the flats I saw in that price range were either very small or very shabby, or both. Something more affordable meant a commute, from Sharjah or even farther away. And that meant buying a car. Which was another additional expense.

There was also the matter of what Jennifer would do. If in America there was no shortage of unfriendly work environments for her, Dubai was going to eat her alive. There were some volunteer possibilities at the British Council, where I'd talked to some people. But paid work seemed out of the question. Things were just too harsh here, and everyone was in too much of a hurry.

And then the government passed a decree raising the minimum salary requirement for foreign workers who wanted their spouses to join them. And my monthly wage fell several hundred dollars below it.

"You shouldn't have to worry about that," someone told me. "You're an American, and I'm certain they won't apply the rules to you."

Well, yes, probably not. But with my American-sized bills beginning to come due—no one from India or Pakistan had student loan payments the size of someone's monthly pay packet—I had visions of getting trapped in Dubai's squalor. Maybe I was wrong, and should have taken the chance, but it seemed like there was simply no upside to staying.

I was unwilling to take the chance that my nationality alone would be enough to get Jennifer to Dubai. And I'm not sure I wanted her there anyway.

So I decided to leave.

It was a complicated decision, in part because I was haunted by leaving the army early, and by the way I left. I did not want this experience to be a mirror of that. I wanted to be good at something other than absconding.

Leaving early meant abrogating my contract. It meant I was on my own to get home. And paying *Khaleej Times* back for my ticket there.

My presence in Dubai had always been something of a puzzle to those I worked with anyway.

"Why are you even here?" one of my Indian coworkers asked me one day.

Before I could answer, Robin Arthur stepped in.

"Because this will look good on a résumé. Because this will help him stand out when he looks for work back home. This is the beginning of his career, and not the end. That's where he's different than the rest of us."

He was right. He was also probably right the day he told me I needed to assert myself with the newspaper's managers.

"Look, I don't understand you, complaining about your salary. You need to walk into the editor's office, pound your fist on his desk, and tell him in so uncertain terms, 'I am a white man, and you need to pay me like a white man!' You do that, and you'll have him quaking in his boots, and they'll pay you what other Westerners are paid in this place."

I looked around the room. There was an embarrassed silence from my other coworkers, but some of them nodded in agreement.

Robin may have very well been right. I don't know. I had a hard time imagining such an approach would have ever worked. I do know there was no way on God's good and dusty earth I could do that. Not me. Not given where I'd been.

Something interesting happens when you surrender privilege. No one cares. No one says thank you, no one throws a parade, no one sings God's praises, no one slaps you on the back and says "welcome." The most you might get is solidarity, the kind that acknowledges a willingness to live as someone without privilege, as someone with a "slave name."

Now, that solidarity is a lot, but it's also understood that it's conditional, since everyone knows you can walk away, into the wider world, and live as if nothing has changed. I could always walk away from the Muslim community when I got tired of being a part of it, take my skullcap and my long shirt off, and no one would know who or what I was. Unless I told them.

So, what you generally get is confusion. Those with privilege wonder why you aren't one of them. Those without wonder why you aren't using the privilege you have. From both sides, it's as if you've violated the natural order of the world. It can be the ultimate no-win situation. Act the part of the privileged white man and everyone glares at you for using the power that skin color and social standing have given you. Lay that privilege down and everyone glares at you in disbelief, thinking you must be crazy.

Or very, very stupid.

As I was getting ready to leave, *Khaleej Times* suddenly made things difficult. It turns out that my ticket to the UAE wasn't valued at the market rate, but rather had been obtained as part of a swap with KLM for advertising. The advert space was worth twice the price of the airline ticket.

That's what I owed *Khaleej Times*. And I couldn't leave before I paid it.

That would leave me with no cash to return home with. I was willing to do that, but I didn't want to.

Unsure what to do, I called an American consular official I'd had some previous contact with.

"That's a private contract matter. We don't have any jurisdiction, and there's nothing we can do. You're on your own to deal with that; we can't really help. I'll make a phone call or two, but I can't make any promises. Sorry."

"I understand," I said. It looked like I would have to bite the bullet.

I came to work the following morning, and Robin Arthur got up and looked straight at me.

"What the hell did you do? You've got everyone terrified and pissing themselves over at the main office!"

So much for not making any promises. I told Robin about the phone call I'd made the previous afternoon.

He looked around the room.

"Amazing. Do you think my government, or the Syrian government, or the Philippines government would have this kind of power? Or that they'd even take our phone calls? No one would care. My government would not care."

"That, my friend, is power," Emilio said. "That is real power." I couldn't disagree with him.

This was awkward. And embarrassing. I hadn't wanted this. I hadn't wanted any of this.

Later that morning, the phone rang. It was the business manager at *Khaleej Times*. He was both sheepish and angry.

"The price for your ticket was the price we first quoted you, and not the advertising price," he said. "And you didn't have to call your consulate and get your government involved. That wasn't necessary."

It seems, over the years, I'd acquired an interesting skill—maybe it was a gift, even—the ability to wriggle out of really bad situations. I wasn't proud of this skill, in fact I was somewhat ashamed of it. I wish that things had worked out differently, that I was a different person, someone who didn't need to do this.

If there was an upside, I was going home to Jennifer. But that was about the only upside I could find.

Not long before I left Dubai, I was out with Emilio as he escorted a Filipino diplomat around. The consular official was going home. The Philippines couldn't pay its diplomats very well, but it could give them a fairly good perk when they left a foreign posting—they could bring back a full shipping container duty free that they could then sell.

Emilio was helping the diplomat deal with various merchants, and on that particular afternoon they were negotiating the price for bulk carpets. I just tagged along, watched and listened.

At some point, I got tired of standing and sat down on a huge stack of carpets, all about three feet by five feet. They were comfortable, and I started flipping through the carpets and reading the labels.

All the labels read, *Made in Belgium.*

I asked Emilio about it. Why would a rug merchant in Dubai have a shop full of Belgian-made carpets?

"They aren't made in Belgium. They're all made in India, in Kashmir probably. They're shipped here to Dubai, where they get new papers. So they can enter the European Union duty free. They sew those Belgian labels on here."

And that's everything you need to know about Dubai.

Some months later, Jennifer and I were browsing through a J. C. Penney in San Bernardino when a stack of carpets in the home furnishings department caught my eye. It was a dead ringer for the stack of carpets I had sat on in the little Dubai shop. I turned the top one over to look at the label. And then a few more, to see if they were the same.

Made in Belgium.

That afternoon, after we had finished filling the diplomat's shipping container, Emilio looked at me with his tired eyes—Emilio always looked tired—and took a long drag on his cigarette.

"Don't forget how fortunate you are. You can leave. We can't. Remember that."

Robin Arthur was right. Having *Khaleej Times* on my résumé was enough to get me noticed by editors. My résumé and my clips stood out. It took only a few months to find a job, this time as the agricultural and rural correspondent for *The Herald Journal* in Logan, Utah.

That's what spending summers on a farm will do for you.

It turns out my father had lived in Logan as a child, when Grandpa ran the Indian School in Brigham City for a year, preparing for his Bureau of Indian Affairs job in Alaska. Until I'd been offered the position, I'd had no idea.

The job was fairly typical of small newspaper jobs. I was responsible for covering a lot—agriculture, business, county government in Cache County, Utah, and even reporting on Preston, Idaho (where the movie *Napoleon Dynamite* was filmed) and Franklin County, Idaho. But my job took me as far afield as Boise (for Idaho National Guard maneuvers) and Wyoming (something related to water use issues, though I don't exactly remember). I put well over thirty thousand miles on my pickup that first year I was at *The Herald Journal*.

Logan was about the right size for Jennifer. Easily walkable, laid out on a grid, it had a cafe and a library, and what else did Jennifer need? She worked a little, in a greenhouse, and volunteered with Bridgerland Literacy, a library program that helps teach people how to read.

There was a tiny Muslim community in Logan, and they owned a small house they used as the Logan Islamic Center. This group of Muslims, mostly Arabs and Africans working on advanced degrees in hydrology, was by far the most centered group of Muslims I'd ever encountered. No one wanted to wage war, or blow stuff up, or impose Islamic law on the world; no one was angry at what women wore in public. They were studious, faithful, and serious about being Muslim without being too obnoxiously pious.

"It's because the Mormons are as conservative as we are," said Aref, a Kuwaiti who was not typical of the Muslim students at Utah State University. He was working on a bachelor's degree in accounting, his assigned role in his family's business. "The women all dress modestly, and a lot of the undergraduates are married. It feels more like home here than the other places I've been in the United States."

Aref didn't just talk from the pious imagination. He'd begun his undergraduate studies at San Diego State University, but had dropped out after a year or two.

"Oh, the girls there," he said, smiling. "I had . . . too much fun. I paid no attention to my studies. It was very bad."

He took a couple of years off, got married to a good Kuwaiti Muslim, and then found a more socially conservative part of the United States to study in.

"There are fewer distractions here," Aref said. "It is easier to study."

None of the other Muslims had Aref's experience, but all agreed—the Mormons helped make Logan feel like home, regardless of whether home was Gaza, Cairo, Khartoum, or Mogadishu.

I became deeply involved in this tiny Muslim community. After the disappointment of Dubai, they had redeemed being Muslim for me. They were a community, and everyone mattered here. We were serious, and not too hypocritical (well, I was, since I took to brewing beer in Logan), and confident about who we were. There may have been tinier religious minorities in Logan, but I was hard pressed to figure out who they were.

One afternoon, sometime in the middle of spring (spring comes late in Cache Valley), we were all sitting cross-legged in a circle, in the main room of the Islamic Center, after Friday prayer. Somehow, the conversation turned to where we'd each grown up.

Aref said he'd grown up in a walled villa in Kuwait, with a garden but no yard. Muhammad talked about the flat in Gaza where his family lived, rubble piled where parks should have been. Yards were something the Israeli settlers had, but not the Palestinians.

The answers were similar for everyone else—the Somalis who grew up in pre-civil war Mogadishu, the lone Egyptian, and the Saudi. There were parks and gardens, but no yards.

"So, Brother Umar, tell us about where you grew up," Aref asked.

I told them I spent most of my teenage years in a big house with a corner lot, and we had a huge yard that my father and I mowed every other week.

There was a bit of silence. Aref smiled, and placed a hand on my knee.

"So it is settled. Brother Umar will mow and water the yard."

Settled? I was unaware we were even discussing this.

I looked at Aref.

"Why me?"

"Because, Brother Umar," his smile broadened. "You are the only one of us here who grew up with grass."

Sometimes this, and not the lightning strike in the middle of the head, is the call of God.

So, I mowed and watered the lawn at the little Logan Islamic Center for two summers. I enjoyed it hugely and looked at my work as a kind of prayer. I even fooled a bit with the grape vines in the backyard, though I knew nothing about grapes and they weren't my responsibility.

At the same time, Jennifer became very involved with the little ELCA Lutheran church in Logan, helping with worship. We also became good friends with the pastor, Barry Neese, and for a time, Jennifer was so enamored of Pastor Neese that she again considered a call to ordained ministry.

But as much fun as wandering around Cache County was, I found touching cows, standing in the midst of smut-infested barley fields, and trying to master federal dairy policy and state water use laws tedious and a little boring. A job I could do for a bit, but not a calling.

I had no idea what I was called to do, and no real plans. I had some dreams and desires. I wanted to be important. I wanted to be a Middle East expert, get paid to write and talk. I wanted to be a columnist. Maybe even the next Tom Friedman. That's what I wanted.

They sound like dumb dreams now. I had no idea how to go about doing any of these things, only that I wasn't going to get anywhere near them in northern Utah.

So, I looked at Middle East Studies programs. And for some reason, I focused on Georgetown's Center for Contemporary Arab Studies. I also wrote to Georgetown's National Security Studies Program (a longtime interest, largely thanks to my father's work), but I knew that with my political inclinations, I would be utterly unemployable with a National Security Studies degree.

I didn't expect Georgetown would take me. But they did.

I remember telling my friend Patrick Visel, who had been my boss when I worked at Ohio State's Middle East Studies library, the good news. He was glad for me and invited me to stop by to see him on my way through Columbus. He was also a little stunned.

"I'm not surprised they accepted you," he said. "But I am surprised you even applied."

12

Force Majeure

IT WAS NOT A typical press conference.

First, the venue was a big room on the Senate side of the U.S. Capitol building, and not the tiny Senate press gallery a floor or two above. Second, the room was stuffed full of people other than reporters, which was unusual for any kind of press conference. Third, the vice president of the United States, Al Gore, was there. Which explained why the room was full. It was both a legislative press conference and an event in support of Al Gore's 2000 presidential campaign, which was very nearly at full boil late that summer.

I'd managed to secure a seat in the second row, and saw a few reporters from rival agencies—Reuters, Bloomberg, Dow Jones. But it wasn't like we would be able to ask questions, so I suspect some of my colleagues/rivals stayed behind in their offices to watch the whole thing on C-SPAN.

Honestly, it was just as easy to report that way. Especially if you were writing wire service copy, since no one was paying for color anyway.

A group of senior, farm-state Democrats were rolling out a major new agricultural policy initiative. I dealt with most of these senators, or rather their staffers, on a fairly regular basis: Byron Dorgan and Kent Conrad of North Dakota, Paul Wellstone of Minnesota, Tom Harkin of Iowa, Dick Durbin of Illinois, Blanche Lincoln of Arkansas, Max Baucus of Montana, and Senate majority leader Tom Daschle of South Dakota. Occasionally, they would be joined by Patrick Leahy of Vermont and Herb Kohl of Wisconsin, especially if the agricultural policy in question affected milk, cheese, and butter in any way.

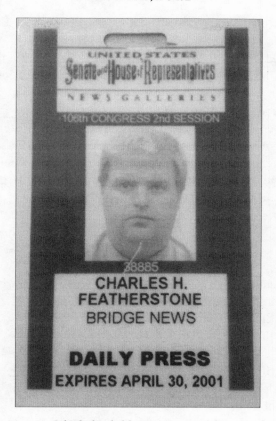

It looks kinda like my tie is too tight.

I looked around. Aside from a few cynical and impatient reporters (almost nothing in Clinton-era Washington ever started on time), the room was full of young congressional staffers and sparkly-eyed true believers, many brought here from the hinterland to be the living props in support of the policy the senate Democrats were unveiling.

That was the way of things.

I forget who started speaking. People whose lives would be changed by the proposed piece of legislation were named, pointed at, asked to stand. Eventually, Gore was introduced and he stepped forward.

If ever there was a day when I should have made extensive notes, this was it. Gore began to speak about his childhood in Tennessee, helping on the family farm, the goodness of the earth, the dignity of tilling the soil.

But what had begun as a gambol through Gore's childhood idyll quickly veered into a swamp. His speech became muddled and incoherent. Things he said didn't make much sense, and it seemed clear—at least to me—that he'd not given a lot of thought to what he was saying.

I looked around the room. Does anyone else here see that the vice president of the United States is making an ass of himself? Reporters scribbled and shiny eyes sparkled.

Apparently not.

Not even the senators sharing the rostrum with Gore were fazed. Perhaps they'd had a lot of practice looking confident and assured during moments like this. Somewhere, knee deep in the muddy of confused metaphors, Gore took a big breath, like he was trying to arrange his thoughts and think of the next thing to say.

Tom Daschle stepped forward.

"What the vice president means is this," he began, and then proceeded to quickly, clearly and coherently explain the need for whatever legislative initiative they were proposing. Without skipping a beat. Even Gore was visibly undisturbed by Daschle's act. Whether he was angry or relieved, I could not tell. There was nothing but a safe, blank look on his face, and the spotlight quickly shifted to Daschle.

When the press conference was done, I went outside to phone in my story to my editor, Avi. But a Secret Service agent carrying an automatic weapon angrily ordered me back inside the Capitol building—the vice president hadn't left yet, and security was always tight wherever the president or vice president went.

"What's the headline?" Avi asked me. He was the most skilled of the people on the copy desk, and the back-and-forth with him, while sometimes difficult, always made for a better and more focused story.

"VP Gore Endorses Democrat Farm Proposal," I said.

"Well, he would. That's not news," Avi said. "What else is there?"

So we went with the actual proposal itself. Sent out a headline, then a first paragraph, and then I returned to the BridgeNews bureau on 14th and F St. to finish the story.

It was the only story I ever got any flak for from my boss, Ros Krasny, the BridgeNews senior grains correspondent in Chicago. She called me up the following day, a little perturbed.

"Was Vice President Gore at that press conference you covered yesterday?" she asked.

"Yeah, he was."

"Then why didn't you lead with that? Reuters did, and it looks like we weren't even there."

I took a breath.

"Well, I intended to. But Avi at the copy desk said that wasn't news. So, we went with the proposal itself."

I don't remember exactly how Ros responded. She was a good boss and would call me up occasionally to say I was doing good work. So, this was a big deal. But the general conclusion was, if the vice president was speaking, that was news, regardless of what he said.

Or what the copy desk said.

But the whole thing added to my nagging sense that this is all a game. One I couldn't take as seriously as I needed to in order to make a career of it.

That conclusion would be affirmed one day as I bounded up the steps on the Senate side of the U.S. Capitol—I spent more time on the Senate side than the House side—and, as reached the third floor, came face to face with a bust of Spiro T. Agnew, Richard Nixon's first vice president, the former governor of Maryland who had resigned in disgrace in 1973 for tax evasion.

I stood there and laughed. A bust of Spiro Agnew, staring straight at me. His vacant eyes looking right into my soul. For a moment, this whole place, the U.S. Capitol, felt like an absurdist carnival, a circus, put on solely for my benefit. It was somewhere between a Kafka novel, a Dali painting, and Monty Python's "Confuse-a-Cat" sketch. I felt like I was Jaroslav Hašek's *Good Soldier Švejk*, wandering almost accidentally from scene to scene surrounded by pompous Austrian generals and overeager sergeants thinking I should love the army and the war as much as they did.

While all I wanted was a cold beer, a hot meal, and a dry place to sleep.

After about a year as a reporter in Washington, I'd found it almost impossible to take any of it seriously. At least not for very long.

Which is funny, because this job was exactly why I came to Washington.

I loved my two years at Georgetown. I really did. The work was hard, the language study was intense, the reading and the writing almost constant. As one of my fellow students from Spain, Virginia Tortella Canyelles, described it later, Georgetown was "reading and more reading, some Arabic, more reading and writing papers. Boring and some suffering. Done."

But I liked it. I liked being surrounded by smart people, I liked the discussions on theory and literature, the examination not just of history itself but how we examine and conceptualize history, the back-and-forth with professors and other students. I liked being a very tiny fish in a giant pond. And I really liked the fact that I was not always the smartest person in the room.

Because people have held that against me for almost as long as I could remember.

The Master of Arts in Arab Studies program was part of Georgetown's School of Foreign Service and was a two-year "professional" master's program. We were being prepared—I don't really want to use the word *trained*, because it doesn't quite fit here—for very particular kinds of jobs, the middle- and upper-middle-level analytical and managerial positions of the late twentieth-century liberal-bureaucratic state. This included the government, but also "nongovernmental institutions" committed to doing well by doing good (mostly by finding and funding projects hither and yon), as well as the whole massive edifice of global finance, which was just coming into its monstrous own during the Clinton years.

Playing a homemade didgeridoo on a bench in Georgetown University's Red Square, probably mid-1998. The didgeridoo was made and given to me by Mike Wennergren, my editor at the *Herald Journal*.

Finding a job after I graduated was going to prove interesting. Intelligence work, which a few of my colleagues pursued, was out of the question. I couldn't, in good conscience, draw little red circles on maps and tell someone, "Bomb here." There was also the matter of my past—I probably couldn't get a security clearance, and I didn't want to try.

The same was true of the rest of government work. I was simply not interested.

But the professional do-goodery of Washington, DC, was also out of the question. It just seemed like fraud to me to try to "help" people by writing position papers, lobbying the government, raising money, and whatnot. It all seemed like pretend to me. It still does.

Work in the "private sector," that nifty little euphemism for anything that isn't government or that makes a profit, held out a few more charms. I'd done some temp work at Friedman Billings Ramsay, an Arlington-based investment bank, and I saw the hours analysts and brokers worked. Did I love money enough much to work those hours? Not really.

Besides, working for a corporation usually meant professing some kind of loyalty to the company and its mission. And it was hard for me to be loyal to anything I couldn't love.

So that left journalism. I may not be doing good, but I didn't see myself doing obvious evil, either.

In my last semester, I started doing some research. And I tried getting my résumé and clips out to whomever might be interested. I had invested in this specialized education about a region and its people, studied a language, and I hoped that would be of some value to an editor or two looking to expand or improve coverage of the Middle East and Islamic world.

What I discovered was dispiriting. Almost no one was interested, and those few who were suggested what I really needed was some solid experience on a midsize daily newspaper somewhere. Which made me angry. I hadn't come to Georgetown and learned Arabic and economics only to go to work in Toledo covering cops and courts.

I should have just set out for the part of the world and taken my chances. But I didn't have that kind of courage.

At some point during my final semester at Georgetown, I came across postings for a couple of news services specializing in business and finance—Dow Jones Newswires and BridgeNews. I'd sent a résumé to Dow Jones in response to a very specific job ad, and a résumé to Bridge as an introduction. "Can you use someone with my skills?" I asked.

Dow Jones wanted an interview. And Bridge showed some interest. So, I made a trip to New York and stayed with my friend Vince—we'd met at San Francisco State many years before, and he was currently living on Staten Island.

My first real experience of New York came at the PATH station underneath the World Trade Center. I stood, looking up at the giant map of the PATH train system, wondering how it worked.

"Where you going?" a voice from behind me asked.

"Exchange Place. I have an interview this morning . . ."

"Take any train and get off the first stop. Can't miss it."

I turned around to thank the man who'd helped me, but he'd already moved on. I always found New Yorkers to be amazingly kind and helpful. But they were also always in a hurry—and had no time for the pleasantries of introductions or social negotiation. If you aren't moving, or if you're opening a map, the presumption is you need help. And help descends.

So I arrived at Dow Jones Newswires in Jersey City. The office had the ambiance of a Phoenician slave galley, and no one working there looked happy. Several people gave me looks that seemed to say "Kill me now" or "Run! Run as fast as you can from this place!" It had little personality and almost no soul. It was not the happiest place on earth, and it certainly wasn't a place I saw myself working.

Nevertheless, they offered me a position on their energy desk. I told them I would think about it.

I had told Pam Conway, the senior energy reporter with BridgeNews in New York, that I was coming up that week. Would it possible to meet? To see if Bridge was a possibility?

"Sure. Just don't come up here if this is all you have," she said.

I walked into the BridgeNews offices in Three World Financial Center and right away could see how different the whole place felt from the work camp atmosphere of Dow Jones. The place was more brightly lit, and cubicles were personalized in a way Dow Jones wasn't. One editor had hung rubber deep-sea fishing lures all around, and a reporter had decorated her workspace with little Star Wars Lego sets. There was a liveliness to this place that Dow Jones didn't have. No one looked at me with fear in their eyes, with a "please take me with you" look.

Yeah, I could work here.

"Hi, Pam? I'm Charles Featherstone. We had an appointment this morning."

She seemed a bit flustered as we went into an office.

"Thank you for meeting with me," I told her.

"Not a problem," she replied. "So, why are you here again?"

About a month before I graduated from Georgetown, BridgeNews offered me a position as an agricultural policy and trade correspondent in

Washington, DC. Because I'd covered agriculture for *The Herald Journal* in Logan, Utah. Because I'd spent a couple of summers as a teenager on my grandfather's farm, greasing a combine and driving a truck.

BridgeNews had been put together by St. Louis–based Bridge Information Systems, which had a global fiber optic network and proprietary trading software. At some point, the company decided, "We have this network, let's sell our own news on it!" And so they created BridgeNews, borrowing a great deal of money to glue together bits and pieces, like KnightRidder Financial, that no one else wanted.

I'm certain it seemed like a winning business strategy at the time.

BridgeNews was a finance and commodities news service, and we specialized in covering anything that was either traded on a market or could move a market. My job involved covering the U.S. Department of Agriculture, where we had an office; keeping tabs on the activities of farm and trade lobbying groups; watching Congress (I thought the Cache County Planning and Zoning Commission was dull, but it was a regular circus compared to the House Agriculture Committee); and following around the secretary of agriculture (and other senior USDA officials as necessary, such as the chief economist) and phoning in their utterances. Because anything they might say—Russian food aid, disaster assistance (there was almost always a disaster somewhere), policy proposals, anything—could move wheat, corn, or soybean futures.

And those traders were our customers. They paid for our news.

My first big scoop came a few weeks into the job and involved a major donation of U.S. beef products to Russia, which was then reeling from the dismantling of the Soviet Union and the collapse of the Soviet economy. Someone in the bowels of USDA told me the Department of Agriculture was giving Russia twenty thousand metric tons of beef livers and thirty thousand tons of beef hearts.

"Can I have your name?" I asked the source.

"Oh, no, you cannot use my name," he said, in a bit of a panic, as Bill Tomson, a much more experienced reporter, shook his head and silently screamed "no!" at me.

These were the rules—a civil servant or a congressional staffer somewhere with the power to leak something would give it to a reporter, or several reporters. In return, you could never use the source's name. "According to a USDA source" or "said a source in the Department of Agriculture familiar with the situation" was all you could say.

I tried to visualize thirty thousand tons of beef hearts, sitting in open-topped containers, throbbing and beating and squirting little misty jets of blood. Or twenty thousand tons of beef livers, glistening and jiggling in the bright autumn sun. It was not appealing.

"Good job, Charles!" Ros told me later that afternoon, adding that we beat Reuters on that particular scoop.

The big agricultural commodities for us were corn, soybeans, and wheat. But I also worked closely with our Kansas City bureau to help them cover anything meat-related—there are cattle and pork futures too. And I also worked with our New York commodities reporters who covered sugar, cotton, and frozen concentrated orange juice.

We each had our own interests as reporters. I became the *de facto* genetically modified crop correspondent for Bridge in Washington, and managed to develop a USDA source to the point where I got some leaked documents dealing with a then-important case of non-approved GMO corn contaminating corn stocks. Most of the important work in journalism is building relationships, developing sources, people who trust you enough to give you things first, or things they won't give anyone else.

Along the way, you figure out who can be a friend and who is merely using you. Because journalism is mostly about using people, and being used. There weren't many friends, and I was never really happy with the using people part.

This using was particularly true of members of Congress, who were as close to the top of the food chain as I regularly got in Washington. For most senators and representatives, we were somewhere between a necessary inconvenience and an inescapable blight on the landscape. We helped them further their agenda, and they helped us further our careers. To the serious working reporter, the typical member of Congress was judged not on the basis of ideology or charisma, but whether they or their staff returned your phone calls. Or whether or not they would they insult you in public.

Once, determined to get an answer to a particular question after repeated phone calls were not responded to, I cornered Senator Dick Durbin in a hallway in a Senate office building as he left a hearing. He was visibly annoyed. But he gave me an answer.

And no, I don't remember now what the question was.

There were a couple of exceptions to this particular way of using and being used. Senator Paul Wellstone always showed up fifteen minutes early to press conferences in the Senate Press Room and chatted with us as if we were human beings, showing real interest in our lives. And remembering the details.

"I like the beard," I told Wellstone the first time we met. "It makes you look like Leon Trotsky."

He blushed.

Dick Lugar of Indiana also did this sort of thing, though not as often. Once, we talked for ten minutes about farming. He told me about his family farm in Indiana, and I told him that I was lucky for a city kid, having a farm and ranch to go back to occasionally and even work on when I was a teenager.

"That sounds really nice," he said. "Eastern Washington, that's good country. Pretty country."

My work schedule didn't really allow for much in the way of daily prayers, and this cut something of a hole in my life. I would pray when I could, which wasn't often. Sometimes I would pray Friday prayers at the Saudi embassy, and sometimes with a group of Muslims who worked on Capitol Hill in a little ad hoc prayer room in the basement of the Capitol.

But mostly what I liked about this work was that when I was done, I was done. I took nothing home. When the markets weren't open, or Congress wasn't in session, there wasn't an awful lot to do.

There was a plan, of sorts, when BridgeNews hired me. I would spend my time in Washington, learning how Bridge does things, prove myself as a reporter and writer, and then, when an opening became available, I would go to New York and work on the energy desk there. If I proved myself capable of that, then I would go on to the global energy desk in London. And if I proved myself at that, then off to Dubai.

But this was only an informal plan, a verbal agreement, and it was subject to change. Or, as just about every commodities deal states, *force majeure*—circumstances beyond anyone's control that prevent the fulfilling of a contract.

And in the month I took a position covering North American natural gas markets in New York, BridgeNews was hauled into bankruptcy court by a creditor in Texas anxious he wasn't going to get his $35 million back.

It turns out BridgeNews owed all its creditors somewhere in the neighborhood of $1.5 billion. The gluing together of all those unwanted bits and pieces had created an unwieldy company that couldn't keep track of everyone it provided services to.

Or bill them properly. And this most definitely is not a winning business strategy.

My job in New York was a lot more sedentary than in Washington, where I was out and about a lot. Covering natural gas futures involved sitting at my computer while the market was open, writing a preview piece before the market opened, a midday review, and a market wrap after it closed. And if anything interesting happened, writing about that.

BridgeNews' New York offices were located in Three World Financial Center, the tallest in a four-building complex constructed on the soil excavated when the World Trade Center was built in the late 1960s. Three World Financial was home to the world headquarters of American Express, and BridgeNews rented the 28th and 29th floors. Bridge also rented two floors for customer support somewhere in the south World Trade Center tower. Pricey real estate with spectacular views of New York and New Jersey (yes, there is such a thing). During my time there, I gained a new definition of smoggy—not being able to see the Empire State Building from the World Trade Center.

There was no need for this company to have such a prestigious New York address. It would have been one thing if, as commodities reporters, we had floor privileges on the New York Mercantile Exchange or the Board of Trade, or if our jobs regularly took us to meetings, but neither of these was true. We could have easily done this job from cheaper digs in Midtown, or Brooklyn, or Secaucus, New Jersey, or somewhere in Connecticut or Pennsylvania.

Same with our help desk.

The work was a daily grind of phone calls and more phone calls. I've never much liked the telephone, to be honest, though it's the most useful tool a reporter has, and I've made an uneasy peace with it. And we had the same deal with the traders, brokers, and analysts in New York that we had with the civil servants and congressional staffers in DC. No names.

But our sources could be a little more colorful. I remember one afternoon the natural gas futures market had moved maybe two cents the entire day. So I called up a broker, someone I hadn't talked to in a couple of days.

"So, how would you describe the market today?"

"Like watching clams fuck," he said.

I laughed.

"Can I quote you on that?"

"If you can get that past your editors, you may use my full name!"

Bridge found some other uses for me in New York. We put together a daily story during the height of the California power crisis following the state's botched deregulation of wholesale electricity prices, and one day I caught the young traders of Enron—who always struck me as grown-up, amoral versions of Spicoli from *Fast Times at Ridgemont High*—playing fast and loose with overnight power prices thanks to some insider knowledge that one of the nuclear reactors at Arizona's Palo Verde power plant was going to be down that night.

And Bridge put to me work as their UN correspondent.

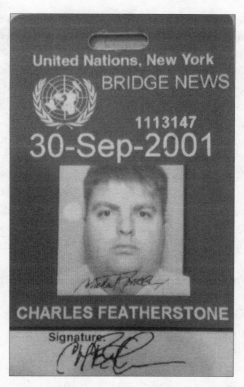

I hate this picture. I look like an angry, redneck Kim Jong-un.

In the summer of 2001, the system of sanctions imposed on Iraq following its annexation of Kuwait in 1990 had fallen into such disrepute, and the UN oil-for-food program was so riddled with corruption, that the Security Council was struggling to replace it with a technology control regime, similar to what the West imposed on the Soviet Union in the 1970s. There was a lot of wrangling over the details, of course, with the United States and Britain arguing for the tightest system possible while France and Russia wanted something much looser.

Our interest, of course, was oil markets. How much Iraqi crude would flow, and when. And under what conditions.

While I sat through a couple of public debates, most of what the Security Council did was in private. Which meant reporters stood around and waited for the ambassadors to come out of the chamber. It wasn't much different than trying to ambush the Secretary of Agriculture, or a member of Congress.

But I got a couple of scoops by being able to talk to Iraqi UN Ambassador Muhammad al-Douri. I'd ask him in Arabic, and while he fingered his prayer beads, he'd always answer me in English.

One day, I was sitting in the diplomat's lounge reviewing my notes and taking a breather when a junior Iraqi diplomat came and sat down with me. I'd seen him trailing Ambassador al-Douri. He was joined by a heavyset Libyan diplomat I'd never met before.

We had coffee and a long conversation on Islamic history and the nature of government in the Arab world.

"The problem is," the Iraqi summed things up, "our governments are not accountable to the people they govern. It is a big problem."

"Yeah," I responded rather flippantly, "but this is a problem across the world. You saw our recent election. We have this problem too."

"But not like us," the Libyan said. The two junior diplomats looked warily at each other.

"Something will break eventually," the Iraqi added, the Libyan nodding in agreement.

He looked at his watch and downed the last of his espresso.

"Thank you for this. I need to go."

"So do I," the Libyan added.

I don't know why those two diplomats trusted me that day to have this talk in front of me, or what they expected me to do with it. I never told my editors. Two weeks later, a rumor swept through the UN building that an Iraqi diplomat had defected to the United States. I tried to find out if this was true, but the diplomat I'd had the very frank conversation with was unwilling to answer anyone's questions.

When Jennifer and I arrived in New York, we were given the keys to the company apartment in Jersey City and told we could stay until we found something permanent. Which was usually two months.

And Jennifer and I did look at a few apartments, in Queens and Brooklyn. But the Bridge bankruptcy quickly morphed from a reorganization into a liquidation. So I asked Pam Conway, who was now my boss's boss, how long Jennifer and I should stay in the corporate apartment.

"Until they throw you out," she said.

Jennifer and I loved New York. It was a wonderful city to wander through, to walk around in, even—or maybe especially—at two in the morning. Manhattan sparkles and glows at night, and there were times when wandering around was itself almost intoxicating.

Before we arrived in New York, I got Jennifer her own cell phone and put my number on speed dial.

"I want you to feel free to wander the city on your own. And call me if you get lost. Give me the intersection you see, and I'll find it on a map"—I made sure to have all the New York transit maps—"and give you directions. Okay?"

But for some reason, the New York subway system made intuitive sense to Jennifer, and she found it easy to make her way around the city. It also seemed like she scoped out every cafe with decent coffee and Pellegrino water south of 14th Street.

One evening, as we were crossing the street—in a proper crosswalk— in the East Village, a taxicab inched its nose forward. Jennifer, who was walking right beside me, looked at the driver and pounded on the hood of the car.

"I'm walking here!" she shouted.

"Who are you and what have you done with my sweet, shy little wife?" I asked her on the other side of the street.

She smiled.

"Well, I was walking there."

I loved what New York did to and for Jennifer.

By early summer of 2001, it became clear Bridge was going to die. Bits and pieces were being sold off for much less than they'd been bought for. The whole thing was coming undone.

For a long time, the managers of BridgeNews tried hard to save the news operation, to find a buyer who would keep all of us, or at least most of us, employed. But it made no sense to buy a whole news agency if you could simply buy the company's contracts to provide news and hire whomever you might need to fill out the coverage.

Eventually, we learned Dow Jones had bought those contracts. And had promised to interview a select number of BridgeNews reporters.

I was one of those reporters.

The ambiance at Dow Jones Newswires hadn't changed. It still felt oppressive, fearful, and unimaginative. On the other hand, they were solvent, and making a profit. Which was something. So, I agreed to the interview. But I really wasn't interested.

"Why do you want to work for Dow Jones?" the interviewer asked me when we were done.

"I don't," I said. And that was that.

It was also the truth. While I may not have been praying that much—I would occasionally duck into an old synagogue in Jersey City a group of Bangladeshis were slowly refurbishing as a *masjid*—I took the demise of BridgeNews as a signal from God that I had no business being a journalist anymore. I could find the work amusing for a while, but it did nothing for my soul. And my soul had to be able to find nourishment and rest in what I did.

I still had no idea what that was, however.

I called Amatzia Baram, an Israeli expert on Iraq and a professor of mine from Georgetown who had taken an interest in my career thanks to a paper I'd written comparing Iraqi and post-WWI German disarmament, and he set up a phone interview for me with Patrick Clawson at the Washington Institute for Near East Policy. Clawson and I talked for the better part of an hour one afternoon, and his suggestion was that I pursue work as an intelligence analyst for a few years, and then consider something at a think tank.

It was kind of Clawson to take the time to talk to me. But as intriguing as the possibility was, I was still unwilling to seriously consider intelligence work. I wasn't sure it was something my soul could live with. And there was my past. I was unwilling to subject myself to that kind of scrutiny. I didn't imagine it going well. Or ending well.

So there I was, in the summer of 2001, stuck. I had no idea where to go. Or what to do.

Sometime in the middle of the summer, I decided to start wearing shorts, a T-shirt, and sandals to work. To a professional job in the American Express corporate headquarters building. I figured, if anyone objected, I would go right back across the Hudson and change. It's not as if my day was busy or anything. Most of us by midsummer were just marking time, waiting for our layoff notices. Or some other opportunity.

The new hires at American Express, all fresh-faced college kids, looked at me funny from behind their stacks of binders and books.

"At least they have jobs. That must be a nice feeling," I said to a Bridge-News editor one morning in the elevator.

"Have you done their job? They work eighty to ninety hours a week. Most of them won't have that job in two years. You don't want it."

But no one said anything. No one made me go back home. No one even seemed to notice.

Except Pam Conway, when she came back from her vacation. "So, these are the shorts I've heard so much about." But she didn't send me home either.

A few of us played hooky, taking long lunches, going to baseball games and movies. One afternoon, we all switched beats, and I covered the sugar market. Our coffee reporter took Jennifer and me on a tour of the coffee tasting room of the New York Board of Trade, and a couple of coffee tasters gave us lessons on slurping and spitting. Jennifer loved it.

This is what happens when you work for a dying company. The rules slowly evaporate.

By early September, I was writing one story a day—on the status of U.S. nuclear power plants. It was an easy thing to write: just take the template, look at the Nuclear Regulatory Commission website, and update the status information—down or running—and the date. And any additional information. It would take me all of five minutes. The rest of the day was mine.

And by late August, those of us who hadn't gone someplace else all got our layoff notices. Our last day of work would be September 15, 2001. With health insurance continuing until the end of October.

That was it. We were done.

I miss BridgeNews. It was an amazing place to work, full of brilliant misfits, incredibly talented and very smart people who didn't quite fit with corporate culture but knew their stuff. Had Bridge not collapsed, I suspect I would still be working there, maybe even made bureau chief by this point, in some far-flung corner of the world, reporting on bamboo futures. Or some such.

13

That Beautiful Tuesday

THE MORNING OF SEPTEMBER 11, 2001, began as most mornings did: the radio went off at 6 a.m., and I lounged in bed, somewhere between consciousness and sleep, until about 6:30.

I love lying in bed in the mornings listening to the radio in that in-between state. Because I love that in-between state, not quite asleep but not quite awake. My wife hates it. She hates getting up in the mornings, and she always grumbles when the radio goes off and she's forced to wake up. What typically woke me in the morning was the BBC World Service on the shortwave. But that summer, the BBC had finally abandoned its last English-language service to North America, and the Caribbean signal I could occasionally leech off of was only really good for about fifteen minutes.

Especially this close to the World Trade Center. The twin towers were murder on shortwave reception, scrambling frequencies and showering much of the shortwave spectrum with noise.

So, I'd learned to settle with National Public Radio. I wasn't happy about that—I missed World Service—but it's what there was.

I showered, made coffee and had breakfast. I thought about getting Jennifer out of bed. After all, a group of us from BridgeNews were planning an outing to A Salt & Battery Fish and Chips in Greenwich Village for lunch. But she looked so sweet sleeping there, and she always got so cranky when I woke her up.

So I let her sleep. It would have been nice to have coffee and breakfast together at American Express, or at one of the many cafes in the World Financial Center, but it wasn't necessary.

I put on a pair of khaki shorts, a striped blue T-shirt, and my sandals, and grabbed my backpack. I had a few books in there, as well as my shortwave radio. Since I'd been at San Francisco State, I almost always took a shortwave radio with me everywhere I went.

"Little one," I said, using my favorite nickname for Jennifer. "Remember we have a lunch outing today. So, go ahead and come over whenever you want. Just lie in bed for now."

"Okay," she mumbled drowsily.

I took the elevator down from our 26th floor apartment—we were still in the Bridge corporate flat in Jersey City—and walked out the front door. It was beautiful that morning, and the sun was just beginning to inch above the skyline of lower Manhattan. The sky was clear blue, a blue I remembered from winter mornings in Southern California.

PATH train or ferry this morning? Oh, it was too beautiful to take the train under the Hudson. This morning was clearly a ferry morning. I walked the short walk, about five minutes, from our apartment to the ferry slip, handed in my ticket, and got on the next boat across the Hudson.

The blue of the sky, the brightness of the sun, all struck me intensely. I stood on the bow of the ferry, pressed myself up against the railing, and felt the spray of the river on my toes and ankles. And the warm breeze in my hair. Trying to take it all in.

"The world is so beautiful today," I thought. "What an amazing, strange and wonderful life I've had."

I looked at the Manhattan skyline. The rising sun had come up behind the South Tower. The World Trade Center did something that morning I'd only ever seen mountains do before—the shadow it cast was visible in the air. I looked up and saw that shadow cut through sky above me. Like that shadow was actually a thing you could touch, something you could grasp and hold in your hands.

Sunrise over Lower Manhattan was almost always spectacular, especially on cloudless mornings like this one. And sunset, especially as the setting sun was reflected in pinks, oranges, yellows and reds in all the steel, glass, polished granite, and burnished aluminum of Lower Manhattan, was very nearly always a thing to behold.

I inhaled. And exhaled. I thought of the fact that Jennifer and I would soon have to leave.

"Remember this sight always," I thought. "It will not be with you much longer."

The ferry docked. I walked past the New York Mercantile Exchange, into the Winter Garden, up an escalator, swiped my ID badge, and took an elevator to the 28th floor of Three World Financial Center. The last week of Bridge. I went to work early, out of habit. Because my one and only story was an early morning story. And, well, just because.

I walked through the maze of cubicles, saying hello as I went. Deborah Kinirons was there. Deb was young, only a couple of years out of college, a graduate of one of the SUNY schools, and she'd been hired as our frozen concentrated orange juice (FCOJ) correspondent. I'd worked with her on a Brazil orange production story once when I was in Washington. FCOJ is where Bridge tended to start commodity reporters who were brand new, and it's where the New York Board of Trade also tended to start traders. It's a fairly simple and stable market, not prone to wild fluctuations.

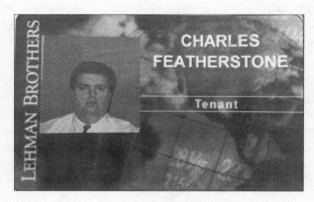

The key to Three World Financial Center.
Note that I'm not wearing a T-shirt in this photo.

My heart would often skip a beat when I looked at Deb. She'd smile and, for a brief moment, I'd see Lauren. When she spoke, though, it was all Long Island.

And Scott Reeves was there too. Scott was a hard-bitten old-timer, a reporter from the days of Underwood typewriters and ever-present Scotch bottles. He'd started his career with the Associated Press in Mississippi, then graduated to covering California government for *The Sacramento Bee* in the 1970s and 1980s. He'd become somewhat notorious after showing up drunk to a press conference—and asking questions—of then-Governor Jerry Brown. He gave up drinking completely not long after.

Scott was opinionated, irascible, and absolutely wonderful to be around. He covered initial public offerings for BridgeNews and had a stuffed cloth doll of Hillary Clinton he kept at his desk. So he could stick pins in her.

He was that kind of conservative.

I sat down at my cubicle and turned on my computer. I made a note of the things I needed to do this week before Bridge was done. Mostly, I needed to grab copies of all my stories off my computer before I left so that

I'd have samples of my work. I'd kept some, but I didn't have a full archive. And I wanted one.

I browsed my e-mail. Nothing new there. I went to the Nuclear Regulatory Commission's website and opened the template for the power plant story, preparing to do my one and only thing for the day.

That's when we heard it.

It's a hard noise to describe, a kind of muffled, oscillating whoosh. It went in and out, going from silent to loud, like very slow helicopter blades or something. And it got louder. Whooosh! Whoosh! WHOOSH!

Then there was a very loud grinding sound.

Heads popped up from behind cubicle barriers.

"What the hell was that?" somebody asked.

I turned around to the side of the building that faced the World Trade Center, where the noise had clearly come from. Suddenly, burning debris fell just outside our office windows: giant chunks of steel, huge twisted pieces of metal. They weren't identifiable as anything.

Between the noise and the shape of some of the debris, I thought at first a helicopter had hit the North Tower. Several reporters who sat at window desks and had seen the whole thing happen were at a loss for words to describe it.

The best view was in our corner conference room, which overlooked the intersection of West and Vesey streets and had a full view of the World Trade Center. I wandered over to the conference room and saw a giant hole on the north face of One World Trade Center. Whatever had hit the building, it had gone clear though.

I looked down. On the ground, thirty floors below us, shards of glass and bits of metal sparkled in the early morning sun. The city began to fill with the sound of sirens.

What about Jennifer? She might have gotten out of bed, might be on a PATH train or somewhere under the World Trade Center. I grabbed my cell phone and punched her speed dial number.

Nothing. The phone was dead.

Then I remembered: that antenna on the top of the north tower. That's not just TV and radio for much of New York. It's also cell phone service. My phone didn't work.

Which meant Jennifer's likely wouldn't either. And I didn't remember the land line number at the corporate apartment.

So, I had no way of getting ahold of Jennifer. For some reason, though, I wasn't worried. I don't know why.

It was not even six in the morning in California, but I called my mother.

"Hello?" she said sleepily. I had woken her up.

"Mom, you probably haven't seen this yet, but something has happened here in New York. We think an airplane has crashed into the one of the World Trade Center towers. I just wanted to let you know I'm okay."

"Mmmph, okay," she said, still not entirely awake.

Scott and Deborah joined me in the conference room. We stared up at the giant hole in the building, sixty floors above us. It belched fire, smoke, and great billows of paper.

"Well, they finally did it," Scott said. As much as I liked and admired Scott, he had a dismal opinion of Islam and Muslims. We would spar on this subject occasionally, and while I was never entirely sure how far I could take the sparring, he always seemed to enjoy it.

It didn't seem to lower his opinion of me.

"I hope not," I said. And I did hope that.

In fact, for those twenty minutes we gawked at that hole, I hoped and prayed fervently that this was just an accident.

"Attention!" The rarely used PA system crackled to life. "This is American Express management. A plane appears to have crashed into the North Tower of the World Trade Center. There is no cause for alarm, and there is no need to evacuate the building. We ask all employees to remain calm, and we will keep everyone updated on the situation. Thank you."

Ambulances and fire trucks gathered on the ground below. They were everywhere, red lights flashing in the cool shadows of Lower Manhattan's deep canyons.

We gawked. We stared. We talked. We tried to make sense of it all. And then we heard it: a roar that came out of nowhere, the roar of a second plane. There it was, a United Airlines jetliner in blue and gray, not far above us. The plane banked, and I could see the sunlight stream through its windows and glint off its shiny metal skin.

The roar got fiercer, as if in that very last moment the pilot was gunning the engines. And then the plane simply disappeared, vanished in fire and smoke as it crashed into and through the southwest corner of the South Tower. Tongues of fire blew through the building.

And that sound. I will never forget that sound—that horrific snap of metal, that shattering of glass. I felt it as much as I heard it.

I turned around. There was a look of stunned horror on Deb's face. There was no mistaking what we'd just seen.

No one waited for American Express to give the evacuation order. Everyone who, just a moment before, had been gawking at the great big hole in the North Tower moved en masse to the center of the building. To leave as fast as we could. I went to my desk, grabbed my backpack, and made my way to the elevators.

"Don't take the elevators!" yelled the same Bridge editor who'd told me not to be envious of the new hires at American Express. "We're in the next tallest building, and if there's another plane coming, we're the most likely target! Take the stairs! Everyone take the stairs!"

Another plane. That possibility had to be taken seriously.

The stairway was crammed with people but everyone was moving quickly. I want to say that people helped those who couldn't move fast, and I think there was some of that. But it was really everyone for themselves that morning.

And so I ran down twenty-eight flights of stairs. As fast as I possibly could. It was surprisingly easy, and I don't remember having to stop or even getting winded.

On the third floor, I knew an alternate way to get to the entrance, one far less crowded that went through American Express's cafeteria. So I took it.

Once I'd left the building, I found myself on the corner of Vesey and West streets. It was chaos. A panicked FDNY captain was directing everyone to go west, to the retaining wall along the Hudson River, and then walk north. I had to get to a ferry, to get to New Jersey, to Jennifer.

As I walked quickly toward the ferry slip, I noticed that the FDNY had set up an ad-hoc triage and treatment station in the space between Three and Four World Financial Center. I saw a man sitting, propped up against the granite wall, covered in blood and holding a bandage or towel or something to his head. He was dressed in what looked like a white chef's shirt and black slacks or jeans. There wasn't much blood on the cloth he was holding, and I looked at the way the blood covered his shirt.

The blood covering him was not his own.

I walked past the New York Mercantile Exchange. There was a huge crowd there at the ferry slip, and New York Waterway, the company that runs the ferry service, hadn't quite figured out how to respond to the situation and was still taking tickets from anyone wanting out of Manhattan.

I looked up. Both towers belched fire and smoke. And heaved billows of paper into the wind, paper that fluttered off to Wall Street and across the East River to Brooklyn. The sun, which earlier had shone so brightly in that clear blue sky, turned a sickly gray-orange behind the smoke.

The fire in both buildings was steady.

The gathered crowd murmured and gasped. And then someone would either slip and fall or throw themselves out of one of the buildings. And the crowd would cry out in unison, "No! Don't! Stop!" A pathetic and powerless plea made as bodies tumbled end over end to the ground.

I watched six people die that way.

At some point, I remembered I had a radio with me. I got it out and fiddled with the dial. The New York CBS affiliate had its broadcasting tower on the Empire State Building, so it was one of the few radio stations still transmitting that morning.

People gathered around me.

"What's happening?" someone asked.

The Pentagon had just been hit by a jetliner, and another plane, believed to be headed either for the White House or the Capitol, was somewhere over Pennsylvania. The FAA had just grounded all air traffic, but two more jetliners were unaccounted for.

And there were reports a bomb had gone off in front of the State Department building in Washington.

"This is the end of the world," someone said.

It felt like that.

I knew I had to get out of southern Manhattan. Because those towers were going to come down, and when they did, they would respect neither power nor position. By this time, New York Waterway had given up on taking tickets and had started moving its entire ferry fleet to the little slip in front of the New York Mercantile Exchange.

But it took a bit. So I stood there, looking up at the burning buildings, the drifting paper, the falling bodies.

And then, as had happened twice before in my life, there were words in my head. Words I knew were not mine. *My love is all that matters.*

But this time there was no electric shock. Nothing turned blue. No breathlessness, no halted prayers. Just these words, gently inhabiting me, words given to me—spoken but not spoken—in the midst of death, terror, and destruction. In the midst of the worst thing that I and everyone else standing there beneath the fire and smoke had ever experienced. *My love is all that matters.*

There was no time to think about this, to contemplate what this might mean. Not that morning, not in that moment. I finally got on a ferry, stood on the stern as it pulled out, watching a couple of NYMEX floor traders, one standing next to me and the other still on the ferry slip—each wore the same company's coat—give each other hand signals as the ferry pulled out.

I stood on the stern of that ferry and wept.

The terrible thing was that the burning buildings in front of me, the hijacked airliners, all made sense to me. I understood this act, the anger behind it. There was a time in my life when I myself could have done it, been part of it, eagerly supported it. I could have learned how to fly a plane only to crash it. I never cared about virgins in the afterlife, but I was angry enough once to believe that this kind of act was a perfectly valid, legitimate way to make a political or even moral point.

To be honest, though, I suppose I would have found myself, at the very last moment, as the building loomed in front of me—when it was too late—saying, "Well, this was probably not the best idea I've ever had."

It was as if God had grasped me by the scruff of the neck and made me look. "Behold what you could have done. See what you once wanted. See what it *means*."

I was living through someone else's violent vengeance fantasy. I'd had so many of my own. And now I was being shown what that kind of vengeance led to. What it really meant to want to get even with the world. The pain, suffering, destruction and death that could bring.

Because whatever ideological and religious reasons Muhammad Atta, or Khaled Sheikh Muhammad, or even Osama bin Laden himself would give for this day, at bottom it was all about vengeance. About inflicting pain. About getting even.

When the ferry got to New Jersey, we all hurried off. The police were ordering everyone to move on. I walked home to the corporate apartment, took the elevator up, and found Jennifer watching a fuzzy television signal, a look of sorrow and fear on her face.

I held her. And wept. For how long I don't remember.

"I don't know why, but I didn't worry about you. I just knew you were okay," she told me.

There was a knock on the door. It was Frank, our next-door neighbor. Frank had been an engineer for Grumman in the 1960s, where he helped design the lunar lander. Currently, he worked for a venture capital firm. Frank had been working out in the gym in Six World Trade Center when everyone had been ordered to leave, and his wallet—with all his credit cards—was still there. Now it was under several stories of rubble.

"You need to see this. The South Tower has just collapsed."

We looked at his television. He had cable, so his picture was clear.

Frank placed a call to his bank; we left him as he was wrangling with a representative. We went out to a little park that jutted into the Hudson River and sat together. The sight we beheld was strange. One lonely World Trade Tower stood there in the late morning sun, framed by haze, still belching fire, smoke and paper.

"It's going to come down," I told Jennifer. "Watch."

We sat for a few minutes. And then the top five floors of the North Tower wobbled from side to side for a bit as weakened steel began to give way. And the top just came straight down, the antenna flopping about and falling as the collapse began, leaving a cluster of columns in the center—as if the building were being peeled—that themselves collapsed just after the rest of the building.

A man in a NYMEX trading jacket stood on the shore in front of us, shouting and waving his fist.

We sat there, Jennifer and I, watching the dust rise over southern Manhattan. The World Trade Center, which had loomed so large and seemed so permanent, like a pair of mountains, just hours before, now was gone. Flattened.

All that remained was smoldering rubble.

The first fighter jets roared over New York Harbor about twenty minutes after the towers fell. I was sitting in the apartment, stunned, when I heard them.

The sound put me into an absolute panic. I scrambled for cover, looked for a place to hide, tried to find something to crawl under, until I realized what it likely was. Jennifer tried to calm me, but there were tears in her eyes as she saw how frightened I was.

It was the first time the sound of jet planes drove me into a terrified frenzy. It would not be the last.

A little after noon, the wind shifted, and all the smoke, paper, and debris that had been blowing over Brooklyn since a little before eight that morning suddenly started falling over Jersey City. The smell was horrific, like burning styrofoam and plastic, with odors I'd never smelled before and haven't smelled since. The smoke was full of soot, like a forest fire, and some of it fell on our balcony.

But this wind shift didn't last long. And soon it was blowing back on Brooklyn again.

Jets roared over New York Harbor every twenty minutes or so. Try as I might, there was no getting used to the sound.

Anything that could float was being pressed into service—ferryboats, tugs, yachts from North Cove Harbor—and people, all of them covered in the gray dust of the World Trade Center, clamored over the retaining wall to get on board. The large yacht I'd always seen berthed in the little cove came across to New Jersey covered in people, all gray with dust except for the orange of their life vests.

And even then, not all wore life vests.

That afternoon, the New Jersey National Guard began assembling a field hospital in Liberty State Park. A U.S. Navy ship came and anchored off the Staten Island ferry terminal. Ambulances began arriving from cities across the Northeast, from as far away as West Virginia. People anticipated a huge search and rescue operation.

But there was almost no one to rescue. And that became clear by Tuesday evening. The ambulances that had come so far began to leave.

I called people—my mother, my father, some old friends—to let them know I was okay. The talk I had with my father was the most memorable one. He'd been dealing with the trauma of Vietnam for a few years, and he talked to me differently that day—and has ever since.

As if we now shared something, something bigger than words, that we'd never shared before.

As the sun set, I looked at the commuter parking lots behind our apartment building. Usually, by this time, they were almost completely empty.

But there were still cars there. Not many, but enough to remind you that there would be some who would never go home.

That night, the Red Cross set up an aid station near the ferry slip in Jersey City. Jennifer and I, wanting somehow to help, went down and schlepped a few things. But there were so many hands, so many people aching to help, that there was little for us to do except watch and get in the way. Some of the ironworkers who'd been busy building the new Goldman Sachs headquarters had their gear and were waiting to cross the river to Manhattan.

"They need people who know how to deal with steel," one told me.

The sun rose over New York and New Jersey the following morning and it was dead quiet. Quiet like it was out in the fields of my grandfather's ranch. You could sit outside and hear nothing but the wind. That quiet, punctured by the roar of fighter jets flying low over New York, prevailed all day.

And now I had time to think.

The world had changed. Things that had never made any sense to me now suddenly did. I'd always thought the Christian doctrine of original sin was silly, even illogical. "No bearer of burdens can bear the burdens of another," the Qur'an says. And I believed that. We were accountable not for the sins of others but for our own.

Now, though, the confession "We are captive to sin and cannot free ourselves" made sense to me. Not intellectually—I still think many attempts to explain this are silly—but intuitively. It isn't a thing to be explained. It is an explanation, a confession. It explained the world.

No one deserved to die that day. No one had it coming. The bond traders of Cantor Fitzgerald who had arrived for work that morning at their top-floor offices in One World Trade Center had done nothing to earn their deaths. But there will come a day, for all of us, when there is no getting out alive, no making it to tomorrow. I'd known this—this is one of the realities of human existence most religions try to deal with—but I didn't really *know* it. Until the morning of September 11, 2001.

And there was what God had told me in the midst of it all: *My love is all that matters.*

I still wasn't sure to make of it. But I knew that in the midst of suffering, fear, violence, death, and destruction, what really mattered was love. God's love for us. This was new to me. I think I'd spent my entire life getting ready for this message, but it was completely new to me.

I didn't have a religious language to deal with this. The Qur'an is about many things, but it isn't about love. Muslims certainly do care for each other—love each other—and for non-Muslims around them, and God clearly cares for humanity, but the Qur'an lacks a language of love. I had been given something amazing, something I had no idea what to do with.

On Thursday, Jennifer and I met with some friends from Bridge. We had lunch. We went to Central Park, rented some rowboats, and later walked madly through streets empty of traffic. That evening, I stood with Jennifer in Times Square as President George W. Bush drove through.

It was the first time in my life I felt safe, even comfortable, in a crowd.

The following week, while taking a bath, I slipped in the tub and tore open my right knee shattering the soap dish. Jennifer nearly had a breakdown. She'd already come face to face with my mortality. Our friends Vince and Jessica drove us to the nearest hospital, where Vince had to step in and make sure I was seen. The wounds were pretty deep, and I had a towel wrapped tightly around my knee to make sure it didn't bleed.

Something I learned in the army, actually.

The internists on staff that night were not sure how to deal with my injury. As I let go of the towel, and they unwrapped it, a thin mist of blood squirted from one of the cuts. They wanted to take X-rays, to make sure there was no porcelain left in the wound. In their uncertainty, they called an orthopedic surgeon.

He angrily charged into the emergency room about five minutes later.

"Who called me?" he demanded. As if he'd been roused from a nap.

One of the internists explained the situation. The surgeon didn't even talk to me. I was just a wound to him, and a wound he referred to solely in the third person.

"You don't need an X-ray," he said, putting on a rubber glove. "You want to see if there's anything left in the wound? Just run your finger through it."

Which he then did, and it felt very weird.

"See, he's not screaming. There's no porcelain in the wound." He tore his latex glove off and tossed it on the floor. "Now don't bother me!"

When I related the incident to Dr. John Hartwell, he laughed. "Yep, that sounds just like the bedside manner you get from an orthopedic surgeon."

We had scheduled a last-day-of-Bridge get-together that Friday. It was still on, and Jennifer and I showed. I went to get a beer—and found Mike Wallace of *60 Minutes* tending bar. Apparently, important people were upstairs being interviewed.

"I hear you've had an additional adventure," Pam Conway said to me after I sat down.

"Yep. Wanna see my stitches?" She said no, but I showed them off anyway.

A little later, over the din, I looked at my now former boss.

"Thank you for hiring me," I said.

"Really? You don't regret coming to work here?"

"Nope. I've done some amazing things, been some amazing places, met a lot of really interesting people. Even after all this, I wouldn't trade any of it. For anything."

I don't remember how she responded to that. She did suggest, however, that Jennifer and I might want to sue the building over my wounded knee.

A few days later, Jennifer and I packed the truck and left New York. We didn't really know where were going, not in any real sense. But somehow, that didn't matter so much anymore.

❧❦❧

Actually, we knew exactly where we were going. After September 11, my mother invited Jennifer and me to come stay with her in Southern California. I didn't really want to. I had my heart set on renting a cabin somewhere in upstate New York and holing up for the winter.

But both Jennifer and my mother had been shaken by recent events, and my mother especially wanted to see me. So, we headed west.

I was still not entirely sure what to do with myself now. But one thing had changed—I was willing now to consider intelligence work with a seriousness I never had. I still knew that my past would be a problem, and any security clearance process would be an excruciating excavation of my life. I was under no illusions about any of this.

However, the events of Tuesday, September 11, made all of that a risk worth taking. I figured I knew some things that might be worth knowing, things that would help in tracking down the people who had attacked us.

And yes, I said *us*. For the first time in my life, America actually felt like my home, as opposed to some place I accidentally found myself in—some place that didn't seem to want me. People had attacked the city where I lived, right across the street from where I worked, and I had watched others die.

If there was something I could contribute, then I wanted to. I knew it would be difficult and unpleasant, but I didn't care. I was willing. There would come a time, I thought, when as Americans we would need to seriously ask ourselves what we brought to this, because September 11, 2001, didn't come out of nowhere. There was a lot of very real anger toward the United States among Muslims, and a lot of it very justified. But I also thought that needed to wait.

So I did some looking online and found that a group of CIA recruiters would be at a job fair at Cal Poly Pomona. I readied a couple of résumés and made my way to their recruiting table. I handed my résumé to the recruiter, who took one look at it and became very excited.

"We'll give you a call. I can almost promise that!"

And they did, inviting me to a special orientation for candidates held in a hotel in El Segundo, just south of Los Angeles International Airport.

The drive in was a typical Southern California freeway excursion. I think I took the 10 to the 110 to the 105. I do remember being on the 105, passing by the airplanes at LAX and then seeing the tall buildings of downtown Los Angeles in the distance. I had to pull over and just weep for a bit. It was the first time I'd seen both together since . . . well, since that day. And it was hard to take.

I don't remember much about the actual orientation session. It was halfway between "we're interested in you" and "we'd like to offer you a job." Mostly, it outlined what the hiring process would look like if we were selected. We'd made it this far, so we'd already passed some level of pre-screening. There'd be more screening if we were actually selected.

A week or two later, I received a formal offer from the CIA as a Central Asia analyst at the Counterterrorism Center. I looked at that letter and thought, "Of all the jobs they could offer, this looks like something I could, in good conscience, do."

They also invited me to visit the Counterterrorism Center. The people I was going to work with were interested in meeting me.

So, Jennifer and I packed the truck and headed back east. We rented an apartment in the same complex in Alexandria, Virginia, where we'd lived when I worked for BridgeNews in DC. And got the rest of our stuff out of storage in Jersey City.

I called the CIA and arranged the visit. Once that was done, they would arrange the security interview. So, I drove to the CIA headquarters in

Langley, passed through security, and left my cell phone and PDA in the car. Just as the signs told me to.

I looked at the main building, and with its antennas and dishes on top of the roof, I suddenly thought of the Naval Postgraduate School in Monterey.

My first reaction: "This is my father's world, and I have no business being here."

I got a nice tour of the Counterterrorism Center, a somewhat chaotic cube farm in one of the Langley building's many basements. I talked with a few future colleagues and had a lengthy sit-down with the person who would be my boss. It was strange, as most of the work would involve using a computer all day long, and it didn't look much different than sitting and covering a traded commodity for a wire service. The computers were nicer, and the information sources broader, and a lot of cubicles had been personalized. Not as chaotic as Bridge (no deep-sea fishing lures or Lego kits), but it didn't feel like a slave galley either. They didn't let me loose in the place, and the tour was over in about ninety minutes, but there was nothing in that one main room, or the little offices where the managers worked, that they weren't willing to let me see.

Within the week, I received instructions for the security interview. I showed up at a nondescript office building in northern Virginia with a slip of paper that I was supposed to give to someone when I arrived there.

There were a lot of forms to fill out. There was a medical exam (I discovered I have a 15 percent hearing loss in my left ear), and a half-hour conversation with a psychiatrist.

"Well," I said with some sense of embarrassment, "there's the matter of my military discharge. I'm not that proud of what happened."

He looked at me from behind his desk, a big man with thick glasses and a beard that looked a bit like a vacant lot overgrown with weeds.

"I wouldn't worry about that," he said, looking through my paperwork. "We've seen it, and we understand that things happen when you're 19."

And then came the security interview.

I was escorted to a small blue room without windows or mirrors. The woman who interviewed me that afternoon had a thick folder with her. Apparently, that was me. She explained to me how the polygraph worked—hers was a laptop computer—and that she would be asking me a series of questions, all of which had one correct answer: no.

At this point, I need to say I take all of this at face value. It is possible they knew more about me—about my past, where I'd been, whom I'd known—than they let on. But nothing in those two days more than vaguely suggests that they did.

I don't remember all five questions. Three were fairly mundane, but two involved terrorism. One dealt with providing financial support for terrorist groups and organizations, and the other I don't remember. Membership, maybe.

And she told me that I was failing the two terrorism-related questions.

The moment of truth. So, much of what I have recounted in this book, I told her. What was supposed to take an hour took three. She took fairly copious notes.

She worked with me to reword the questions so that I could effectively and "truthfully," according to the polygraph, answer "no."

And it wasn't working.

"I've had people confess to murder in these sessions," she told me. "So there isn't anything I haven't heard."

But her eyes told me different. This she had not heard.

She got up and left. She was gone for a while before coming back.

"You'll need to come back tomorrow so we can continue this," she said, handing me another piece of paper.

So I came back the following day. And was escorted to a different office, a larger one, painted white with a large mirror along one wall. And my interviewer was different. He was tall, thin, with a mustache that didn't quite seem to fit. He also didn't look much like the photo on his ID badge. Which didn't bother me, since my father would go years between ID badges at General Dynamics and so didn't always look very much like the younger self in the photo.

He hooked me up to the polygraph.

"Feet flat on the ground. Relax. Don't try to control your breathing," he said.

That morning was much like the previous afternoon—trying to make all five answers come out "no." And failing—at least according to my interviewer.

But he began asking different questions, and about an hour before lunch, I got a very uneasy feeling. This felt less like a security interview and more like the beginning of a criminal investigation.

"Did you know any of the 9/11 hijackers?"

"Not that I know of," I said. Which was true. I had scanned their faces closely, wondering if I'd ever come across any of these people. Not that I knew of—but then, I'd met so many people, and was so bad with names, that I couldn't be sure.

"Did you ever meet John Walker Lindh?" he asked, referring to the young American who had been captured while fighting with the Taliban in Afghanistan.

No, I said, I'm a lot older than he is, and had left the Bay Area long before he became Muslim.

"What were you doing at the World Trade Center on September 11?"

I worked there. An answer I'm not sure he really believed.

After lunch, he gave up any pretense that this was a security interview and began asking for names, dates, places, people. I answered every question I could, but I wasn't sure any of it was going to be enough. I began to wonder whether I would even be going home that day.

In the late afternoon, after taking a short break, he came back in, sat down in front of me instead of at his desk, and looked at me.

"Is there anything you might learn about CIA that might make you leak information to the press?"

What do you mean? I asked.

"Is there anything CIA might do that would make you question your loyalty to the organization or your oath of allegiance?"

I wasn't sure how to answer this question.

"You mean like if Alex Jones is right and Usama bin Laden is on the payroll? That kind of thing?"

He didn't respond. I think he took my question as answer enough.

And then he asked me two questions that hit me hard.

"Why should we trust you? And what made you change?"

The answer to the first question was easy. You shouldn't trust me. I was stupid to even try this. I knew it was going to end like this. I had wasted my time and theirs.

But the second question I hadn't given a lot of conscious thought to. Why had I changed? Because God met me in the midst of terror and death and told me that the real purpose of human life—of my life—was love. Because over the years, love had slowly transformed an angry young man eager to douse the world in gasoline and set it on fire to someone who, while not entirely stripped of anger, was able to find, to see, to experience the love of God in some of the most barren, loveless places human beings could make.

And even to begin to love back.

But that day, electrodes attached to my limbs and wrapped around my chest, I couldn't give that answer. And I'm not sure that answer would have mattered. Not there. Not in that place.

Quitting time—5 p.m.—arrived. He unhooked me.

"We're done today."

"I'm free to go?" I asked. Truly uncertain if I was.

"Of course," he said. "And you can come back, and we can keep trying, but really, given your situation, I can make no guarantees about the success of this."

No. Of course not.

Still, I got home and wanted to curl up in a ball. I spent the next few hours wondering if the FBI would show up at my doorstep and haul me away. Of course not, my rational mind said, they already had me and didn't need to let me go. But I was drenched in fear.

The following morning, I called a special phone number.

"I'd like to withdraw my application for employment," I said.

The person on the other end of the phone seemed incredulous.

"You mean you wish to self-terminate?"

What a nifty little bit of jargon. It sounded so brutal, so permanent. I had visions of sitting cross-legged in a Pentagon parking lot, dousing myself with gasoline and setting myself on fire. No, I did not want to "self-terminate," thank you very much. I just no longer wanted to go through this process.

"Sure, yes, fine, please, whatever," I said.

When I called my mother to tell her what I had done, she told me she was relieved. Her father would be too.

"Grampie thought there would be nothing but trouble for you in working for the CIA," Mom said.

She was probably right. I'm not a company man, and my sense of loyalty extends only to the people I love, and who love me, as well as the ideas and ideals I cherish. It is almost impossible for me to be loyal to institutions or abstractions, largely because I have found them so much like school—intolerant and brutal. Loyalty to these things has always meant "you must love us, regardless of how we treat you." Had I come across something I thought the world should know, I would have wrestled with it for a bit but more than likely leaked it. I don't believe governments should keep secrets, especially from the people they govern.

And because of this, I likely would have ended up in very real trouble, trouble I could not have even begun to wriggle out of.

Five days later, still feeling a little paranoid, I came across a job advert on a journalism website from the Saudi Press Agency in Washington that looked like it was written straight from my résumé.

"Someone's fucking with me," I said to Jennifer. I sent them a résumé and some clips anyway, and got the job.

Not long after all this, Jennifer and I were sitting, drinking coffee and reading. I put my book down and looked at her.

"I think we should find a church," I said. I had no idea where this had come from.

Jennifer gets this sweet little grin on her face when something good happens to her. With this question, her eyes sparkled. And her grin got very big and very sweet.

"Okay," she said. I'd rarely seen her this happy.

We tried a couple of places, all Lutheran because of Jennifer's background, but nothing fit well. Then, one afternoon, while out driving, we saw a Lutheran church that advertised all of its worship services.

Including an Amharic language service on Saturday evening.

"I didn't know there were Ethiopian Lutherans!" I said to Jennifer while we drove past. "That makes them interesting. I think we should try this church out."

We fell in love with Peace Lutheran Church in Alexandria, a congregation in the Evangelical Lutheran Church in America, almost immediately. This was an amazing little community of people, incredibly open and accepting, many of them "refugees" from other churches—Roman Catholic, Baptist, more conservative flavors of Lutheranism—because they felt unwanted where they were. They were, most of them, simple, gentle people who loved and struggled with God, who worshiped and prayed and tried to make sense of the world. And how God was active and present in it.

In this place, with these people, I slowly learned that we'd all met the same God, a God who proclaimed love to the world in the suffering and pain of human existence. Even as we struggled with that suffering and pain. It wasn't any one single thing we liked. It was just being with them, being accepted and loved in that place.

And they taught me who it was I'd really met that day underneath the World Trade Center—it was the risen Jesus Christ who had spoken to me that morning, who had met me in fire and fear, who had told me, "My love is all that matters."

For a time I lived in two religious worlds. On Sundays, I worshiped with Jennifer. At work for the Saudi Press Agency, I prayed with the tiny group of Muslims in our office, and then when we moved to the Saudi embassy, I prayed there. I was such a regular that when I got a job with the *Saudi Gazette* in Jeddah, the consular officials in the embassy stamped my work visa "Muslim" without even asking for the requisite proof that I actually was Muslim.

I'd worshiped for more than a year without taking communion. It didn't make any sense to me, and I wasn't going to do something that made no sense.

But one Sunday, it just did. And for the first time, I ate the bread and drank the cup. Jesus was here, with us, offering himself to us.

"Thank you, Charles, for joining us in the meal this morning," Pastor Mark Olsen said to me after we were done.

It also didn't take much time at Peace Lutheran for something odd to start happening.

"You should be a pastor," someone told me one morning after worship. "You would make a very good pastor."

I'm not sure where this came from. Jen and I had only been there a month, and I wasn't even baptized. But several other people told me the same thing.

I didn't really know what it meant to be a pastor. I wasn't raised with it, as Jennifer was, and I didn't grow up in a church. What did it mean? And who was I that God would call me to this? No, I tucked this in the back of my mind. It was not something I was willing to consider. Not seriously.

And yet. It was a call that wouldn't stay tucked away. Something about this really spoke to me, even though I had no idea why.

After a year with the Saudi Press Agency, I took a job as an editor with the *Saudi Gazette* in Jeddah, Saudi Arabia. I had few, if any, expectations of life in Jeddah, and so I enjoyed being there a great deal more than I did Dubai. However, the *Gazette* hired me to do a job—business editor—that was already filled. And I was more or less on my own to figure out what else to do. And I wasn't very good at that.

I was one of several Americans brought in to help relaunch *The Saudi Gazette* as a tabloid, and we were all brought in on visit visas. The hope was they could be converted to proper work visas through connections the paper's owners had with the interior minister, Prince Sultan ibn Abdul Aziz. As the process dragged on, our visas expired and we were asked to stay on— to work and live in the Kingdom of Saudi Arabia illegally. Which we did.

Then *The New Yorker* published an exposé of life at the *Saudi Gazette*, and suddenly no one in the Saudi government wanted to be responsible for expediting our work permits. We would have to leave, apply for permanent visas in the U.S., and then come back that way. Through the proper channels.

I took the opportunity to say thank you but no, there's no point to my being here given there's not enough for me to do.

Which was a pity. I wanted very much to go on *umrah*—the minor pilgrimage—to pray in Makka with thousands of other Muslims, to see the center of the Islamic world. To walk around the *ka'aba*. To see Makka. And we tried to make it happen, but concluded that my visa limited my movements to Jeddah governate. It was possible that the soldiers at the checkpoint on the Jeddah-Makka highway would let me go through, but they could just as easily detain me.

And no one wanted that.

Upon returning to the United States, I quickly got a job as assistant editor at *Oil Daily*. But this was it for journalism, I told myself. The last couple of jobs had been to pay rent, buy groceries, provide coffee for Jennifer, and keep my student lender at bay.

One evening, Pastor Mark Olsen visited our tiny apartment in Alexandria.

"So, what needs to happen to get me baptized?" I asked.

"How soon do you want that to happen?"

And I was baptized a couple of weeks later, on Pentecost Sunday, 2004. Jennifer never looked so sweet or beautiful as she did that day.

"You look like you've gotten everything you've ever wanted in life," I said to her.

She smiled. "Just about!"

And I slowly began to surrender to this call. All throughout my last year at *Oil Daily* I struggled with the sense that God was asking me to become something more—something much more—than I was. I had no idea what that meant, what it would entail. Only that I had gone as far as I could on my own.

It became clear to everyone that I would go to seminary. Even me.

"I look forward to the church that gets you," said Christine Howlett, one of my biggest supporters in the congregation. The folks at Peace knew my story—or most of it. And she laughed, taking great joy in just how different I was.

"And they're going to say, 'But he *looks* like one of us!'"

I filled out all the paperwork for candidacy for ordained ministry in the ELCA and took the psychological tests I needed to take. I met with the candidacy committee for the Metropolitan Washington, DC Synod. All fourteen or sixteen of them. It was very intimidating, almost terrifying, meeting with all these stoic Lutheran pastors and academics, trying to answer questions asked in their strange church language.

On our way to seminary . . .

Still, they accepted my candidacy for ministry.

Mark Olsen and I sat in his car afterwards. We prayed, and then he looked at me.

"He is a chosen instrument of mine to carry my name before the Gentiles and kings and the children of Israel," Mark said, quoting Jesus's words to Ananias from Acts. "For I will show him how much he must suffer for the sake of my name."

I don't know whether Mark Olsen was perceptive or prophetic.

Or a little of both.

14

"And This Is Who I Am"

WHAT STRUCK ME MOST about Uptown Lutheran Church was the smell—
the smell of unwashed bodies, of unwashed clothes, of stale cigarettes, of
hard-edged coffee, of cheap cleansers tasked with hiding all of the other
smells. The smell of a wet that could never quite get dry.

I'd walked into this place near the corner of Lawrence and Sheridan in
one of Chicago's more troubled neighborhoods one cold January morning.
Uptown was a storefront outreach church, somewhere between actual worshiping congregation and social service agency. It was a warm place where
the homeless or the neighborhood poor could stay when it was cold, a cool
place to stay when it was too hot out. And most of the people who came in
through the doors were poor, or homeless, or mentally ill, struggling with
demons great and small.

And they knew they could find something resembling a safe place
here. They could find someone who would listen, who would take them seriously, who would talk to them about a God who loved and cared for them.

Tell them they were not alone. That they had not been forgotten.

When I first walked into Uptown to do several months of clinical pastoral education (CPE), my heart sank. I had worked on Capitol Hill, been to
the White House, covered the United Nations, had an expense account and
wandered the edges of Wall Street as a reporter. I'd traveled the world. And
here I was, brought down, reduced to dealing with junkies and drunks, the
very poor, people who probably couldn't have told you who the president of
the United States was, much less say they'd met him.

And to boot, this was the last place in the world that wanted me. I had
not been able to get into CPE during my first year at seminary—one hospital
supervisor, at the end of our interview, told me she was afraid she was going

to spend the entire summer fighting with me—and I wasn't sure afterward that any program would take me.

If I couldn't finish one unit of clinical pastoral education successfully, then this whole adventure, this ridiculous call from God, would be over.

So, I was very grateful when Sister Barbara of the Urban CPE program in Chicago accepted me. Most seminarians do clinical pastoral education in a hospital or a similar setting. But the Urban CPE put seminarians in a very different kind of place—mission outreach churches like Uptown, halfway houses for those recently hospitalized but with no safe place to recover, even community organizing and advocacy.

Uptown was the only place with an opening that January.

"Yeah, we'll take you," the pastor, Robert Lesher Jr., told me over the phone. "If you can deal with being here, we can deal with having you."

Lesher was a tall, lanky man who looked like he could have been one of my father's younger brothers. He was kind, gentle, and authoritative, the kind of person I wished my father had been.

As soon as I let go of my ego, abandoned the sense of who I was that I'd held to so tightly, and simply lived into the fact that this is where I was going to be, that God had called me to be here, I found Uptown to be a wonderful, amazing, Spirit-filled place where the love of God shone in some of the most astounding ways.

One morning, after an Alcoholics Anonymous meeting, I was sitting at the front desk when Eileen, who almost always attended the morning AA meetings at Uptown, approached. Eileen had been beautiful once. But a life on the streets, a life as an addict, had worn her down. It was impossible to tell just how old she was. She could have been my age, or younger, or much older.

She leaned in, almost whispering what she wanted. The room was noisy, and it was hard to hear. She spoke up, but clearly she didn't really want anyone to hear what she was asking.

"Um, I want to know, how much, um, how much would it cost to get a priest like you out to my house to visit my mother," she said.

Cost? Where did you come from that getting a priest to make a home visit cost money?

I said, "It won't cost anything. I'd be glad to come visit. When would be a good time?" Eileen thought for a moment.

"I need to ask my mom. She has cancer, and she's very sick, and I'm taking care of her." She stood up. "Thank you. Oh, we're Catholic, by the way. I hope that's okay."

"It's fine," I said.

I had no idea what I would do. I'd never made a home visit before. Plus, I was a Lutheran seminarian visiting a Catholic home. What prayers would be appropriate? I looked through my *Occasional Services* book and trolled the library for anything similar from the Catholic Church that I could possibly use.

"The worst thing you could do," said a seminary colleague of mine whose mother had once been a nun, "is to pretend you are a Catholic priest. You won't be able to, and she'll likely figure it out. So don't."

The apartment where Eileen lived with her mother was small, carved out of the first floor of what had been—maybe a century ago—a very nice two-story Chicago house. Eileen told me she was taking care of her mother as a way of showing her family that she was finally serious about staying clean and sober. Trying to make up for the time she wasn't.

Mary lay in a big wooden bed, a tiny, white-haired and very pale woman writhing in pain. She looked up at me, in my clerical collar, and managed a weak smile.

"Thank you, Father, for coming," she said, her voice a sweet but tired Irish lilt.

I sat down next to her and she took my hand. I was in over my head—I had absolutely no idea what to do. But I was here, committed.

"Father, I'm dying," she said. "I don't know long it will be, but it won't be long now. And I need to know . . . I need to know that I'm forgiven. I've done a lot of things, bad things, in my life, and I need absolution."

I squeezed her hand gently.

"Well, I can assure that God does forgive you for whatever you have done," I said, fumbling with my service book, finding a prayer, and saying that prayer with her. But she needed a ritual, a ritual she had probably seen many times in her life, one that would give her comfort and assurance. And I could not, and would not, do that ritual.

"Well, there might be a problem," she said, wincing with the pain. "I was never confirmed, so I don't think I'm a proper Catholic."

Oh my dear Mary, I wanted to say, that's okay. I'm not a proper priest, either.

"That doesn't matter to God," I said. "But I will need to find you a priest who can do what you need. It's . . . It's not something I know how to do. Is that okay? I'll make sure he gets here."

She nodded. The silence felt awkward to me. I prayed again, made the sign of the cross over her, and then said I needed to go.

"Thank you, Father," she said. "Thank you."

Several weeks later, Eileen told me her mother had died. She thanked me for the time I came to visit, told me that several priests had been to see her, and invited me and my wife to her mother's wake.

It was fascinating to see Eileen with her family, to get a glimpse of who she could have been. The people we meet at Uptown almost feel like pod people, all of them born in a zucchini patch, out-of-the-womb addicted or mentally ill, without family or roots or community. Atomized individuals with no past and no future. People who belonged to no one. One afternoon, I looked out upon the dayroom and thought to myself, "No mother ever held a baby and said, 'I hope you grow up to smoke crack and have schizophrenia and live on the streets in constant fear for your life.'" All of these people were once the focus of someone's hopes and dreams.

And here was Eileen, with brothers and sisters. A teenage son who was clearly hers, a boy she long ago gave (or was forced to give) to an older brother to raise, and a five-year-old ginger-haired girl, her face full of freckles. Eileen was a gracious and gregarious host, and there was a hint of the physical beauty that life on the street had long since worn away.

Yet her family seemed wary. How long would this last? Perhaps she'd been clean before, made promises before, only to find the street, the drugs, far more attractive.

The truth is, so many at a place like Uptown show up because they are people without a past, a family, a community. For so many, the drugs, the alcohol, or the mental illness set fire to their lives and destroyed everything. By the time they walk into a place like Uptown for warmth, for coffee, for clean socks, for one more attempt at rehab, there's nothing left.

As Jennifer and I sat at a small table sipping beer, her older brother walked over.

"Thank you, Father, for seeing our mum," he said. "And thank you for looking after our sister."

There was something right about Uptown, about my being in this smelly, miserable little storefront church. I had no idea what it was. It just felt right. This was the ragged edge of the world, and somehow I understood I belonged here in a way I'd never belonged anywhere else in my life. Proclaiming God's love to people who felt themselves so terribly unloved and abandoned.

"Pastor, I have question for you," began an all too typical conversation with so many of the people who wandered through Uptown. "Do you think God is punishing me for my sins by making me homeless? Is God punishing me by making me mentally ill? Because it feels like God is punishing me. It feels like God hates me."

No, I would say. I don't know why you are here. I don't know why you struggle with voices in your head. I do know your sins cannot be so bad that God has singled you out and put you here because of them. Others have sinned far worse, and they aren't here. So, I don't know why you're here. I do know that even here God is with you. God is here, in this place. God loves you. That love, and not your sins, is what matters.

I know it makes no sense, I'd say, given where you are. But trust me— God loves you. God's love is all that matters.

So many of the people I have known—beginning with my wife—have seen the pain, abuse, and suffering in their lives as God's judgment. And they are inclined to despair, believing themselves beyond the love of God, beyond any human mercy. They don't need a word of judgment because they live with that word every day.

They need a word of love.

It's a simple thing, a word of love. But it's no small thing.

In his final evaluation, Lesher put it simply: "Charles is a natural at this."

Lesher left to take a call in Wisconsin, and I was hired for two months as interim pastor. A couple of days after this started, I was in the dayroom, sitting at the front desk, looking at all the people sitting in the room.

And it came to me. There was something else Jesus told me on September 11, 2001. Something I had not heard that day, something I was unable to hear that day, something I could only hear because I was in this place. *And this is who I am.*

Fear. Death. Suffering. Utter powerlessness in the face of terror and destruction. Poverty. Addiction. Helplessness. Mental illness. Cast aside. Clinging to life on the raggedest edge there is. This is how God is most incarnate, enfleshed, *here*, present with us in the mess that is our world. This is our God, aching and weeping and cowering and bleeding with us, dazed and confused and frightened and uncertain. *My love is all that matters. And this is who I am.*

I'm still working on what that last bit really, truly means.

Seminary was the hardest thing I've ever done. By far. Even harder than army basic training, which up until I started at the Lutheran School of Theology at Chicago (LSTC) in the fall of 2006 had been the most difficult thing

I'd ever attempted to do. I was able to finish basic training in the allotted eight weeks. But my four-year seminary program took six years.

Seven, actually, if you count the extra year I had to take to wait and redo candidacy for ministry.

The academic work wasn't hard—a whole semester at Georgetown was more intellectually and academically challenging than all three years of classes at LSTC. Even the language classes weren't all that hard, though I found Koine Greek to be a mess of a language that made Czech and Russian, with their handful of case endings and zillions of pronouns, seem easy and intelligible by comparison. Hebrew was a something of a refresher for Arabic, though I had to be careful with vocabulary, as Hebrew and Arabic words might share roots but not necessarily share meanings.

No, it was hard because I was still very much a stranger, though that was no longer obvious. Blue eyes are not so unique among the Lutherans. I was an outsider, almost completely unfamiliar with the customs and the culture, but because I was here, studying to become a pastor, there was an expectation that I understood it all, that I knew all the rules. So any difficulty or failure was not indicative of ignorance or unfamiliarity, but rather a sign that something was terribly wrong with me.

American Lutherans place a great deal of emphasis on conformity and life in community—things that had never, ever worked very well for me. I had only two real experiences of community life—school in Upland and my life as a Muslim—and both were shaped by a very intense experience of outsiderness. There was no belonging in or to Upland, and no point in trying. As a Muslim, I was accepted, but I was also very clearly an outsider even as I worked to conform to social expectations. There weren't special rules for me, but there was special consideration.

LSTC also felt, especially during my first two years, like school. So much so that I didn't feel entirely safe.

I'm not sure it would have been different anywhere else. Ministry candidates from the Washington, DC, area tend to go either to the seminary in Gettysburg, Pennsylvania, or to Southern in Columbia, South Carolina. Neither of those places interested me.

Jennifer and I picked Chicago for the oddest of reasons. In January 2006, Jennifer was riding her bicycle home one evening when, as she crossed an intersection while the light was green, a DC Metro bus failed to stop as it made a left turn and ran Jennifer over. The bus came to a stop on her right foot, and I remember coming to her that evening in the emergency room as the surgeon stitched her foot up.

It looked like an overripe tomato that had dropped on the kitchen floor and split wide open.

The wounds didn't heal easily—she'd been run over by a city bus, after all—and Jennifer was hospitalized for two weeks, had to have a small portion of her right foot removed, and then two more months of very difficult recovery at home while complex and expensive medical equipment helped her mend her foot.

We contacted an attorney, who told us that Virginia's tort laws made any kind of lawsuit difficult. But we had a good chance at a fairly substantial settlement.

One that would pay for seminary, Jennifer and I thought. And so we chose Chicago, because we'd never lived there before, because LSTC was close to the University of Chicago, and if money was no object—it looked like it wouldn't be—then classes at the University of Chicago would be an option.

It didn't work out that way, however. We were never informed of the court date when the bus driver appeared. Jennifer, with her walker and her wound vac, would have made a very sympathetic figure to a judge. But we weren't there. So the judge simply dismissed the case. Without that, no settlement was possible.

We were fortunate that between Blue Cross and my auto insurance company, all of Jennifer's medical bills—the total came to about $65,000, including the plastic surgery needed to put skin back on the wounded parts of her right foot—were covered. But that was it.

The injustice stung, but it wasn't strange. It was familiar. It was something we'd long lived with, both at home and at school. People could do whatever they wanted to us—humiliate us, abuse us, hurt us, mistreat us, lie about us, treat us like objects—and nothing ever happened to them. Our suffering didn't matter to anyone. And we weren't allowed to object—that just got us into trouble. We had no rights anyone was bound to respect. There was no justice in this world, not for us. We didn't like it, but we'd come to expect it.

"Someone can run me over with a bus and it doesn't matter," Jennifer sometimes says in angry, tearful moments.

Seminary felt like school for a number of reasons.

First, much of the language used at seminary had a touchy-feely element to it, an echo of *Free to Be . . . You and Me* and "I Am Lovable and Capable." And I had learned long ago that those were words no one really meant when they said them. They were things people would say in between calling me stupid, or telling me no one liked me, or threatening to hit me, or letting the bully shove my nose into a corner. The language of seminary constantly had me on edge for a long while, because I was never sure exactly what would follow once the words stopped.

It also didn't help that I am a big man and can be loud, boisterous, and even sometimes obnoxiously cheerful. I have a larger-than-life personality and can easily fill a room. This apparently frightens people, and if I seem oblivious to this sometimes, it's because it simply makes no sense to me that anyone would ever be afraid of me. *I* was the frightened one.

But I quickly noticed how similar fear and the kind of contempt and hatred that leads to bullying are. They look and feel the same.

And a lot of that fear was justified ideologically. It was at LSTC that, for the first time in my life, I socially became a "straight white male" and was expected to see myself that way, feel some guilt over it, atone for that "reality," and retreat from some amount of public space in order to give others room.

It angered me that I was being made accountable for social power and social position that I'd never really had. In fact, I'd never really had any positive experience of personal power, especially in a community like this one. It felt like a no-win situation—and I was familiar with those—based solely on who people thought I was because they'd taken a quick look at me and had made a judgment founded on stereotypes and assumptions.

Honestly, I've never met a people who use stereotypes so readily, or who cling to social expectations and use them so ruthlessly and mercilessly, as do Lutherans. If you aren't who you are expected to be—insider or outsider—that's your problem. And it is made to be your problem.

But the ideology assumed that merely being a white man meant that somehow you'd lived a very typical (or stereotypical) life of bourgeois "privilege," oblivious to the lives of others—especially those significantly less privileged. It assumed many (perhaps most) of its seminarians were good, honest, decent, compassionate, empathetic and earnest women and men, people of good conscience who were curious about the world. What LSTC strove to do was to take those people and crack open their heads a bit, to show them a wider world. To give them a "guided tour" of a world of want, of significantly less privilege, power, and position, so that as students became pastors, they could be the kinds of people who tried to help their congregations be less insular, less afraid, and more welcoming of strangers and outsiders.

LSTC didn't know how to deal with my life. We didn't even know where to start. I didn't need any exposure to the wider world. If anything, I needed a guided tour of the culture, needed to know how it worked, desperately needed someone to say, "If Charles is going to become one of us, we need to teach him what that means."

Instead, they just assumed I would assimilate. I can't really blame them. After all, why else would I even be there?

Because of all this, I was far too afraid to tell my story. Who would understand? Who would believe me?

But it was these people—who could be both incredibly welcoming and thoughtlessly intolerant, so open and yet so very narrow-minded—whom God had given me to. To learn how to love. And to teach me how to love.

The worship class I took during my second semester at LSTC encapsulates all of the problems I had. By necessity, teaching Lutheran seminarians worship basically says, "This is what you've been doing your entire lives. Now we'll show you why you've been doing it."

Except that I hadn't been doing it all my life. I'd been worshiping God this way for barely two years. It was still strange to me. When Muslims pray, *every* Muslim prays. There are no spectators, no space for different roles, no dishes or fair linen or distribution. So it was a profoundly disorienting class. I studied, but it didn't help much.

Jennifer came to class with me occasionally. One evening, Dr. Mark Bangert, who taught worship at LSTC then, handed out a quiz. He knew Jennifer was a pastor's daughter and gave her a copy.

"You can take it if you want," he said.

Jennifer asked me for a pen.

When we got the tests back the following week, I noticed the grades. Jennifer got a 73. I got a 56. She was very happy, and a little embarrassed for me.

"Your wife did better than you did," Dr. Bangert noted.

"I should hope so," I replied.

Now, I appreciate that a class like this by necessity has to be structured this way—this is what you've been doing your whole lives, now we'll show you why. For just about everyone in the class, even the refugee Catholics and the fugitive Missouri Lutherans, this whole way of worship is not strange or new. I doubt anyone like me will go through this process anytime soon. It would be pointless to try to arrange the class for someone like me. And I get that.

But it meant the entire class was a struggle. Groping to try to make sense of everything. Jennifer was a little help, but like many church things, it all just made sense to her. She couldn't explain it well.

I did better than pass the class, largely because worship is about leading. And this I can do. I catch on fast. It feels both good and right to lead worship this way, and apparently those things that lead some people to fear me—a loud voice, a large presence, the ability to fill a room—can work in my favor when I'm chanting liturgy or reading scripture. But I'm still a bit of an outsider when I do it.

"You lead worship like a Greek priest!" one Palestinian Christian doctoral candidate happily told me one day after chapel. "I like it!"

At the same time, I failed to get into a summer CPE unit. And that didn't help.

I'm hard pressed to explain what clinical pastoral education actually is. The goal, near as I can tell, is to have seminarians (and ordained clergy) develop their gifts for ministry—the ability to be present, to listen, and to think theologically—during "supervised encounters" (according to the Association for Clinical Pastoral Education's website) with people who are suffering, in pain, or dealing with crises. Some synods in the ELCA view CPE as a kind of therapy, a way to help people figure out their own issues as they deal with the pain and suffering of others.

But like everything, CPE existed in a cultural context, one that assumed the student spoke, or at least understood, a language very specific to the institution that is mainline Protestant and Catholic clergy in North America today. And that the student appreciated the guided nature of the process—that while some things could not be anticipated, everything was "supervised." It also assumed a certain kind of self-awareness. So, I'd get questions like this from potential supervisors: "What do you hope to learn in CPE?"

And I was flummoxed. It was a puzzling question, one that made no sense to me. What do you mean "what do I hope to learn"? Um, I hope to learn things I don't know? And if I knew what it was I didn't know, I could go out and learn it. Because that's what I'd always done.

This answer, however, was seen not as an honest admission but as a lack of self-awareness and proper self-reflection. Which, again, puzzled me. Clearly, there was something I was missing.

The other important part of CPE is "person in crisis." CPE itself arose in the late 1920s after studies showed that too many clergy found themselves unable to articulate any kind of theological meaning or understanding in situations of pain and suffering because such experiences were becoming increasingly distant for so many clergy. I find that odd, given how recent the

Great War was then, but it was decided that clergy should spend time with those in difficult situations—in hospitals and prisons, mostly, though other places where "persons in crisis" could be found were added—learning to care for people who were sick, suffering, or dying.

In describing Anton Boisen, an early twentieth-century hospital chaplain and one of the important founders of CPE (who himself suffered from depression), Stephen D. W. King notes the following in his history of CPE, *Trust the Process*:

> Boisen's writings asserted that Liberal Christianity could be naïve and overly simplistic. Clinical training was a means to expose students who were inexperienced in hard life experiences to the "terrible reality of the dread abyss where there is weeping and gnashing of teeth, of what is far worse, the contentment and apathy which is the adaptation of death." Clinical training was a means to disturb the consciences of those stuck in a blissful or superficial life world. Studying the mentally ill would enable understanding of (or at least exposure to) tough spiritual struggle and basic needs that a spiritual and religious caregiver or caring community should address. Clinical training sought to remove some of the blinders so that students might see, feel, and understand the human situation more clearly. It taught observation, perception, and understanding through supervised experience, goals of progressive education.

Now, there's an interesting assumption in all of this—that one's faith did not arise in, is not the product of, pain and suffering. That there is an ordinary faith trajectory that is grounded—maybe *swaddled* is a better word—in some amount of love, care, and compassion from family, congregation, and community. And maybe that assumption is correct. I was struck quite early by how many of the people I attended seminary with came from families and communities in which they knew, and understood, and believed that people did, on some level, love and care for each other. If nothing else, there should be some amount of care in the world. And something was wrong if there wasn't.

Oh, to live in such a world, to even believe such a world—where people care for each other—was possible.

That was not my life. I did not live with that assumption. I had not been bullied or tormented as an adult, and that was always a matter of some wonder and amazement. But I was always deathly afraid that, at any moment, I would find myself in the fifth grade again, tormented, unwanted, and absolutely alone, with no one to protect or care for me. I could not expect the people around me to care for me—that was an impossibility, something not even worth striving for—but I could hope simply to be left alone, untormented and unmolested.

Suffering poses no theological puzzle for me. It challenges no long-held assumptions I have about God. Or the order of the world. It is the way of things. People are, more often than not, inexplicably brutal, cruel, and violent. I believed in God not despite my own suffering, or the suffering of the world, but quite possibly because of it.

I *did* need to learn how to sit with, how to listen to, how to be present with "persons in crisis" like Eileen and her mother, Mary. I may be a natural at this, but even natural talent, or God-given gift, has to be worked and honed into a proper skill.

But I'd spent my whole life reflecting, to one extent or another, on suffering. Little of what I came across at Uptown shocked me. It certainly didn't challenge me. People can be cruel and abusive toward each other. Especially in families. People can find their lives torn to shreds, and largely by their own doing. So what? I already knew this.

A seminary colleague of mine who had been abused as a child and as an adolescent told me something similar once as we compared our CPE experiences. She had been at the University of Chicago hospital and found dealing with families mourning the loss of children from Chicago's rampant gun violence grueling, but something she already emotionally and theologically knew what to do with.

"You just grit your teeth and get through it. It's not fun, but it's not hard," she said. "What we really needed was a CPE full of nothing but puppies, kittens, rainbows, unicorns, and Care Bears, a CPE of love. That's what we needed. That's what would have really challenged us."

And that's true. Once I got past the smell of Uptown, very little fazed me.

But the right thing would. It was a food pantry morning, and something we did with everyone who came in for groceries was to sit and talk with them, as long as they wanted (or their English-language skills permitted), just to see if there was anything else they needed.

I don't remember the name of the fiftysomething African American man who sat down that morning in my office. The youngest of ten children raised in rural Mississippi, he was an amazingly cheerful man for all the difficulties he faced in life.

He told me all about his family, his life in Chicago. We must have talked for thirty to forty-five minutes. But then he talked about his mother.

"My mama was the best mama, and how she loved us!" he said, smiling, relating how hard she had worked to care for all her children, even after the family relocated north.

She had been dead many years, he said, but he didn't say this with any sadness.

"I keep her love here, with me, everywhere I go," he said, tapping his chest and smiling brightly. "My mama is with me, everywhere I go. Her love is always with me, and it never leaves me."

I sat there in awe of this man, wishing at that moment I could have what he had.

"You are truly blessed," I told him.

"Don't I know it!" he said, smiling. "My mama is with me everywhere I go. My mama will love me forever!"

To have that kind of love, to know that kind of love, to live with that kind of love. I felt small, petty, foolish. I am nothing, I have nothing, in comparison to that.

❧❧

In the midst of the crisis caused by the confusion of worship class and my failure to get into summer CPE, I decided I needed to finally tell someone. Who I was. What had happened to me. Aside from Jennifer, I'd never told anyone. I had simply been too afraid. And too ashamed.

But something had to change. This nagging sense that I was being called, even compelled, to become something more—was this it? I had to tell somebody. Someone had to know who I was. I could no longer reasonably be angry that people didn't know who I was if I didn't tell them.

I picked Rosanne Swanson. I had taken a pastoral care class from her in my first semester and had gotten a good vibe from her. She was married to Dr. Mark Swanson, my academic advisor, a pastor who had lived and taught in Egypt for many years, and a specialist in Islam and Middle Eastern Christianity. (Yes, LSTC is a very small place.) There was something about her, something I felt I could trust.

Ever since I was twenty, when I sat in Tom Johnson's newswriting class at San Francisco State University, wishing there was more to my relationship with Tom than there was—or could be—I realized I wanted someone to be my daddy. I'd managed this desire fairly well for many years. But this desire to be parented, to be loved and cared for, to be protected, went absolutely haywire at LSTC, surrounded as I was by kind, authoritative male professors and a few exceptional families.

"This took a lot of courage," she told me when we met. "I'm honored that you did this. Your story is safe with me."

That voice I heard when I was ten years old, that voice giving me the will to go on? That was the Holy Spirit, she said, urging me on long ago. I had never been alone, because God was there in my life. It was hard for me to see, but Rosanne helped me understand.

If I'd been paying any attention, or perhaps the right kind of attention, I would have figured out that I really wanted Rosanne to be my "mommy." I couldn't see that until later. I lived with daddy hunger for more than twenty years—I knew how that felt and how to deal with it.

But this. This was completely new.

Rosanne suggested I seek some counseling, in order to start talking all about my life. And I took that to heart and had a couple of first sessions with counselors. But they wanted to focus on family, and I wanted to talk about school. That, for me, was the far bigger wound, the one that mattered more to me. So, I didn't follow up with anyone. Maybe I should have, but I'm not sure it would have mattered.

That summer, the summer most of my classmates were busy or away at CPE, I spent my time biking around the South Side of Chicago, seeing what there was to see.

I found a little enclave of Arab Muslim immigrants near the corner of 63rd and Kedzie—including a restaurant, a grocery store, and a *masjid*. This was nice, since I'd long hoped for someplace closer than Devon St. to pick up red lentils and spices, though the ride along 63rd St. could get a little daunting in places.

As I went into a little grocery store, the smell of the place hit me hard. It was familiar, comforting, and yet no longer mine.

I got some groceries and talked in Arabic with the storeowner, who was impressed with both my accent and pronunciation.

"*Anta muslim?*" he asked. Are you Muslim?

And I stood there, realizing that for the first time in my life, I had to think about how to answer this question. What would he understand?

"*La,*" I said. No.

The only people who ever really wanted me. And who ever really knew what to do with me. Or how to treat me. And I'd been yanked away from them. For the first time since September 11, 2001, I was deeply saddened by this.

Becoming a pastor in the ELCA isn't simply a matter of going to seminary and graduating with a master's of divinity. It also involves going through "candidacy," which is a process supervised by each of the ELCA's numerous synods. Seminaries and synods are supposed to cooperate in the process, and mostly they do, but in the end the synod has the final say.

Along the way, the candidate has to fulfill several requirements, including one unit of clinical pastoral education and a successful pastoral internship.

These requirements were overseen by LSTC's field education program. And one of the things field education constantly told seminarians was to "get out of your comfort zone." For most of my fellow seminarians, that meant going to the edges of the church.

For me, that meant going straight to the center.

At least that's what my academic advisor, Mark Swanson, and I concluded. We looked at an international program, one that had the possibility of spending a year at an evangelical Protestant church in Cairo.

"You would do very well there," Mark said. "You'd have no trouble with the culture and have fun brushing up on your Arabic."

"But," he continued, "there isn't an awful lot for a seminarian to do there, and while you'd pass, I think you'd be bored. And I'm not sure you'd have the chance to learn the pastoral skills you really need to learn."

Nope. I needed to find a typical, average, ordinary American Lutheran church.

After LSTC's usual mix-and-match process in which I—along with all my classmates—interviewed with a number of potential internship sites, I picked a church in rural northern Wisconsin. I'd liked the supervisor. He was young, energetic, and we seemed to click theologically. Because of his relative youth, I knew I wouldn't have any daddy issues in dealing with him—something important to me, since I didn't want to have that struggle on top of all the other things I had to do during my internship.

And he picked me.

But as Jennifer and I packed our things and prepared to go, we were afraid. Afraid these people wouldn't accept us. Or worse, that the things that had led people to abuse us when we were younger were somehow just waiting to become obvious again. And we'd have to deal with a year of alternating cruelty and indifference.

That, however, is not what happened. They welcomed us with amazing warmth and openness. In fact, it was overwhelming how welcoming the congregation in that little town was.

On the second day of my internship, as I moved into the half office I shared with the pastor, my phone rang.

"Hello, is this Charles, the new intern?" a female voice asked.

"Yes, this is. Who is this?"

She told me her name was Samantha. "And I'd like to come over later this week and kidnap your wife. We'll have some fun!"

It was an odd introduction, one that should have warned me of something, but the three of us quickly became close. Samantha regularly invited us over for dinner, offered to try to fix my rubber boots when the zippers failed, did a number of small and very kind things for us, and even made us a quilt with matching pillow cases. She was kind, the mother of a clutch of daughters (four, I think)—I believe I had become the son she never had.

In turn, she became the "mom" I never had. Yes, I have a mother, and I love her very much—she even came to visit us during my first internship—but I'd never had a "mom," not in the "please have another piece of pie, dear" kind of way. Jennifer and I got a kind of emotional care and acceptance from this woman that we'd never gotten before.

And it felt really nice.

I am a very emotional and expressive person. And a very physical one as well. With Muslims, this was never a problem, and I always had to remind myself that the level of physical affection among Arab Muslim men—holding hands and even kissing on the cheek—that I had grown comfortable with was not something I could even begin to contemplate with American Lutheran men. (And yes, I missed it.) Women were also completely out of bounds—there's something to be said for the virtues of Islamic prudery.

But one afternoon, during an annual dinner at a neighboring church, Samantha's mother came up behind me while I was sitting down and hugged me tight.

"Would you like to be our priest?" she asked me.

"Well, I'm not part of this denomination," I said, trying to loosen her grip around my neck.

"It doesn't matter," she said, speaking into my ear. "We'd be happy to have you!"

What she did seemed to me to be permission. This kind of embrace was something that was okay to do.

At some point, I don't remember when, I did exactly the same thing to Samantha, coming up behind her, wrapping my arms around her, and kissing her on the top of the head. Several times. I forget how many.

She never told me this made her feel incredibly uncomfortable. And I don't fault her for that. But she told my supervisor, and then he sat on this for something like eight weeks. Without telling me. It would have been easy to handle. I would have stopped and, to the extent that I could have apologized, repented, and made penance for the wrong I had done and the hurt I had caused.

Except he didn't want to deal with it. So I couldn't deal with it either.

And then one Monday in late February 2009 he told me to come in for a meeting. And that's when he told me the internship was over. In his communications with the seminary, the supervisor had lied about things. Not about what I had done but what he had done; he made it seem as if he'd talked to me several times, but that I was completely out of control. Rosanne Swanson, who was now the director of field education, was on her way up to make it formal.

We had a week to get out of the apartment.

"Where are we supposed to go?" I asked.

"I don't know," Rosanne said. "Can you go stay with your parents?"

"No, we can't. There's no place we can go."

Rosanne sighed, exhaling what seemed both exasperation and pity. I'd become someone's problem again.

"Well, you can't come and live in student housing. Officially, you aren't students anymore. So, you're on your own."

It's hard to explain just how angry I was with Rosanne. I trusted her, and I thought she understood something about me. To have this happen, without even being asked—I was *never* asked; the seminary just took the supervisor at his word without even asking me what happened—it hurt more than I could say.

We were alone, adrift, abandoned. We would soon be homeless. When I most needed some care, some sense that I still mattered, there was no one. The people God had called me to weren't talking to me. I had no idea if I was one of them anymore. It was my worst adult nightmare. I felt like I was ten again, in fifth grade, powerless and disregarded, surrounded by mean kids and a few abusive adults.

Thanks to our friend (and fellow seminarian) David Barnes, who had some connection to the Bethel New Life organization, a community development agency on the West Side of Chicago, we got a housesitting gig in the West Garfield Park neighborhood. It wasn't the safest neighborhood for a couple of white people, but Jennifer and I had found refuge in such places before.

And we were a short walk from Bethel Evangelical Lutheran, one of the ELCA's most celebrated African American congregations.

Black folks. Even though they were Christians, I knew the rules for behaving and belonging here. At worship that first Sunday at Bethel, I had not felt so comfortable, so at ease, so at home in a while.

At the end of that service, I introduced myself to Pastor Maxine Washington—she would later become one of my mentors—and explained to her where we were and what had happened.

"Remember who called you!" she said. "Remember who called you!"

Right after my internship ended, I had flung several dozen resumes in the direction of Washington, DC. It was the only place where journalists were being hired in the immediate aftermath of the near-collapse of the banking system, and had an editor expressed any interest, Jen and I would have gone.

Running away seemed an easy thing to do. After all, I'd done it before. I had run away from the army, from Dubai, and from Saudi Arabia. I was good at it.

But something was different about this. First, the stuff I was dealing with was the stuff I think I was called there to deal with. I might as well tough it out. I didn't yet know if any of the people at seminary really cared about me, but they said they did. They spoke a lot about being welcoming and open to strangers, and while I was inclined to view those words as non-sense—lies no one really meant, things said mostly to make people feel good about themselves, designed to be discarded once the strangers proved to be too strange and dealing with them either too difficult or too uncomfortable—part of me said no, stay, make them prove it.

"Their words of welcome have consequences, and they need to understand what those consequences are," I thought. I'd never felt anything even remotely like this before. I have no idea where this came from.

And there was the little matter of God. God had called me to this church, this place, this people, and I was not being called to leave. Everyone—including me—was going to have to deal with that.

❧❀❧

Both the seminary and my home synod in Washington, DC, required that I begin therapy. It seems to be the only recommendation church people have these days, and while I don't believe it's imposed as a punishment, the way the ELCA talks about therapy and counseling almost makes it punitive (I suspect this is true of other confessions too).

Still, it was something I needed to do. So, I found a counselor—an ordained Lutheran pastor with a specialty in trauma and, oddly enough, experience helping seminarians whose candidacy processes had gone off the rails.

"I'll have you know," he said to me after our fourth session, "that I usually only have two or three pages of background on someone. I have nine so far on you."

And it was amazingly helpful. He told me I was an impulsive person who only really trusted my feelings because for a significant portion of my young life, what I heard from the world around me had been so thoroughly negative that I had learned not to trust it. This was not unusual for someone with my experience. I knew these things about myself, but I didn't really *know* them until I heard him tell me.

He also concluded fairly quickly that there was nothing wrong with me that merited an official diagnosis. We had talked about post-traumatic stress disorder, and while that was close, it didn't fit.

We plumbed some depths—school, family, the internship experience—but mostly my counselor and I worked on mindfulness, learning to be a little more aware of what I'm feeling and putting some space between feeling and acting.

Especially when those feelings were overwhelming. As the feeling of being accepted and belonging had been.

And he also helped me with some social and cultural pointers, things that no one was going to explain to me and that I wouldn't know because I hadn't been raised in the culture. That was tremendously useful too.

With all this, however, Jennifer and I still felt very alone. None of the pastors I knew where I was doing my internship had asked us if we were okay, or came to pray with us, or even to say, "I'm sorry." The lack of care, of concern, only furthered our sense of rejection and isolation.

The same was true of my home synod. No one wondered if we were okay, no one prayed with us, no one asked, "Is there anything we can do?"

Only a couple of professors at LSTC expressed any concern—Kadi Billman and Kurt Hendel. I had been corresponding with Kurt, who taught Lutheran confessions at LSTC, since the previous spring, when I decided to "poke" him with some awkward questions, just to see what would happen.

What came of it was an intensive and persistent engagement. Kurt would not let go of me, and I would not let go of him. Over the next few months, Kurt and I hashed out what had happened, why, what it meant to live in a community, and why I didn't really know how to do that. He was also clear about what many of the unstated social and cultural expectations of a Lutheran pastor were, and the need for the pastor to conform to the standards of the community but also for the community to accept—and be formed by—those who have been called into its midst.

These were hard exchanges. But important. It wasn't as kind as what Abdullah al-Hamdan and Ibrahim al-Khuweiter had done—there was literally no handholding. But finally, someone had concluded that if I was going to become one of them, I needed to be taught what that meant.

Which was hard. For them, not for me. Because most American Lutherans seem to be convinced that how they behave is how normal, well-adjusted human beings behave—or ought to behave. The idea that a grown adult would need to be taught, or could be taught, social skills strikes them as odd. Even unthinkable. If you don't know this stuff, well, something's just wrong with you. Something that cannot be fixed.

The truth is that in my early forties, I was having to learn a whole bunch of things that many people more or less learn in their teens. And I was doing it under harsh lights and almost constant supervision and adjudication.

And this is when something unexpected began to happen. I had always seen conformity as a one-way street, as a demand by those around me that I do and be what they expect me to do and be. I had nothing of value to contribute. I was nothing of value. But this was different. The faculty at LSTC, and many of my fellow seminarians, not only saw something of value in me, but they were also being changed by my presence, and my persistence.

I didn't think such a thing was possible.

In the process, they began to see—really see, and help me see—my gifts for ministry. My being an outsider, a stranger, was actually an asset. A gift, even. It had value. It meant I could and would go places most of my colleagues could not go—tough places, marginal places, difficult places, even frightening places. And feel comfortable, at ease. As if I belonged there.

"You cross the color line with an ease and lack of self-consciousness that I've never seen in the ELCA," one ordained faculty member told me. "We talk about being on the margins, but you really know how to live there."

I'd been bumped into another class, and I became closer with many of my new classmates than I had been with the class I'd started seminary with.

"You know, a lot of people are kind of scared of you," Angela Nelson, who walked with me throughout much of this, said to me one day.

"I know," I sighed. "I wish it weren't true. I have no idea what to do about it."

"Well, let me help you. I'll be your press agent. After all, you aren't frightening once people get to know you," she said. "You're just a big dork."

I'm not sure I particularly liked that description. But it's probably true.

I did get a second internship. It was an arranged situation with a small church in rural northern Illinois. It was not optimal. I wanted something closer to Chicago. I still was not entirely sure I could trust Rosanne Swanson.

"If you don't take this, I cannot guarantee anything this year," she said.

But our relationship had changed. I no longer saw her as a possible mommy. My desire to be parented had abated, in part because Jennifer and I had taken care of a ten-year-old Russian boy for two weeks while his mother, who was earning an MBA at the University of Chicago, traveled to Europe for job interviews. That little boy hungered for a daddy, and I became that for the time he was with us. And in doing so, I had discovered that when you give away what you don't have, you are filled with it. That changed me completely. It's the economy of God, and it makes no sense to me. But it's true.

The most important thing Jennifer and I took with us was the expectation that parishioners would care for us. And they did, though they didn't know quite what to make of me. Truth is, almost no one ever does. I don't like it, but it's been true for almost as long as I can remember, so I've accepted it. They were kind. And they seemed to appreciate what I brought to their congregation.

And no one tried to become my mom.

I was a little stiff for the first few months. Truth is, I was terrified of making the least little mistake. There would be no third chance.

All seminarians have to do a project. At my first internship, I organized the county's program to give gifts to poor kids. I'm not much of an organizer, and it was a tough project. I kicked around a few ideas with my second supervisor, but none of them really struck my fancy.

"Why don't you write songs for the confirmation class? To review the Bible lessons for the week?" he suggested.

I thought it was a joke. But when I ran it past Rosanne Swanson, her eyes grew wide and her face serious.

"Do it!" she said with an intensity I'd never heard from her before.

This meant a whole new kind of songwriting, where I would have to communicate something rather than simply express my feelings as opaquely as I could. No more "in-jokes for one person." And I would have to do this on deadline, even. Could I do it? Was I up to it?

Oh God, was I up to it. There were weeks I could not stop writing songs about Bible stories.

Some of the grown-ups in the congregation may not have known quite what to do with me, but the kids figured me out pretty quickly. I might be big, and a little loud, but I wasn't scary.

"You're just a big pushover," Jennifer told me the afternoon I'd spent more than an hour playing songs on the ukulele for the pastor's granddaughters.

It was as if my life had been blown up in an incredibly powerful explosion, and as the pieces slowly began plunging to earth, they were beginning to fall perfectly into place.

I don't know if any of this could have happened without the mess, without the pain, without reliving and going through some of the worst feelings I've ever had about myself and the world. But how true was that for me generally? Could I have started asking hard questions about myself without being hooked up to a polygraph in a nondescript CIA building in northern Virginia? Could I have met Jesus—I mean really met Jesus—without the mass death and destruction of September 11, 2001?

Anything could have happened. But we don't live in a theoretical world. I met God, learned to love, learned to be loved, in the things that actually took place. In the history that happened.

It was after my first internship went kablooey that I truly fell in love with the Bible. Especially the Hebrew Bible, the story of Israel's calling, its conquest, exile, and God's promise of redemption. This is where the grace of God, a God who simply will not give up on God's people, meets the real mess and ugliness of human life. Where God's never-ending faithfulness and persistence meet human sin and faithlessness.

Unfortunately, as amazing as things were in Chicago, they were not going well in Washington. My candidacy committee had always frightened me—I always felt like a ten-year-old child facing a host of fifth-grade teachers. The meeting we had after my first internship, however, almost put me into a panic.

I understand and appreciate the church's concerns about pastors and seminarians who don't know proper boundaries, especially when it comes to matters of inappropriate physical affection. Pastors must know better, in large part because they have to be doubly aware—not just of their own feelings but of whatever feelings the people they deal with might have. Managing my own feelings at that point was something I was only beginning to do, and I can appreciate how troubling that was to the members of the committee.

But I was too frightened of them to handle the committee well. I felt ganged up on. No one was particularly compassionate, and it felt like several of the committee members treated me as if they were hunting a potential predator. Our first meeting after the first internship ended went particularly badly.

"What if the person who had shown you affection had been a child?" one committee member asked me.

I got defensive. And sharp. I did not like the implication of the question.

"I don't even like children," I said. Which, at the time, wasn't true. I was more frightened of children than anything else.

"I would never touch a child in any wrong way," I said. "I know what it is to be touched."

And when asked about forgiveness, I responded by saying, "I don't even know what forgiveness is." Which, unfortunately, was true.

I'm hard pressed to describe how the committee responded, but it was something akin to "Does he have any idea what he's just said? How he looks?" All I wanted to do was to shut the questioning down and make everyone go away. There was no thought, just fear. A sense I was cornered. I just wanted the conversation to end.

It did. The committee decided I needed to take another unit of CPE. Because I was "insufficiently self-aware."

Culturally, I think self-awareness here is more than just knowing what you are feeling. It's knowing how to act on those feelings. Kurt Hendel and I had a long conversation and he managed to convince the committee that knowing what I felt wasn't the problem. Acting on what I felt was, and CPE wouldn't really help that.

That encounter, I think, set the tone for all my subsequent meetings with my candidacy committee. They took the description from my first supervisor of an out-of-control intern, mixed it with their perceptions of an incredibly frightened, anxious and even somewhat angry me, and formed their opinion. They did give me the benefit of some doubt—after a very long and heated discussion in which I could tell some harsh and loud words were exchanged, they did agree to let me go on a second internship.

But they never fully trusted my counselor or the seminary. And they never really communicated what their concerns were. Not to me, not to my counselor, and—so far as I have been told—not to the seminary.

During my final year of seminary, the faculty at LSTC recommended approving me for ordination. As did my second supervisor, though he tossed in a little line in his final evaluation that read, "Parish ministry may not be the best use of his gifts." I was concerned, but the seminary was not.

That line was enough, however, when combined with the committee's other perceptions and experiences of me. At our last meeting, I tried to steer the conversation toward ministry, but members of the committee kept bringing it back to some version of "So, tell us what's wrong with you and why."

As the pieces of my life began falling back together, I became less afraid of the committee. I realized I was no longer a defenseless ten-year-old, and they were no longer a committee made up of uncaring and malicious teachers. (There were times when I felt this whole process with the Washington synod was abusive.) The problem is, the flip side of fear is not love. Or even courage. It's contempt.

And it was hard to stifle that.

"We have decided not to approve you for ordination," Bishop Richard Graham told me in a Tuesday afternoon phone call in early February 2012. "It's a matter of fitness, and we do not believe you are fit to be a pastor in the Evangelical Lutheran Church in America."

This decision came as no shock. By that point, I'd been expecting it for the last two years. I was a little angry—it seemed the last six years were all for naught. But more than anything, after years of wrestling with the folks in Washington, DC, that part of it was over.

Throughout this process, I always tried to imagine how difficult dealing with me was for most of the people in this process. And how bad I really looked, given what I had done, given how I appeared.

"We think we've seen a part of you that the seminary hasn't seen," Graham told me later. "And that informed our decision."

But more than anything, the Washington committee simply saddened me. They struck me as an incredibly incurious group, unwilling or unable to engage me and ask any questions. The head of the committee later wrote in a letter, "you seem to think you're different" and "you need to deal with your authority issues." All true, all things we could have talked about had they really been interested; they could have really helped me. If they'd wanted to.

Instead, it was like being tossed in the water while a small crowd of people stood and took notes, watching me flail and drown.

It felt like they were saying, "Our job is to see if you can swim, not to help you learn how."

❦

"Doesn't this bother you?" Jennifer pointedly asked me about the decision the following day. "Because it bothers me."

I sat there mulling over her question. No, it didn't bother me. Why didn't it bother me? I began to ponder that.

It wasn't as if I didn't have a ready-made narrative to describe what had happened, to give the whole experience sense and meaning. My childhood experience at Citrus Elementary had given me a coherent story—I was the child brutalized and abused by cruel kids and wicked grown-ups.

Or, to put it another way, "People could run over us with a bus and it didn't matter."

But for some reason, that Wednesday, that story no longer worked. I couldn't make it work. It didn't want to.

This was a staggering realization. It left me somewhat breathless. My past no longer had any say in what my present meant. And it could no longer determine my future.

I was free. For the first time in my life, I was free.

That afternoon, something incredible happened. There's a story of the Prophet Muhammad as a child. Two angels came and washed his heart, to purify it, with water from Zamzam, the well in Makka that gushed forth water for Hagar and her infant son, Ishmael. That's the only description I have for what happened that afternoon. For about two hours, it felt like there was something inside me, washing me, cleaning me. It was intense, overwhelming. The light in our apartment was different, fuzzier, like it was coming through a filter. I felt like I was glowing. It was all I could do to just sit with this and feel it.

I was not in control. I belonged to someone else. My body and my soul were no longer mine.

All my life, I'd struggled to have control over who I was. What my life meant. I, and I alone, would determine that. And now, I was finding my life was more mine when I was no longer in control. When I gave all that up. It made no sense, but it was so clearly true that I simply surrendered to it.

Thursday was a day of recovery. This overwhelming encounter with God left me somewhat bleary and feeling every breath I took.

But it wasn't over.

The following day, sometime in the middle of the afternoon, I walked out of the LSTC building. Snow was beginning to fall, and I stepped out into the blowing snow and raised my arms.

"Holy Spirit, take me. Fill me."

I stood there for a moment with the snow blowing around me. And then I started walking home to our apartment.

And then it came to me. All at once. Forgiveness suddenly made sense.

To forgive those kids at Citrus Elementary, to forgive Ms. Johnson, it all felt like weakness to me. I held them tight because I felt that if I didn't, they would win. To forgive felt like powerlessness. And more than anything, I wanted what they did to me undone. I knew that was impossible, but the ten-year-old boy was not reasonable. He wanted to have the last word. To be powerful. He wanted impunity.

But that isn't how it works at all. By holding them so tight, I gave them—these ghosts long gone—the power to tell me who I was. And I finally understood, not in some intellectual way, but in a deep, true, emotional and spiritual way, the truth of forgiveness. Forgiveness is power, the power to say "you do not get to tell me who I am."

And so I said the name of each David, of each Mike, and all the others, their first and last names—because I still remembered them after all these years—of Ms. Johnson and "Toni Tenille," and after every name, I said, "I forgive you."

"I forgive you." Over and over.

And as I walked through the blowing snow, I smiled.

"And now, you all have to walk," I told them when I was done. "Because you all have been with me for too long, and I am tired of carrying you."

I had a new story. Not that of an abused, bullied, frightened and powerless ten-year-old. I was now Jacob at the Jabbok, wrestling the mysterious stranger. That stranger had grabbed me and would not let me go. I had grabbed back, fought all night, demanded a blessing, and was so persistent in my struggle that in order to overcome me, the stranger—God—had to wound me.

15

More, Please . . .

José Escobar was dead.

He'd been killed by a single gunshot early on a Sunday morning in late September 2012, while waiting to get something to eat at a twenty-four-hour restaurant near the corner of 35th and Morgan in Chicago's Bridgeport neighborhood.

The shooting was, according to a spokesman for the Chicago Police Department, "apparently gang related."

Jennifer and I had just moved into the neighborhood that month, into a little apartment on Carpenter Street. José was apparently one of our neighbors. We lived a couple of blocks from where he was shot.

And he was also a member of the Latin Kings, one of Chicago's oldest street gangs.

A fair number of Latin Kings lived on our little street. They were not well liked as neighbors, and the Chicago police had made it a policy to drive them out of Bridgeport.

"What happens when you do that?" one Bridgeport resident asked at a community meeting.

"Then they will become some other district's problem," the police spokesman replied.

That Sunday afternoon, as the sun was setting and a breeze with just a little bite of cold on it was blowing, a number of Latin Kings were gathering about five doors down from where we lived, lighting candles and pouring libations of Corona and Mad Dog to honor their fallen comrade.

Jennifer and I saw this gathering as we came home. We parked, hauled in our groceries, and I thought about the scene outside. I felt the tug and didn't think twice. I put on one of my clergy shirts, grabbed my occasional services book and my keys.

"I'm going outside. I have to. I just have to," I told Jennifer.

She nodded. She understood.

"Don't forget your phone."

I walked over to a chain-link fence around an empty lot and stood in front of some candles dripping wax on the sidewalk. And I prayed there, alone.

But not for very long. A young man in sagging pants and a parka several sizes too big came over to me. He grabbed my hand.

"Show me how to pray."

So we prayed. I said a line, and he repeated it carefully and slowly. He held on to my hand tight. And when we were done, when I'd said "Amen," he squeezed my hand and let go.

"Thank you," he said, hugging me.

Men and women began gathering around me. As I had on that afternoon with Eileen's mother, Mary, I knew I was in over my head. But I also knew that I had to be here, that a word of love had to be spoken here. And that if I didn't speak it, it would not be said.

"I'm not a Catholic priest," I made sure to tell them. "I'm a Lutheran pastor"—because there was no time for the complexities of my situation—"and you all need to know that. I hope that's okay."

There were nods.

"We're just glad you're here," someone said.

So, I turned to the service, "Remembering Those Who Have Died," and began.

"Blessed be the God and Father of our Lord Jesus, the source of all mercy and consolation . . ."

There was some jostling. "What about Buddha?" someone asked.

"Shhh, the priest is talking!"

The rest of the short service went on like that, as I read from the Bible and recited prayers, the folks were a little rambunctious but generally respectful.

"We have gathered here to remember José . . ."

"Escobar!" someone prompted me. I had forgotten.

"Your friend and comrade José Escobar, whose life was taken this morning. José mattered, he mattered to you, and he mattered to God. So, I ask you all to take a moment to remember him."

I'm not sure what I expected. What happened was a collective caterwaul, about thirty seconds of howling and wailing, from everyone around me. And it looked as if some of the young men we pulling at their shirts as if they wanted to tear them.

And we recited the Lord's Prayer. Which just about everyone knew by heart.

"Almighty God, bless us, defend us from all evil, and bring us to ever-lasting life," I said, ending the "service" while making the sign of the cross over everyone.

"You showed us respect," several people told me afterwards. "That means a lot to us."

"We didn't choose this life," a couple of girls told me, trying to explain who and what they were. "It chose us!"

A calling. That I understood.

I had no illusions about these young men and women. Too many of my neighbors had told me stories of break-ins and assaults. But they were neighbors, mourning a loss. And I knew the sense of outsiderness when I felt it. It was palpable on that sidewalk that evening. They were all each other had. I knew how that felt too.

Besides, I dislike it when people are treated like problems. Even if what they do is problematic. I too had felt like I'd been little more than someone else's problem for much of my life.

And then the Chicago police showed up. How badly this could have gone I do not know. The Kings were fairly well behaved, and the police were taken aback by the presence of a "priest."

"I think your being there was a good thing," one of my neighbors later told me. "I think it calmed things down and prevented something really bad from happening."

Everyone scattered fairly quickly. I should have stayed around a little longer, just to make sure everything went well, but it was getting a little cold and I wasn't quite dressed for it.

I wanted to see where this would lead, and over the next couple of weeks, there were some conversations. But the arrival of cold weather and a police crackdown made continuing impossible.

More of this please. Because this is what I'm called to do. Everything in my life has prepared me for it.

My situation still had not changed. I was not approved, and in a meeting I had with Bishop Richard Graham a couple of months later he made it clear that they were done with me. There was the possibility of transferring to another synod—say, Metro Chicago—after waiting a year, and he said he would not stand in the way if I chose to do that.

"But I don't think you'll be successful," he said.

And for some reason, I was okay with that. To quote a Scott Miller song, "I'm okay with things not being okay." I had no idea what I was going to do with my life—the music ministry, maybe. But I'd lived with this feeling since the summer of 2001, so this was nothing new.

It wasn't a comfortable place to be. But it was a familiar one.

The faculty at LSTC, however, were angry. They'd walked with me throughout this whole process, and they'd seen how I had changed. How I had been formed. They'd also come to see me for what I was, the gifts I had, rather than focusing on what I wasn't or what I lacked. There was a strongly worded letter to the Metro Washington Synod, a letter I've never seen, asking them to reconsider.

During my last couple of years at seminary, former Metro Chicago Bishop Paul Landahl had become one of my greatest supporters. He wanted to get my candidacy transferred from Washington to Chicago. But the rules were clear—I had to wait a year. And the Chicago candidacy committee wasn't even going to consider the possibility until a year had passed. Even then, there were no promises.

"I have nothing to lose," I told him. "If they don't approve me, or don't even take me on, nothing has changed, and I'm no worse off than I am now."

A couple of things happened in the meantime. I got involved as an occasional preacher at a tiny little church in Watseka, Illinois, loosely associated with the Presbyterian Church in America, and two weeks of preaching at Grace Lutheran in Westchester, Illinois, led to a job offer from the church, a Sunday job helping with education as well as occasional preaching.

I knew a lot was riding on the work I did at Grace. At the same time, I was not being graded and I didn't have to fill out paperwork. It was somewhere between a call as an associate pastor and a third internship, and it was wonderful. I fit in amazingly well—far better than I ever imagined—and was accepted far better than I ever expected to be in this little white suburban church.

In the pastor, Roger Crum, I found another mentor, advocate, and friend.

Once the year had passed, Metro Chicago decided to meet with me in early April 2013. To see, I suppose, if I was all everyone—Landahl, Crum, the entire faculty at LSTC—said I was.

We talked. Not only about me, but about ministry. They asked me about my experience with Metro Washington, and at some point, my evening of ad hoc worship with the Latin Kings came up.

"How come," one committee member asked me, "you were afraid of a group of Lutherans but weren't afraid of a street gang?"

I took a breath—something my counselor had taught me to do as I measured how best to answer a question.

"I'm looking for the words to answer this question," I said.

One of the committee members got a little angry.

"You measure your words too much, and you're too careful," he said. "Just say it."

This was new. Okay, fine. I can do that.

"People who looked like the Latin Kings had never tried to hurt me before," I said.

They even seemed to appreciate my impulsiveness. Some spontaneity would do some congregations a lot of good, one committee member said.

This conversation went as well as my encounters with Washington went badly. I had to wait a few weeks, but at the end of April, they decided to accept my application for candidacy.

At this point, I expected that a six-month timetable would be the best I could hope for. And I was even prepared to take a whole year—to get to know committee members, so they could get to know me.

"We've scheduled you for early August approval," I was told. Which was more than I could have possibly hoped for.

And then . . . I was approved.

I felt a little like I had been redeemed from exile. Or maybe raised from the dead.

❧

To be honest, I feel like a fraud writing this memoir, having only lived half a life. I've accomplished so little, and I truly feel like I've failed at just about everything I've tried. I have no fortune, no great accomplishments, won no prizes, own no property, have no long tenure anywhere, and no children bear my name. I've no advice to give, no wisdom to dispense, no secrets about life to reveal. Nearly everything Jennifer and I own can fit in a seven-by-fifteen-foot storage space.

All I have is this story, the story of a love that grabbed hold of me and simply would not let me go. A love that transformed me, remade me. But it only did so by dragging me to the edge and making me look hard into the abyss—the abyss of human indifference, cruelty, rage, and violence. It made me look at what people could do, at what I was capable of doing, of believing, of wanting. It made me see. It made me understand what it really means not to love. It showed me what that could lead to.

This love has at times been a harsh love. It has not waved away the cruelty and violence of the world, or my own cruelty, nor did it carry me away from loneliness, despair, and terror. It made no promise to do so, and I never expected it would. It is the love I find most starkly and intensely on Good Friday, a love in suffering and death that demands we look and not turn away, a love that tells us, "This is who I am, and this is who you are. You have done this." It is a love that strips us bare of any pretenses. Standing at the foot of the cross, staring up at what our fear and our anger have accomplished, we cannot escape ourselves. We cannot escape what we have done. There is no place to run.

And we cannot escape God.

At the same time, this love has been amazingly gentle and kind. I have experienced it most in the sparkle of Jennifer's eyes, the warmth of her smile, the gentleness of her touch, the softness of her skin, the beauty and innocence of her soul—a soul that seems so comfortable, that fits so well, with mine. She loves me without condition or reservation, and that love slowly taught me how to love. And to be open to love. I love easily and readily, very extravagantly and intensely. Because love, the kind of love human beings can show to one another, still feels like a miracle, like something that really shouldn't happen in the world we inhabit.

That anyone would love me, for any reason . . . still makes no sense to me.

The love I have is a wonderful shambles, a glorious mess, and it needed to be given some order, some boundaries, some coherence. All of the people who helped form me as a pastor at LSTC, and the churches I have served, helped me learn how to discipline that love.

Especially if it is to be experienced as God's love for the world.

I needed to learn that discipline. Especially if I was going to become what God had called me to be. It was difficult, because for part of the time, it was hard to distinguish the love I have found among the Lutherans from the indifference and cruelty I'd experienced when I was younger. It looked and felt much the same. But as this love had grabbed me and not let go, so I had grabbed back and held on. Persistence can be a kind of love, too, and it is certainly one way God has loved me.

And in that persistence, I came to see how they truly loved. I came to know, and to feel, how they love.

Have I been wounded in this long night I have wrestled with God? Absolutely. It was agonizing. I'd long felt alone, unloved, unwanted, abandoned. But I think of Jesus appearing to the frightened disciples at the end of John's Gospel, showing his hands and his side to Thomas, who had demanded just this display: "Put your finger here, and see my hands; and put your hand, and place it in my side. Do not disbelieve, but believe."

Our risen Lord still bears his wounds. The wounds we gave him when we humiliated him, flogged him, tortured him, executed him. Wounds that could testify to the cruelty of the world. "Look at what you did to me!" Jesus could just as easily say.

As I had said, silently and aloud, for many years.

But instead, those wounds now testify to something very different. The worst we can do to each other has no meaning. The pain, suffering, and death we so easily inflict can accomplish nothing real, nothing permanent. The murderous mob of Good Friday is overcome by the resurrection on Easter. "All your anger, fear, and violence have no meaning. They are not the last word." I am part of this love now, made one with the risen Lord Jesus Christ, and in that new life I now have my wounds testify to the reality of a love far greater than I am, a love that defeats death and suffering by going through it with us.

"Feed my lambs," the risen Jesus tells us, we who betrayed, imprisoned, tortured, and murdered him. "Follow me."

We who are called to follow are also called to bear our wounds, to invite others to muck around in them. To have them testify to risen, resurrected life. To take that risk, knowing that in this place between death and resurrection, it could hurt. A lot.

Because not everyone will respond as Thomas did, with "My Lord and my God!" Some people will say, "Oooo, nail holes! Does *this* hurt?"

More than anything, however, this love showed me what love could really do. What love was truly capable of. It has redeemed the world.

"God's actually talked to you," Jennifer told me one afternoon. "Why has God never talked to me?" Some years later, my foster daughter, Michaela, echoed the sentiment, adding—in her charming and captivating way—a pointed demand.

"I want God to speak to me. I want what you have had."

I wish it were that simple. I wish there was a toll-free number, or a catalogue, or something to bid for on eBay. Really. Then everyone could have their word—or two, or three—from God. And I wouldn't feel like such a freak.

"Yours is a chrism-soaked life," my friend and seminary colleague Angela Nelson told me one day. And she is right.

The truth is, I've never wanted this. Never wanted God in my head, never wanted words that weren't mine imprinted on my soul. I've never asked for it, never prayed for it, never sought it out, and I would be content—possibly even very happy—if God never, ever had God's way with me ever again. Was never again inside my head, never again washed my heart and soul, never again zapped me senseless and breathless from the inside.

I wanted to serve and love God, yes, but as a monk in a desert somewhere, praying and contemplating, maybe. But love people? I'd rather not, if I didn't have to. I have been given no choice, however. And it's glorious.

There are times when God has made me feel like a Holy Fool, the kind of character who populates Russian folk tales and clutters up Catholic novels. Holy people, touched by God, but driven to something akin to madness in the process. Whether madness is the result, or merely the prerequisite—the condition necessary for that kind of openness to God—is beside the point. God speaks to them, acts through them, lives in them, in ways God simply doesn't for most people.

The very power that makes them conduits of the divine also makes them misfits. Even dangerous.

Holy Fools are a reminder that God is a fire we cannot control.

I think this is one reason Protestantism has no patience for fools. Protestants want a domesticated God, one easily boxed and wrapped, a serene and abstract majesty, the pilot light on a gas stove, easily controlled, easily lit and extinguished. Protestantism is the perfect faith for modernity—calm, cool, measured, reasoned, and reasonable. Protestantism lives in Isaac Newton's well-ordered mechanical universe, in which all things move with perfect mathematical predictability. God's blessing is in the good order of the world, those equations that tell us with absolute certainty where the moons of Jupiter will be on a given afternoon in August some ten thousand years from now.

And a God-blessed life is a well-ordered, well-planned life. It is a life that conforms easily and well to expectations, institutions, and ideals.

When Protestants sanctified ordinary human existence, they elevated marriage, family, and vocation as holy callings. And they were right in doing this. But in doing so, they also set into motion a process that annihilated the possibility that any other kind of life was possible. Or acceptable.

There would be no monks. No nuns. No itinerant holy men and women wandering from place to place. No dervishes. No mendicant friars. No people who seemed strangely touched by God. No lives devoted to prayer. No holy poverty.

And no fools.

Protestantism tolerates no ecstatic visions, except those of the social reformer. All others are irrational and unreasonable, to be explained away by a resort to soft science or medicated into oblivion.

Because in Newton's cosmos, in the Protestant imagination, there is no God in disordered lives. Such people are, at best, the subjects of much sympathy, charity, and even professional management (whether from social workers or prison warders). But if they cannot get their act together, well, that must be proof that God doesn't really bless them. God blesses ordered lives, lives in which people make all the right decisions, plan the right plans, want the right things, save and acquire and achieve.

Believers earn their blessing through their hard work, their patience, their adherence to expectations and norms. Because that's how God blesses the world.

There's still a lot of this in Protestantism. Lutherans speak a great deal of God's unearned grace. And we are actually living that out here and there. But for many, our lived confession, how we really treat each other, is actually much harsher: "If you really, truly need God's grace, you clearly have not *earned* it."

We are not kind, or as kind as we should be, to people whose lives are, for whatever reason, a mess. We don't want to see God—or God's call—in the mess. And we should.

My life has been a big, sprawling, disordered, haphazard, glorious, wonderful, and incredible mess. I have planned very little, and almost all of the plans that I have made—BridgeNews comes to mind—have been blown up, set on fire, and the ashes doused and drowned. So much of what has happened to me, for good and ill, has come about entirely by accident. Because I have been willing to go someplace I should not have gone, wanted something I shouldn't have wanted, simply had no idea what I was doing and followed impulse, intuition, or just plain curiosity. This book is itself the result of a happy accident, and not hard work or much planning on my part. It's not something I sought out. Or even gave much thought to. It just happened.

I didn't choose this life. It chose me.

I have no idea where I'm going or what comes next. I am waiting patiently upon the Lord—upon the ELCA's call process. I have waited for much worse, for things far less certain.

However, every time we meet, my dear friend and fellow pastor David Barnes keeps telling me, "You don't need anyone's permission to do ministry."

And he's right. There may come a time when I am called to rent a storefront and put up a sign: "The Apostle Charles H. Featherstone, Bishop and Founding Pastor of Waters of Babylon Missionary Lutheran Church" (sorry, I have spent far too much time wandering around the South and West sides of Chicago). But that time has not arrived yet.

I don't see it as permission. Rather, I see it as being true and faithful to the people I am called to pastor. Church historian Kurt Hendel, one of my mentors at seminary, constantly says, "God uses means." That is, God uses lowly things—bread, wine, water, sinful human beings—to be the means by which God's love for the world is proclaimed. The ELCA has been a means for me. An imperfect one, and one I'm still not certain has room for me. But I have learned grace and love here.

And this is how they do things. No, this is how *I* do things. Because I am one of them. And here I will stay unless God steps in and decides otherwise. They have made me one of them, for better or worse. There will likely be some disagreements about this over the years to come—I will not be everyone's idea of a good Lutheran pastor. Too messy, too emotional, too sinful, just not one of us.

In fact, it may turn out that the Washington synod was right. I may not fit. Nor be fit. I don't think they're right, but I do keep their judgment tucked back in the corner of my mind. They know the church better than I. But I don't think God has done all this just to mess with me, to waste my time, to have a good chuckle. But honestly, I have no idea. I really don't.

Besides, there are a lot of people who believe I belong here. And they've worked and fought hard to make sure I can stay and be what God has called me to be. They believe this misfit and malcontent has gifts for ministry, the ability to care for God's people, that I have been called by God for ends none of us can quite see. That means a great deal to me. I never imagined being a pastor, but the ministry that I do, whether it's singing songs with children or leading gang members in worship, is the first thing in my life I've ever done that truly makes me feel whole, like a complete human being.

This love, this astounding, incredible love. It blew the breath of new life into me. It called me to follow, and I left everything and followed. This is who I am now.

It is no small thing, this love.

It's even given me the ability to argue with God. Which is a gift. Because Muslims don't argue with God.

Not long ago, I stood in a small clearing somewhere in northern Illinois and shook my fist angrily.

"I'm tired of being called here!" I shouted. "I'm tired of being called to people who don't know what to do with me and aren't very kind about it!"

I didn't want to be called anymore. I demanded that God leave me alone, let me have a quiet life. I swore to God I would find the least moral occupation conceivable—arms dealer and human trafficker came immediately to mind—and do that with as much vicious enthusiasm as I could muster.

Jennifer didn't know what to do. She'd been angry at God for a long time when she was younger. But she'd never seen me angry at God, and she found it very unsettling.

"You'd make a lousy trafficker," she said, trying to comfort me. "One sob story and you'd melt. You'd want to help and protect people."

She was right. But I needed that hour, to vent my anger at God. I'd never been angry with God before. It was new. And I found it unsettling.

God, of course, was silent.

Maybe, though, God was laughing a little and saying, "About damn time."

There were days toward the end of seminary when I thought about who I might have been had not "the disaster" happened. I don't mean September 11, 2001, but rather my childhood. The violence. The emptiness. The wanting to be cared for, valued, and protected and finding so very little.

I would be who I have become. A preacher of the gospel. A singer of songs. A proclaimer of the mysteries of faith. The presence of God's redeeming grace and love to those around me. This is who God made me to be. I'd like to think I'd have become this person much earlier in my life, in my late teens and early twenties, but maybe I'm just romanticizing the lives of my fellow seminarians. Perhaps it was possible, in some better, other world, to be who I am without the pain, the suffering, without the decades of wandering—much of it without real direction.

But I don't think so. The God of Abraham, Isaac, and Jacob does not up and remake the world because our sense of justice is offended or injured. God uses what God has at hand, flawed and broken. God calls the imperfect, the unrighteous, the sinners, the cast off, the despised. We are God's people. We are all God has. We are all we have.

Once, in righteous indignation at a world so utterly defiled and corrupted by sin, God decided to make an end of all living things and start over again. God saved one human family, and a pair (or more than that of a few sacrificial animals) of everything that crawled and flew. Noah was righteous, and would remake the world with righteous people.

But the same God who was so good as to be moved to annihilate all that was sinful in the world came to regret that decision immediately upon smelling Noah's burnt offering.

> And when the LORD smelled the pleasing aroma, the LORD said in his heart, I will never again curse the ground because of man, for the intention of man's heart is evil from his youth. Neither will I ever again strike down every living creature as I have done. While the earth remains, seedtime and harvest, cold and heat, summer and winter, day and night, shall not cease. (Gen 8:21–22)

God would live with human sinfulness. God would, over time, learn to work with and in human sinfulness, to be with us, to gather us, and to call us to follow. Hardscrabble fishermen, tax collectors, zealous Pharisees, Ethiopian eunuchs, prominent businesswomen, the blind, the deaf, the crippled, and even the dead—all given new life in God's love. All called to live as if that love were the only thing that mattered.

For God so loved the world. This world. This sinful, wretched, violent, miserable world.

I can love it too.

Afterword

THERE WERE A COUPLE of months after I was approved for ordained ministry in August 2013 when I thought: finally, I get to live something resembling an ordinary life. The adventures are over, the wandering is done. I will get to settle into something I have prepared for over the previous seven years—Sunday services, hospital visits, council meetings, junior high school confirmation.

The ordinary life of a parish pastor. It seemed to be what I was called to.

I'd even interviewed at two Lutheran churches in the Chicago area, and those interviews went fairly well, I think. No one called me back for a second round, but I never expected it would be easy. The struggle of the last few years had taught me to be patient, persistent, and cheerful.

As I interviewed, however, I was nagged by a sense that I couldn't be entirely honest about who I was. Especially after I started writing this book. And I was haunted by a vision of being called to an ELCA congregation, this book coming out some months later, and being greeted one day by dour congregants angrily clutching pitchforks and torches.

"If we had known that you had done these things, that this is who you were—*who you are*—we would have never called you. And now you need to leave."

It would have been ugly. And unpleasant. Because I have lived an interesting, messy, and somewhat disreputable life. And someone was going to hold that against me.

Some friends advised: don't tell anyone. It's easier to ask for forgiveness than it is to ask for permission. You'll at least be ordained, and they can't take that away from you.

Maybe that would have been the wise course. And if I had much faith in institutions, that's probably what I should have done. But I've never had much luck with asking either permission or forgiveness. Neither has worked well for me. At heart, I'm honest and I don't want to cause trouble. I really don't.

So I told Metro Chicago Bishop Wayne Miller, "There are some things you need to know about in this book, so you can honestly have a better idea of what you are dealing with, and what congregations to give my paperwork to." (Bishops in the Evangelical Lutheran Church in America control the call process for pastoral candidates fresh out of seminary.)

He asked for a list of things a call committee might find troubling, and I gave him one. I was hoping to have a conversation about it, but when the time came, he did most of the talking.

"You will have no credibility as a pastoral leader in the ELCA," he said.

And who am I to argue with him? He's probably right. He knows his church—and his congregations—far better than I ever will.

I could withdraw my candidacy, he told me, or I could let the committee—which had to renew my approval at their next meeting—vote. I didn't give him an answer that day, but after talking with Jennifer, I quickly decided that I would not do their work for them. My attitude was, "You want me out, you're going to have to toss me out."

Which they did, in June 2014.

I was never told what the specific issues were, though some people familiar with the Chicago synod and the workings of the church revealed to me that the biggest issues were my relationships with Anna and Lauren (admitting to relationships with married women, even if they happened nearly thirty years ago, apparently created a legal liability) and my military discharge.

"I see here a lifetime of very poor decision-making," Miller added, somewhat exasperated. As if my life had become a mere administrative inconvenience rather than a witness to something bigger—to grace, forgiveness, and redemption.

Too messy, too interesting, and too disreputable a life for the Lutherans, apparently.

I can appreciate their concerns. Bishops in the ELCA spend an inordinate amount of time dealing with pastors who cannot behave themselves—and the too often horrific consequences of their misbehavior. If someone were looking for warning signs, for red flags, well, it wouldn't be hard to see my life as one giant, rambunctious, and unruly May Day Parade.

But I won't lie. It felt to both Jennifer and me like our future had been yanked out from underneath us. Despair grabbed us hard, held us tight, and hung on for a while. It had been difficult enough waiting for the ELCA's call process to work itself out. Now, we were waiting for nothing. We were nowhere.

The sense of being discarded, tossed aside, even a little abused, hit Jennifer very hard, since she'd seen the Missouri Synod Lutherans treat her father abysmally in the 1970s and had never forgotten it. "You gave up everything to follow Jesus, you were faithful, you did everything that was asked and more, and they do this to you," Jennifer said between tears one morning. The ELCA's candidacy process is tough enough—provides precious little pastoral care—for those who get through it successfully. It is indifferent to the point of cruelty about the well-being of those it throws away.

For me, the toughest thing was having a sense of belonging shattered. I'd ached for so long to belong. For a moment, I thought I'd actually found a community I could be a part of, a people who would want me and even have a place for me. And I'd been wrong about that. And that really hurt.

The bishop told me I could reapply to candidacy after a year. But I have no intention of doing so. I am as done with the Evangelical Lutheran Church in America as they are with me.

I haven't the slightest idea what happens next. A few friends have asked if I've considered seeking ordination through another confession or church body. I haven't, mostly because I don't feel called anywhere else, but also because I don't see another church or organization being any more accepting of me than the ELCA has been. I also don't relish the prospect of trying to conform to someone's idealized (and bureaucratic) understanding of what a pastor is. I clearly can't do it, I'm no good at it, so I should stop trying.

I don't belong. And I never will. And for the first time in my life, I'm really, really okay with that. I know who I am, whose I am, and what I am called to do. My hope is that my life will speak most to the lost, the lonely, the unwanted, and the unloved, those who need to know there is love, and there is even belonging. That despite everything, God redeems, and that redemption is real. That there is no life so messy, interesting, or disreputable that God has abandoned or won't use to speak a word of judgment, grace, mercy, and forgiveness to the world.

Right now, I feel a little like Saul probably felt during the days he stayed with Ananias in Damascus—recuperating, getting ready, knowing that there was no going back (because there was nothing to go back to) and the way forward lay in a darkness that would be illuminated only as he stepped into it.

All he knew was that he would proclaim Jesus: "He is the Son of God."

That proclamation is all I have now. And I have no idea where it will carry me.

Bibliography

King, Stephen D. W. *Trust the Process: A History of Clinical Pastoral Education as Theological Education.* Landham, MD: University Press of America, 2007.

Mailer, Norman. "The White Negro." *Dissent* (Fall 1957). Online: http://www. dissentmagazine.org/online_articles/the-white-negro-fall-1957.

Solzhenitsyn, Aleksandr I. *The Gulag Archipelago, 1918–1956: An Experiment in Literary Investigation I–II,* trans. Thomas P. Whitney. New York: Harper & Row, 1973.